Recovery Meditations
One Day At A Time

Written by members of

The Recovery Group

With Appreciation To:

The Writers

The Editors

The Proofreaders

Overeaters Anonymous

TRG Administration

TRG's Executive Committee

The Members of The Recovery Group

TRG Adm's Administrative Assistant

The Trusted Servants of The Recovery Group

The Daily Distributors of Recovery Meditations

Foreword

Within the next 366 pages of this special book, you will find the experience, strength and hope of men and women from around the world who have come together in a community for a single purpose. That purpose is to recover from an eating disorder they did not ask for nor did they want. Recovery is made possible for compulsive eaters by working the Twelve Steps of Overeaters Anonymous and sharing with one another. There is only one requirement to join The Recovery Group and that is to have the *desire* to quit eating compulsively.

The seed for The Recovery Group was planted in 1995 with the creation of Journey to Recovery and WTS ~ Working the Steps, two online support groups for members of Overeaters Anonymous. Since that date, our growth has mushroomed and today we have over 150 support groups serving thousands of members around the world. In addition to the 12 Step support loops, we also have Big Book Studies, 12 Step Studies, a Sponsor Program, a Newcomer's Program, dozens of Special Focus groups, a Writer's Series, a vast Website and 56 meetings weekly, all registered by and affiliated with Overeaters Anonymous. You can read more details about our history at www.therecoverygroup.org/history.html.

Members of The Recovery Group represent a diverse group and their diversity is reflected in this book. By simply going to our main website at www.therecoverygroup.org you will find every imaginable resource to accommodate all people from all walks of life, cultures, religions and backgrounds. We are not a religious organization but a deeply spiritual one.

Recovery Meditations ~ One Day at a Time did not just happen overnight. There is a very long list of members who have made this book possible. From the writers of the meditations, to the editors, to the proofreaders, the daily distributors and those with technical expertise who put this together with their love, their dedication and their passion, we owe our deepest appreciation.

We hope you enjoy the book ~ perhaps one day your path may lead you to us.

One Day at a Time
The Trusted Servants of TRG

*In the deepest part of our soul is the realization
that recovery begins when we find one another.*

The Recovery Group
www.therecoverygroup.org
www.therecoverygroup.org/meetings/

VICTIMIZATION

*"Within each of us lies the power of our
consent to health and to sickness,
to riches and to poverty, to freedom and to slavery.
It is we who control these, and not another."*
Richard Bach

I have lived most of my life believing that I was a victim of circumstance. As a "victim" I believed I had no power, no options, no choices, no hope and no control in my life. It's so tempting to be a victim. If I'm a victim, I am not responsible for anything. Every pain, every dysfunction, every addiction, every problem was not my "fault" and there was nothing I could do to improve my life. Or so I thought.

One day a friend asked me if I actually wanted to be well and I was shocked to find that the immediate answer flooding from my heart was, "NO." Wow! You would think that a victim would give anything in order to be well, yet I found that I was terrified of the responsibility of being well. If I were well, I would be in charge of my own choices – particularly the most primal choices of all: Life or Death, holding onto powerlessness, or reaching out to grasp hope and health.

I am still tempted to return to the false security of victim-hood. Yet I come to recovery, and keep coming back. I work the program, I learn, I fail, I fall. I rise again and begin again.

One Day at a Time . . . .
I will remember that I have the power, the freedom, and the responsibility to make choices which move me towards health. I will resist the siren call of victimization.

~ *Lisa V.*

Meditation 1

LETTING GO

"He who cannot rest, cannot work;
He who cannot let go, cannot hold on;
He who cannot find footing, cannot go forward."
Harry Emerson Fosdick

Prior to walking through the doors of this program, my goal in life was to set up barricades against possible attacks. My mind was cluttered with battle strategies and defense tactics. I tried to predict every conceivable plot to topple me from my self-appointed throne. I sought to control situations in order to dominate the outcomes. To that end, I would bend over backwards to do for others what I didn't want them to do for themselves. I maneuvered myself into positions of power so that I wasn't presented with any surprises. Every situation was weighed for the probability of failure. I never took chances.

This process took time and vast amounts of energy. My mind was in a constant cacophony. Consequently, there was no room for growth, no space for acquiring new skills and no time to develop old ones. Every day was a constant juggling act between an ever-decreasing energy supply and an escalating demand to feel secure. The more I sought to control, the less I controlled.

Working through Step One brought my whole crusade to an end. I learned to let go of what I had laughingly called control. I learned to relinquish the helm and acknowledge that I wasn't such a good driver. Almost instantly I became aware of a path beneath my feet. I was, for the first time in the longest time, moving forward. The scenery was changing and the outlook was brighter.

One Day at a Time . . . .
I will accept what I cannot do alone, and let go and let God.

~ Sue G

Meditation 2

CHARACTER DEFECTS

"God seldom delivers virtues all wrapped in a package
and ready for use. Rather He puts us in situations where
by His help we can develop those virtues."
C. R. Findley

I have been reading and studying a lot about the Sixth and Seventh Steps lately. I have realized that these Steps are threefold. I must first become aware of the defect of character. Next, I must accept that I own it and it no longer works for me as it once did.

Lastly, I need to surrender that defect of character to my Higher Power. In the meantime, it is my job to act as if the change has already occurred. This means that I may come into contact with some seemingly obnoxious people who will mirror my character defects. I must remember that "Nothing happens in God's world by mistake," and they are here to teach me something. Maybe I am here to be the lesson for them. I may be the only example they ever see of a person trying to work and walk a spiritual path, in a Twelve Step program of recovery.

One Day at a Time . . . .
God, I ask that You continue to help me to be aware of my actions and how they affect others, and to accept and become willing to relinquish my character defects to You.

~ *Jeanine*

HAPPINESS

"Happiness is an achievement brought about by inner productiveness.
People succeed at being happy by building a liking for themselves."
Erich Fromm

It has been said that if one of us ever treated another human being the way we treated ourselves, we would be liable for criminal charges. I did not treat myself as a friend, someone I loved; I constantly fed into my unhappiness.

Alcoholics Anonymous co-founder Bill W. was asked, shortly before he died, to sum up the program in the lowest common denominator. He replied, "Get right with yourself, with God, then with your neighbor." Therefore, it stands to reason that I must start making friends with myself. I must treat myself with love and dignity, and the result will be happiness. To be happy, joyous, and free is the by-product of obedience to the program.

One Day at a Time . . . .
Am I going to try being happy?
Am I going to make friends with myself?
If not today, when?

~ *Jeremiah*

PERSEVERANCE

"Age wrinkles the body. Quitting wrinkles the soul."
General Douglas MacArthur

IT has always been easy for me to feel sorry for myself. My life has been difficult since I was a very young child, and early on I developed a chip on my shoulder the size of a boulder. "Surely no one has ever suffered what I suffer," I often told myself. I used my pain and loneliness as excuses for bitterness, cynicism, arrogance, and harshness. In a twisted manifestation of my sickness, I held onto my suffering as though it were a precious testament to how "special" I was. I was actually proud of my hardships! By doing this, I was mocking James' instruction to consider trials of our faith as reasons to rejoice, and I was sentencing myself to years of immaturity, lack of faith, conflict, resentment, and heartache.

Because I held onto my arrogant, self-defeating attitude, the trials I faced led only to more and more illnesses of my body, mind, soul, and spirit. I was a prisoner in my own mind – ignoring the fact that I held in my hand the key to my freedom.

In the last six months I have been hit with more profoundly chaotic, agonizing, destructive trials of faith than I've encountered in the last ten years. The number, frequency, and intensity of these events did what my rational mind could not do – they brought me to my knees and led me to finally surrender my efforts to control my life.

I thank God for the friends He's given me in Recovery. Trusted Servants have prayed for me, listened to me, and encouraged me. They have shared with me their own stories of suffering and the growth they have gained through it. With God's grace and the support of dear friends, I am learning to release my twisted hold on Suffering, and to instead cooperate with God's work in me. As I focus my attention on the lessons He has for me, I find that even the most painful trials I face can – and will – produce perseverance and maturity, one day at a time.

One Day at a Time . . . .
I will choose to welcome the lessons and growth that God has for me – even when they come disguised as horrific events in my life. I will choose perseverance over bitterness.

~ *Lisa*

Meditation 5

LONELINESS

"Loneliness and the feeling of being unwanted
is the most terrible poverty."
Mother Teresa

I remember being lonely for most of my growing up years. I never had many friends and never felt I fitted in, so I buried myself in studying and became an overachiever. I also buried myself in reading novels and lived in a fantasy world, always trying to escape that terrible empty feeling inside. I could be in a crowd of people or at home with my family, and yet the feeling of loneliness was always there. I didn't realize then that this was a kind of spiritual sickness, and I began to fill the "hole in my soul" with food; I was hoping food would take away the empty feeling. It took me years and a great deal of pain to realize that no amount of food could relieve that empty lonely feeling. Keeping busy couldn't help either. It was only when the pain of the food and the destructive things I was doing to myself became greater than the pain and the loneliness that I was trying to bury under mounds of food that I was brought to my knees and found the doors of my first program meeting.

Even though I wasn't sure that the program was for me at that first meeting, I knew then that I need never be alone. Other people suffered as I did and the feeling of not having to go it alone any more was very powerful. As I grow in the program and have discovered a Higher Power who is with me day and night, I have come to realize that I need never be alone. I can call on that Power at any time when I feel alone and scared. No longer do I have to feel the spiritual emptiness inside that used to drive me to food.

One Day at a Time . . . .
I will remember to call on my Higher Power for guidance and help with my life; in that way, I need never be alone. When I follow the path that God intended me to follow in the first place, the loneliness disappears.

~ *Sharon*

Meditation 6

FEELING OVERWHELMED

"The social workers have named a new syndrome.
It's called 'compassion fatigue.'
Why does it sound so familiar?"
Anne Wilson Schaef

For most of my life I have always cared for others, and have always been in the caring professions. I didn't think that was a bad thing until I was brought to my knees and arrived at my first program meeting. One of the character defects that I found I had was people pleasing. Because I was always trying to help and fix others, I also knew that I had a problem with control and lack of acceptance.

One of the things I am learning in the program is that, because for so many years I had hidden my emotions in food, there are still many layers of the onion that I haven't even begun to peel away. The amazing thing is that it is only when I reach a rock bottom of some sort that I am forced to look deeper at many issues that I have blocked for years. What I realize now is that I have spent so many years of my life taking care of others that I have forgotten to take care of me. No wonder I feel so overwhelmed!

I'm a compulsive caregiver, but in doing that, I have often neglected to see to my own needs. I am so grateful that I have become open to looking further into why I have always put others' needs before mine, and to being able to detach with love from many issues over which I am powerless, so that I can take better care of me.

One Day at a Time . . . .
I will remember that in order to be able to care for and love others, I must first learn to care for and love myself.

~ *Sharon S.*

Meditation 7

RESENTMENT

"You will not be punished for your anger,
you will be punished by your anger.
Anger will never disappear so long as thoughts
of resentment are cherished in the mind."
Buddha

It was not until I came into the program that I learned that resentment is just another name for anger. There are some areas in which letting go of resentment are not so easy, especially when dealing with hurtful words. Word wounds have a tendency to fester. The program shows me how to approach someone and make amends to them for saying something hurtful. That can be extremely healing. Unfortunately, there is no Step in the program which makes provisions for others to make amends to me when my feelings are hurt.

I have learned something that has helped: telling others how I feel when my feelings are hurt. Instead of internalizing my feelings, I am beginning to speak up and ask, "Why did you say that? I felt hurt when you said that."

Doing this releases the negativity and turns it into a positive action for me. Rather than just reacting to a bad situation, I am taking positive action. When I begin to take positive action, I find myself surrounded with positive influences and I am letting go of those friendships which are unhealthy.

One Day at a Time . . . .
I will take positive action and surround myself with positive influences.

~ Marilyn S.

Meditation 8

SEEING CLEARLY

*"If your eyes hurt after you drink coffee,
you have to take the spoon out of the cup."*

Norm Crosby

For so many years I had trouble seeing the obvious. I felt blind when dealing with emotions. I didn't know how to express anger properly. I was either furious (and eating) over little things, or emotionally void (and eating) over big things. I was told my feelings were hurt too easily, so I began to stifle my rightfully hurt feelings, using food to stuff the pain. But the worst was happiness. I was hysterically happy over the stupidest little things, and felt immensely unworthy of kindnesses done for me. Neither felt comfortable, so I always ended up eating.

It all began to come clear in the program. For once I could see my actions and my reactions and begin to understand myself and my motives. As I have worked this program, I no longer feel like my emotions swing on a pendulum from one extreme to the other. I can see things as they really are. I no longer make big mountains out of small hills or make small hills out of big mountains. I can now feel happiness, and express it, in complete comfort with myself. The nicest part is that while I may not be well-acquainted with my new behavior yet, it feels very comfortable, and I no longer have to practice my eating disorders to cover up my feelings.

One Day at a Time . . . .
My eyes are opened by the program to the truth of what is and the feelings that are.

~ *Rhonda H.*

Meditation 9

FORGIVENESS

"Don't carry a grudge.
While you're carrying the grudge,
the other guy's out dancing."
Buddy Hackett

I have spent so much of my life wanting and, in my sickest moments, demanding amends from others. I truly have been treated poorly, wrongly and unfairly. But when I focus on how someone else owes me apologies and amends, I'm keeping myself in a negative attitude while trying to change someone else.

One of the best parts of Twelve Step recovery for me has been to let go of these grudges. I work on forgiving people. It sounds wacky, but forgiving them (not forgetting) allows me to let it go. One way I can find forgiveness is to know they never asked themselves how they could make me miserable today. From there, I can wish them well. It has been an absolute blessing to let go of these things rather than waiting for these people to make amends to me.

One Day at a Time . . . .
I will remember that no one is intentionally doing harm to me. Forgiveness is a much more serene place.

~ *Rhonda H.*

FOCUS

"It takes a long time to become young."
Pablo Picasso

By the time I came to the Twelve Step program, I had forgotten how to have fun. My whole world revolved around food–eating it, planning to eat it, or not eating it (and being very aware of it). When asked to go anywhere, what first came to mind is what foods I could eat there. I would agree to go only if I were in the mood for the kind of food that would be available, and if the person going with me would be interested in eating it too. Parties were all about the food, not who I'd see and meet. Family reunions were about Aunt Betty's specialty dish and Uncle John's grilled meats.

This focus on food made me forget how to have fun. I even forgot what I liked to do, if I ever knew. The truth is that fun came to mean eating, and it was what I liked to do.

In the recovery program, I've learned that I have choices; I just couldn't see them for the food! The first time I went to a party where I didn't even think about the food, but enjoyed all the new people I met while reconnecting with old friends, I was shocked when I ended up at the refreshment table. The party was almost over, and I hadn't visited this area the second I walked in the door! What a relief! And what fun! I came home full of life and love and laughter. I hadn't felt so young in years.

One Day at a Time . . . .
I will pray to keep my focus away from food and instead focus on life.

~ *Rhonda*

GUILT

"Who I am is what I have to give.
Quite simply, I must remember that's enough."
Anne Wilson Schaef

For most of my growing up years, I was fed on guilt, or so it seemed. I always felt that in order to justify being worthy of what others did for me, I had to be the best at whatever I did. I would feel guilty for not meeting others' expectations. My self-esteem was virtually non-existent. I was always there for other people rather than being there for myself. It was no wonder I turned to food to help me cope.

Now, I'm grateful that it took the pain of all those years of compulsive overeating to bring me into this wonderful fellowship of people who accept me just as I am. I don't need to do anything to justify myself. Through working the Steps, I have been able to let go of a lot of guilt and I see that, even with all my character defects, I'm still a very special and unique human being. My self-esteem has improved, and I learned that I need to take care of myself if I'm to be of help to others.

I still struggle with those defects from time to time, but with the support I find in this fellowship, I am becoming comfortable with who I am, and I can let go of the guilt. What a relief that has been!

I don't need to be just the person who is always there for others; I need to be there for myself. I am learning that I am a worthwhile person and that I'm just the way God wants me to be.

One Day at a Time . . . .
I don't need to be just the person who is always there for others;
I need to be there for myself.
I am learning that I am a worthwhile person and that I'm just the way God wants me
to be.

~ *Sharon*

CHANGE

*"If you would truly wish to understand
something, try to change it."*
Kurt Lewin

There is nothing more powerful to me than this one thought. My entire program teaches me to change the fellow who came in or he will surely drag me back out. Without change there is no hope. Without hope there is no peace or serenity.

The "how to" is simply and strongly told in the Big Book of AA. On page 28 it is plain that we must find and maintain a spiritual fitness in order to survive. Change is the key to open the door, and change is impossible without a power greater than ourselves. This, truly, is the easier, softer way. May you find Him now.

One Day at a Time . . . .
I am willing to allow the God of my understanding to change the person I was into the person He wishes me to be.

~ *Danny*

RECOVERY

Survival is nothing more than recovery.
Dianne Feinstein

As a very young child, I had a loving relationship with my Higher Power. I talked to God all the time about the things I didn't understand. I asked for His help in making me a better person, daughter, granddaughter, etc.

Then, as happens in dysfunctional families, things got worse. Being the youngest, I became the scapegoat for people who didn't know how to express anger and pain properly. I, too, learned inappropriate ways to express my feelings. I also began to turn against my Higher Power. Why wasn't He helping me? Why was He letting me be so unhappy? Why wasn't He answering my prayers? Why hadn't I awakened thin yet?

It took me many years to destroy my relationship with God, but thankfully, it only took a few years of the Twelve Step program for me to rediscover my former relationship with Him. As my eating disorders have been lessened and abstinence has become the norm in my life, I am very grateful for the Higher Power in my life today. I truly feel as if I've gained something I once lost. Thanks to recovery, I've also gained things I never had or don't remember having. I have a peace, serenity, acceptance, understanding and love that I can never remember experiencing before. The more I trust in my Higher Power, the more rewards of recovery become mine.

One Day at a Time . . . .
I will work my program and be grateful for the level of recovery I'm currently experiencing. When I feel a lack of growth within myself, I will look at how far I've come and trust that my growth is in my Higher Power's time, not mine.

~ Rhonda H.

GOD OF MY UNDERSTANDING

*"I believe in God, but not as one thing, not as an
old man in the sky. I believe that what people
call God is something in all of us."*
John Lennon

Like many people, I originally came to Program primarily seeking help with my compulsive overeating. My main concern was to gain control of my weight and my appetite. I was expecting some kind of diet program, but I found something quite different.

I already considered myself religious and didn't think I needed much help in this area. I also wasn't particularly interested in working on my shortcomings, but I was willing to overlook these "problem" areas of Program because I was so desperate for help.

Well, I did get my weight and appetite under control, but I got much more than that. Program's concept of being able to work with a God of my own understanding may have been the most radical and personally-enlightening theological tidbit I've ever had the pleasure of tripping over. It changed everything I thought I knew about spirituality and God. Through this shift in my understanding, my Higher Power began to change me and help me with my COE by gradually removing all of my past baggage and encumbrances.

Even though I've now reached my recovery goals, my purification continues daily, as does my spiritual growth. I went searching for a diet that actually worked and instead found a whole new way of life. Whoda thunk?

One Day at a Time . . . .
I will continue to nurture my relationship with the God Of MY Understanding by working the tools of recovery.

~ *Rob*

FORGIVENESS

*"Never does the human soul appear so strong
as when it forgoes revenge and dares to forgive an injury."*
Edwin Hubbel Chapin

I want recovery from my disease of compulsive eating. Part of my program of recovery is asking forgiveness for past wrongs I've committed against other people. It isn't enough for me to make amends just to others, though.

Another aspect of forgiveness is that of forgiving those around me. I need to forgive them for what they may have done to me. Many times people don't know that they've hurt me and maybe triggered a binge, because I've covered up the pain with food. But if I forgive them, then I don't have that pain that I thought could only be soothed with food.

Finally, I need to forgive myself. I can be my harshest critic, and many times I, myself, have been the trigger for my binge. Besides, if I can find it in my heart to forgive others, then surely I can extend the same courtesy to myself.

One Day at a Time . . . .
I will practice forgiveness in all its forms.

~ *Jeff*

PROCRASTINATION

"Procrastination, more than anything else I can think of,
separates those who want to be successful from those who are."
Lee Silber

I would always intend to start everything 'tomorrow.' As a compulsive overeater I constantly promised myself the diet would start the next day, or if a weekend was approaching, then it would be Monday. When I first found this program I still had the same attitude: I would get a sponsor in good time, I would get a food plan next week, I'd read the Big Book and other program literature when I got a moment. I thought if I just kept going to meetings something will happen.

However, I found that procrastination does not work in program any more than it does outside. I no longer wanted to be the member who was constantly sharing what a dreadful week I had with the food and other aspects of my life.

Today I have a sponsor, I have worked through all the Twelve Steps – I am still working and living the Steps – I am in good contact with my Higher Power, have a good food plan which I am following religiously, and I have recovery to bring to my shares.

One Day at a Time . . . .
When I make a decision I follow it through with action immediately.

~ *Lilian*

LOVING WORDS

*"One of the hardest things in life
is having words in your heart that you can't utter."*
James Earl Jones

Many years ago I had difficulty in expressing feelings of love and caring and warmth and concern. Contrary to this, I had no difficulty in expressing criticism, unkind words or constant critiques. Over the years I have learned so much about myself and others ... and now I can express feelings to my friends and loved ones about everything.

Those who are imprisoned by emotional constipation do little to make life better for themselves or for others. To be able to look at someone in your life and tell them you love them is such a beautiful gift. To tell a store clerk that you like something about them makes their heart sing. To look a little child in the eyes and tell them they have a good heart and you admire them takes them through the rest of the day on wings.

One Day at a Time . . . .
Here's to letting the words out of hearts.

~ Mari

OPPORTUNITIES

"Tiger, tiger, burning bright,
In the forest of the night,
What immortal hand or eye,
could frame thy dreadful symmetry?"
William Blake

This quote from mystic and poet William Blake expresses the sense of wonder and awe I have about God, who can make a being like a tiger, an aggressive carnivore. God, who I suppose to be kind and loving, makes beings that are potentially dangerous to me. The question "Why?" stirs in my mind, alongside fears about what God may have in store for me.

"Fear of the Lord, is the beginning of wisdom," says one religious text. I can feel grateful for the stirring fear, and question, as the seeds of new wisdom.

A quick thought enters, "I can also feel grateful for the chance to flex my faith muscles and to increase their strength. Maybe that's why God makes tigers and their ilk."

A habit of staying detached from the emotions life arouses in me heightens my perceptions of what life has to offer, highlights what God has to offer in each situation and the reasons I have for being grateful. This is essential to my recovery. It's the spine of an attitude of gratitude that also nurtures remembrance of God, and conscious contact with Him.

One Day at a Time . . . .
I thank God for what I have already learned, for all opportunities to learn more, and
for the chance to perfect "skill in action" in my recovery way of life.

~ James

Meditation 19

NEW WORLDS

"Each friend represents a world in us,
a world possibly not born until they arrive,
and it is only by this meeting that a new world is born."
Anais Nin

Most of us are so compulsive at almost everything we do, that allowing people in to know our garbage of the past and present is unheard of.

You go to a meeting, find a new recovery friend, and that friend opens a new door. You and that friend step through and WOW, the world in that room looks great! Later at another meeting, you meet another recovery friend and another door is opened. You and your two new friends step through and you find an even better world view. This continues to happen meeting after meeting, Step after Step, room after room and your personal life begins to look much brighter and more beautiful. You find that there really is hope.

Funny how it's still the same world, but friends, recovery and Higher Power make it a much better world view.

One Day at a Time . . . .
I will never end this beautiful cycle of finding new worlds as long as I never lose sight of my Higher Power, my recovery friends and my recovery program.

~ Jeanette

POSITIVE THINKING

*"Positive thinking will let you do everything better
than negative thinking will."*
Zig Ziglar

I came into Twelve Step meetings after descending into a well of negative thinking. It was a vicious cycle, one I wasn't even aware of for the longest time. My negative thinking fostered many resentments, hurts and binges. Once I became aware of this and started to work on changing my destructive thinking, I discovered that letting in just one negative thought opened the door to more negative thinking.

Then one day in a meeting I heard a longtimer say that negative thinking attracted negative (thinking and actions) and positive thinking attracted positive (thinking and actions). That made sense with what I was experiencing. As I walked out of that meeting, I determined that I would do everything I could to keep all my thoughts positive in order to attract more positives to my life.

It worked! The more positive I could keep my thoughts, the better I felt about everything, and the more good things happened to me. My general attitude soared. When a bad thing happened (and they do happen) I found good things about it and focused on the good. Many many times I discovered that the "bad" thing had actually been a new good direction in disguise.

Positive attracts positive. Negative attracts negative. I'd rather attract positive.

One Day at a Time . . . .
I will remember to turn to the program to help maintain my peace and serenity, especially through the bad times.

~ *Rhonda*

Meditation 21

SERVICE

"The only ones among you who will be really happy
are those who will have sought and found how to serve."
Albert Schweitzer

In my first few Twelve Step meetings, I was so angry. On one hand, I didn't think I needed to be there, although deep inside, I knew I did. People were nice enough, greeted me, made me feel welcome, but I kept myself apart with my anger. I was angry that there seemed to be a small core group of members who attended weekly and obviously knew each other well. I didn't think they'd let me in their inner group; I didn't get invited.

Next, I tried to get the program without working the Steps. That inner group talked about the Steps all the time. I'd show them how good I was; I'd get the program, get the recovery they'd gotten, by taking a shorter route. The Steps were for dummies, and I wasn't dumb. I quickly found out the Steps are the only way to get the Twelve Step program, hence its name.

I struggled for a long time. Then I started giving service to my group. It started off by simply straightening up the room because I always got there early. I asked for a key so I could put out the books. I started greeting newcomers, who usually showed up early. When the person who'd signed on to do the topic didn't make it one week, I agreed to lead the meeting.

To my shock, I was giving service. In looking back at my first weeks in the program, I realized that the "inner core" of my home group had become my very good friends. When had I been asked in? Never. I joined when I began to give service and became one of them, the service-givers to the group. I learned why they seemed to have such effortless growth– it came from giving service. With service I always get back much more than I put in.

One Day at a Time . . . .
I will remember to give of myself. I will remember that giving service in the program gives me so many gifts in return.

~ *Rhonda*

Meditation 22

CRITICISM

"To avoid criticism, do nothing, say nothing, be nothing."
Elbert Hubbard

For so many years, I thought I was the only kid who had been raised with criticism. Fear of criticism is one of the reasons I walked on eggshells at home. I learned to fear success in anything and everything. If I could only be "middle of the road," maybe no one would notice me and I wouldn't have to deal with criticism. I did what I had to do to survive.

As I grew older, I received constructive criticism by wise people, but sadly, I didn't know how to utilize such a gift. It hurt me, and I turned away from well-meaning people. I rebelled against their advice.

The program has taught me that all criticism is not bad. I never thought a day would come where I was comfortable with it. I recently took a correspondence course to help me with my work, and naturally the instructor had to critique my work. I worried about that before I took the course. In fact, I'd wanted to take that class for years, but had not been able to handle the cold fear that stabbed at me when I looked at the application. I finished the class last month. There was much criticism to help me to learn, and I didn't shrink from it. I learned from it. It's all in the attitude.

One Day at a Time . . . .
I will pray to remember I have choices. I will pray to keep my attitude in a good place so that I might see all the opportunities available to me.

~ *Rhonda*

POSITIVE ATTITUDE

"Attitude is more important than the past, than education,
than money, than circumstances, than what people do or say.
It is more important than appearance, giftedness, or skill."
Charles Swindoll

I can't remember ever having a consistently good attitude. When I was younger, I usually wore a mask of a good attitude, so many people were attracted to the mask but not to the real me, and I knew it. It didn't help my attitude grow more positive.

Coming into the Twelve Step program, my attitude was all negative. My theory was that if I expected the worst from everyone and everything, if by chance I got something better, I could be pleasantly surprised. This makes me laugh now. With that attitude, would ANYTHING ever be considered good enough to "pleasantly surprise" me? No, and it didn't. I ignored the many good things that happened–or I created a dark side to them.

In a meeting, I once heard that positives attract positives, and negatives attract negatives. This has stuck with me for years. It might be a scientific thing, but for me it refers to attitude. When I make the choice to be in a bad mood, I struggle through the day. Nothing seems to go right, and if it does, I don't notice it or appreciate it. When I make the simple choice to be in a good mood despite whatever problems I'm facing, good things happen to me. People smile back, elevating my mood. I can find humor in things around me. The sun is shining even on a rainy day. It's all up to me.

One Day at a Time . . . .
I will make the choice to be happy for just today. I will look for the good in myself, in others and in the situations around me. I will keep my attitude positive.

~ *Rhonda*

MOVING ON

"Dwell not on the past. Use it to illustrate a point,
then leave it behind. Nothing really matters
except what you do now in this instant of time."
Eileen Caddy

As a child, teen, and young adult, I was sexually, emotionally, mentally and physically abused. I was neglected as well. By the time I was a young woman, the "abuse" was history, and I was left dealing with a very sick family. But I could not let go of my abused past!

The abuse became the topic of every conversation I had. Anything I saw on TV or read in a book or newspaper brought to mind the past. I awoke in the middle of the night to relive my childhood nightmares for a few hours before crying myself back to sleep. I spent entire days staring at the television, eating to numb myself from my pain and anger.

Eventually, I wanted more from my life. I became disgusted with myself and what my life had become. I was led to a Twelve Step group. There I learned how to let go of the past, to work through it, to make amends for my part in things, and to forgive those who abused me.

Today, when I discuss the abuse I suffered, which is seldom, I can do so without the anger and pain bubbling up. I can help others with my story, and then I can let it go. It is my history, but it's no longer ruling my present.

Like Thomas Raddall said, "Don't brood on what's past, but never forget it either."

One Day at a Time . . . .
I will make amends and forgive others, not for them, but for me. I pray to live in today, to make it the best day I can.

~ *Rhonda*

HOPE

"In the hour of adversity be not without hope,
For crystal rain falls from black clouds."
Persian poem

When I was a child, I lived in a fantasy world and dreamed of all the wonderful things that would happen to me when I grew up. I would have a wonderful husband, beautiful children, a fulfilling job and, of course, I would be thin. Unfortunately the fantasy never materialized, and even when I did lose weight my life wasn't the perfect life that I had envisioned. I would lose weight and then promptly regain it. Life in general seemed so empty and futile. No matter how hard I tried, nothing seemed to work. I hated myself and my life; it often seemed pointless to go on.

When I walked into the doors of the first meeting I ever attended, there was something on the faces of the people I met there. I didn't know what it was at the time, but I saw something that I wanted. It wasn't that they were all thin, because many of them were not. So what was it that these people had that I didn't? What they had was the hope of recovery. If they were willing to reach out to a Higher Power of their understanding, and if they would work the program one day at a time, then this would guarantee them recovery.

I didn't know what recovery meant then. Because all I wanted was to lose weight, and because I wanted what they had, I was prepared to do what they were doing. I realized then that it wasn't only about the weight, although that does play a part. These people were learning how to live their life sanely, and even when they struggled with life, as we do from time to time, there was always the hope that they could get through those difficult times by using the tools and reaching out to others in the fellowship.

One Day at a Time . . . .
Even when I am going through difficult times and the future looks gloomy, I have
hope that it will get better if I'm willing to work a simple program.

~ *Sharon S.*

DECISIONS

"We can try to avoid making choices by doing nothing ...
but even that is a decision."
Gary Collins

I can't recall if I ever learned that I had choices. I think it's something a person learns as they grow up, but in my home, it was pretty much Mom's way or the highway, and she had us all so scared of the highway that even THAT wasn't much of a choice!

Imagine my utter shock when I came into the Twelve Step rooms and heard I had choices! I was a married woman by that time, one who had gone along with what everyone else said about anything and everything, and the only choice I seemed to make was how much I'd binge that day, if I'd purge, or if I'd be anorexic. Even that choice wasn't in my hands, but in the hands of my disease.

In these recovery rooms I slowly learned about making choices and the responsibility that went with them. It's been a freedom. It's also allowed me to feel like an adult. As a young child I was put in the position of doing things only adults should be doing. So on one hand, I knew I had done things way before "my time." Yet I still felt immature and naive. Learning to make my own choices and decisions has helped me to feel more mature and confident.

One Day at a Time . . . .
I will not fear making difficult decisions. I will remember I can use the principles of the program to help me make the proper choice.

~ Rhonda

SUCCESS

"Success is the ability to go from one failure to another
with no loss of enthusiasm."
Winston Churchill

My life before program consisted of one failure after the next. I could never master success with my eating, much less with my life in general. Once I came into these rooms and started working the Twelve Steps, with a God of my understanding and the knowledge that God is in control of all in my life, I began to realize that life is NOT a series of failures, only slow successes.

One Day at a Time . . . .
I am a success if I keep on trying regardless of the outcome, because it is truly God's will for me.

~ *Linda K.*

GRATITUDE

"Thankfulness is the beginning of gratitude.
Gratitude is the completion of thankfulness.
Thankfulness may consist merely of words.
Gratitude is shown in acts."
David O. McKay

All the good I have ever been given in life, both before recovery and in recovery, has come from God. Even the ability to learn lessons from the bad has been one of His many gifts to me. I make gratitude lists and offer prayers of thanksgiving, but that is only the beginning. I only express true gratitude by sharing with others. I share it as experience, strength and hope at meetings. I share it by reaching out my hand to the compulsive overeater behind me and sponsoring them or befriending them. I share it by living a life that shows evidence of the realization of all that God has given me. I can only truly express my gratitude through action.

One Day at a Time . . . .
I will show my true gratitude by giving away to others what God has so freely given to me.

~ Vicki B.

NEW BEGINNINGS

"...To dry my eyes and laugh at a fall, and baffled,
get up and start again..."
Robert Browning

When things didn't go my way, I would stamp my feet, lose my temper, and walk away. I was the world's greatest quitter!

The Twelve Step program of recovery teaches me that when I trip over something, I can pick myself up, dust myself off, and start over at any time. I can turn whatever I stumble over into an opportunity for growing and learning.

One Day at a Time . . . .
When confronted by roadblocks to my recovery, I can humble myself and ask my Higher Power, "What do YOU want for me to learn from this?" I can turn stumbling blocks into stepping stones and move on in my recovery journey.

~ *Linda K.*

WORRY

"Worry often gives a small thing a big shadow."
Swedish Proverb

I've spent too much of my life worrying about the future. This was especially true with every diet I was ever on. I was always concerned about how much weight I was going to be able to lose in a certain amount of time. I always thought about tomorrow and what tomorrow would bring instead of staying in the present.

Today, my Higher Power is teaching me to keep my eyes on Him instead of on the calendar. I am more successful and more at peace when I remain in the present and follow my Higher Power's will.

One Day at a Time . . . .
I will keep my thoughts in the present, for my Higher Power will take care of tomorrow.

~ Gina

STRATEGY

"Better shun the bait than struggle in the snare."
John Dryden

Perhaps the most important strategy for beating temptation is to avoid it altogether. Temptation pits me head-on with my disease and all of its cunning and baffling ways. It's so much easier to stay out of its claws and devices than to try to free myself once caught in its web.

What ways do I bring temptation right into my house or provide access to temptation when I go out? Do I keep forbidden foods in my house? Have I ever asked other family members to go without those things because they are dangerous to me or my recovery? Do I go places or engage in activities that increase my desire to eat compulsively? Have I considered that, for now, I just can't go certain places because of the risk to my recovery? Have I considered that I might have to give up socializing with certain groups of people because they lead me into temptation? Does watching TV trigger compulsive eating? Does putting myself in the company of a certain individuals lead to self-defeating behavior of any kind? Do I continually expose myself to stressful situations or people that tempt me to eat compulsively? Do I continue doing the things that tempt me to eat to ease the feelings or emotions that come up over it?

Perhaps I am in an unwholesome relationship, or I overspend, or have another addiction or compulsion. What am I willing to do to recover? What am I willing to change to keep myself out of harm's way?

It is easy to pray for God to keep me from temptation, but I must do my part also.

One Day at a Time . . . .
I must remember to avoid the people, places and things that tempt me to eat compulsively and provide a way for the disease to touch me again.

~ Diane

LOVE

*"The supreme happiness in life is
the conviction that we are loved."*
Victor Hugo

All of my life I felt unloved. Deep in my soul I was also convinced that I was unworthy of love. Nonetheless I craved love deeply.

In a desperate attempt to feel OK, I forsook the God of my childhood and declared that there was no God. I spiraled further and further into the depths of despair, unable to feel or give love. In my downward spiral, I turned to food to block feelings of unworthiness.

I entered Program dying of addiction as well as the deep sorrow of the loveless. I thought I was different from everyone else, that no one could possibly understand me. I had no peers, no real friends.

However, once in Program I found others just like me! I started to belong and to develop true friendships. In my desire to belong, I worked the Twelve Steps as others did and found a God of My Understanding. GOMU is a loving God. This God supports and guides me while as helping me learn to give and receive love. Love has brought me back to life.

One Day at a Time . . . .
Hand-in-hand with my Higher Power, I love and am loved.

~ *Michel*

BEING JOYFUL

"As I stumble through this life, help me to create more laughter than tears. Never let me become so indifferent that I will fail to see the wonder in the eyes of a child. Never let me forget that my total effort is to cheer people, make them forget, at least momentarily, the unpleasantness in their lives. And in my final moment, may I hear You whisper: "When you made My people smile, you made Me smile."

A Clown's Prayer (Author Unknown)

I have made so many people angry with me, so many people cry, so many people worry and despair of me. So many people have been resentful of me. My disease dictated how I lived my life, if you could call it living.

Then I came to this program and I found a new way to live, and I found joy such as I have never found before, anywhere. The program taught me not to take life so seriously. The Big Book of AA tells me on page 132, "But we are not a glum lot. If newcomers could see no joy or fun in our existence, they wouldn't want it. We absolutely insist on enjoying life." I need to remember that. I need to work my Steps, stay in conscious contact with my Higher Power, but boy oh boy, do I ever need to remember that I need to learn that I am not a bad person getting good, just a sick person getting well. Even sick people have fun. I'm a sick person recovering on a daily basis from a terminal disease that was killing me, but recovery snatched me from the brink of death. Now I can't help but see the beauty of this crazy, wonderful world we live in.

One Day at a Time . . . .
I am warmed and my heart sings at the thought that today I have made someone smile. Please, dear God, let me continue to do so.

~ *Marlene*

LAUGHTER

"Laughter can be more satisfying than honor;
more precious than money;
more heart-cleansing than prayer."
Harriet Rochlin

For as long as I can remember I've always been a serious person. I can't remember ever doing something just for fun or to have a laugh. There always had to be a purpose for what I did in my life, or else it was of no value. As for being able to laugh at myself, that wasn't even in my frame of reference. I was so super-sensitive that I'd get upset if someone made fun of me, as it would always make me feel "less than" or stupid.

So when I came into the doors of my first Twelve Step meeting, I was amazed that, even though all the people I met had problems around food, they were still able to look at their mistakes and realize that that didn't make them a bad person. But even more heartwarming was the fact that I heard laughter in those rooms. Before, I'd always thought that when someone laughed at what I said, they were laughing at me, and that would reinforce my feelings of inadequacy.

The lessons I'm learning here are not easy ones and there are still times when my old behaviors of being overly sensitive creep in, but I know that recovery is a process, and as I grow in the program, it will get better.

One Day at a Time . . . .
As I practice the program and work the Steps, I am becoming more able to laugh at myself and not always look at the dark side of life. What a gift it has been to start enjoying life!

~ Sharon

Meditation 35

SELF WORTH

"Your worth is not established by teaching or learning.
Your worth is established by God.
Nothing you do or think or wish or make
is necessary to establish your worth."
Helen Schucman, scribe of "A Course in Miracles"

I have spent the last 30 years of my life wanting more, thinking that in proving myself I would be worthy of the love and affection I deserved and this would determine my value. I was always seeking the best path to take to show everyone what I could do and that I was worthy of more of their love and praises.

Turning my life and my will over to God has allowed me to see that, no matter what I may think, in God's eyes I am worth plenty, and this has given me so much peace. I now know that what others say or think about me is not going to make me worthy or worthless. Allowing God to run the show and doing the next right thing is all I need to do. I don't have to concern myself if I am of value to anyone; I am of value to God, and that is all that counts.

One Day at a Time . . . .
I will continue to turn to God for my strength, knowing that I need not carry the burden of proof of what I'm worth.

~ Maureen

Meditation 36

ERRORS AND ASSETS

*"We grow by our willingness to face and rectify errors
and convert them into assets."*
The Big Book

I have had a paradigm shift in my life. This means that I have begun to see some of my most basic ideas about food and nourishment from a different angle. I never really thought these things through before this program nudged me to have a look at my life with rigorous honesty. Oh, I wanted to be thin, but I barely related that to my feelings about food.

I was on autopilot for years and now realize that my concept of food was reasoned out when I was still a child. I put that childish set of ideas in place and then just stopped thinking about it. That little child wanted the most she could get of everything there was. She wanted the most attention, the most love, the most toys . . . and the most food. And at that time it was exactly the right way to look at the world. When I was a child setting up the system that constantly demands more to calm or soothe or comfort or love, I turned to food because it is simple and I did not possess the skills to get my needs met in other ways. It was a victory really, because I coped, made it through to now. But, to stick with a plan set up by a little child reflects a lack of willingness to face a basic error in engaging the world and change my behavior.

Now I know that eating mass quantities of food isn't about love, or fun, or comfort. Now my adult mind knows that food is a fuel that, if chosen judiciously, helps my body to work efficiently and clears my mind for the task of being a responsible adult in a busy, troubled world. By shifting from "How much food do I get for me?" to "What must I eat today to be healthy?" I change my whole basis for choosing. I take an area of my life that has been a constant error and change it into an asset, one that nourishes me and helps me to do that next right thing.

One Day at a Time . . . .
I am willing to face my flawed thinking about food and change the way I make food choices, meal by meal, so that food is an asset to me and not a liability.

~ *Carol B.*

FELLOWSHIP

"We may have all come on different ships,
but we're in the same boat now."
Martin Luther King Jr.

As a child I never had many friends and I was never one of the "in" crowd. I had many complexes and never thought I was good enough, or clever enough or thin enough. I didn't date much, nor did I often go to parties. Instead I lived in my perfect fantasy world, where I would one day be thin and beautiful and live happily ever after. As a result food became my best friend, and where friends would constantly disappoint me or leave me, food was always there to numb the pain of loneliness, rejection and loss. There was never anyone in whom I could confide the unbearable pain that I felt, and so I would bury myself in books and food, and thought that as long as I had enough food to soothe that great big hole in my soul, everything would be fine.

Finally, however, when the food was causing me more pain than the pain it was supposed to take away, in desperation I found the doors of this wonderful fellowship. The people in that first meeting were from all walks of life, and of all ages, with some being old enough to be my parents or young enough to be my children. Even though they initially appeared so different to me, I realized that in this motley group of people I had found the friends that I had always been looking for. The common bond we shared in our desire to stop eating compulsively and to heal our lives was the cement that keeps this wonderful fellowship going. These friends listened to me without judging me, they loved me even when I couldn't love myself, and they were there for me when I needed them. They have become my best friends and my family. It's a result of this fellowship with other compulsive overeaters, who share with me their experience, strength and hope, that I am constantly able to learn and grow.

One Day at a Time . . . .
I will reach out in fellowship to my friends in the program, as they reach out to me,
and in doing so I am empowered in ways that are truly miraculous.

~ Sharon S.

Meditation 38

DISCIPLINE AND FREEDOM

"Freedom to a dancer means discipline.
That is what technique is for ... liberation."
Martha Graham

I was thinking this morning that keeping in fit spiritual condition was like being a dancer. A dancer knows that without the discipline of frequent training and rehearsal, he or she will not be able to dance freely when called upon to do so. The dancer who is not in shape will look wrong, feel wrong and become injured trying to do something wild and free. The training may be dull, boring and repetitive at times, but when the performance is on, the dancer soars in the freedom of movement.

I try to look at my daily program tasks the way a dancer looks at training. I may not like every minute, but I have the continual blessing of freedom as I go about my day and the hope of great moments of breakthrough into new freedoms as I progress.

One Day at a Time . . . .
I will take each Step of my recovery program with my great vision of freedom.

~ *Q*

BLESSINGS

"There are no mistakes, no coincidences.
All events are blessings given to us to learn from."
Elisabeth Kubler-Ross

I certainly never had a charmed life as a child, and when I was told to count my blessings, I never thought that I had that much to shout about. I was a shy and lonely child, always self-conscious about my shape and size, and everyone else seemed to be far better off than I was. When life started to deal out blows that were far more than I thought I could handle, I wondered why bad things always seemed to happen to me. I would hardly recover from one traumatic event when another one was upon me. I felt life was definitely unfair. Using food seemed to be the only way that I knew to cope.

I was looking for a solution, for some way to make my life a happier one. Fortunately, I was finally brought to my knees by the pain of my compulsive overeating. In working the Steps of this wonderful program, I have come to some amazing realizations. All the time I had railed against my misfortunes, I was being brought to some new understanding.

With the growing openness I now have, I can more clearly see why certain things in my life had to happen, and even why I became a compulsive overeater. Unlike the past, when I used to hate this disease, I now see it as a blessing, from which I can learn and grow. If it were not for this disease, I would not have needed to look at my life, nor would I have had to work at trying to make myself into a better person. I most certainly would not have needed to find a God of my understanding, nor would I have met so many wonderful new friends, who always love and support me.

One Day at a Time . . . .
I will remember that the events in my life are not dealt out to me as a form of punishment, but rather as motivating factors in my life, that spur me on to grow and change as a person.

~ *Sharon S.*

Meditation 40

ATTITUDE

"The last of the human freedoms is
to choose one's attitude."
Viktor Frankl

I have always found someone like Viktor Frankl to be an inspiration. His attitude to life totally amazes me, especially after suffering and losing all his family in the Nazi concentration camps. How could anyone come away from an experience like that and still find meaning in life, much less meaning in suffering? I certainly could never find any meaning in all the years of suffering through compulsive eating which caused me so much pain. Life didn't seem meaningful at the time, and I wondered if it ever could. But one of the things I have learned in the program is that I can allow myself to wallow in self pity, which I did many times, or I can take the lessons from my life's experiences and use them as opportunities for growth. That has not been an easy one for me in my journey, and there have been many times when life just seemed to be too hard. I wondered whether I had the same strength and positive attitude that Viktor Frankl did. Intellectually I know that attitude is a choice I make. There have been times when I've been depressed and full of self pity and I allowed myself to sink into that abyss of despair. But now, knowing that I have a choice, that I can pick myself up and "act as if," I can have a positive attitude. When I make the positive choice, miraculous things happen, and life somehow seems a lot easier.

One Day at a Time . . . .
I will make a choice to think positive thoughts, and try to emulate people like Viktor Frankl and others who have battled enormous difficulties and yet kept a positive attitude. When I do that, I know my life will become infinitely better.

~ *Sharon*

FREEDOM

"Always be a first-rate version of yourself,
instead of a second-rate version of somebody else."
Judy Garland

As far back as I can remember I always wanted to be like – or act like – someone else. I never allowed myself the freedom to be me. I was my parents' child, my husband's wife, and my children's mother. It wasn't until I came into program wearing all of my identities on my body – 150 pounds' worth – that I was able to see how unhappy I really was.

I began my journey to recovery by slowly discovering the real me underneath all that extra weight. Working the Twelve Steps of recovery helped me to peel away the layers of fear that kept me stuck.

One Day at a Time . . . .
I am free to be me ~
And I am enough.

~ Eileen

Meditation 42

POSITIVE THINKING

*"We could accomplish many more things
if we did not think of them as impossible."*
Jean-Jacques Rousseau

I have spent a lifetime dieting. My life can be easily separated into two sections: the dieting periods and the non-dieting, or bingeing, periods. When I first start losing weight, I am positive about it, to the point where, if I go clothes shopping, I even buy things in smaller sizes because soon I won't be as big as I am. This works fine while I'm losing weight, but when I reach a plateau and remain at the same weight level for a while, or even worse, gain a bit, I start to think that I'll never lose the weight I need to lose, that my sticking to a "diet" for the rest of my life is nigh to impossible.

Well, with stinking thinking like this, I'm defeated before I've even started. Through this program, I've learned that anything is possible. First of all, it's true that sticking to a diet for the rest of my life would be an impossible feat, but in program we don't "go on diets." We follow a sensible eating plan, and this plan should be flexible enough that it IS something we can follow indefinitely. Secondly, I have to correct my time spans. Instead of thinking of it as "the rest of my life," I have the option to think of it as "One Day at a Time," and we can do anything for just one day, can't we?

One Day at a Time . . . .
I remember that's all it takes...one day at a time.

~ Marjee

Meditation 43

ADMITTING MISTAKES

*"A man should never be ashamed
to own he has been in the wrong,
which is but saying, in other words,
that he is wiser today than he was yesterday."*
Alexander Pope

Most of my life I had spent in blaming others for all the bad things that happened in my life, and I never learned to take responsibility for my part in anything. I thought that life had treated me unfairly, but mostly it was because someone else had wronged me. I wallowed in self pity and justifiable anger, and not surprisingly, I found comfort in food so I could get through the pain of being treated so badly by others.

When I came into the program and began working the Steps, I was horrified to learn that I was expected to do a searching and fearless inventory of my wrongdoings, for after all wasn't it others who had harmed me and not the other way around? Slowly I realized that I had a part to play in all the events in my life, and that only by clearing up the wreckage of my past and keeping my side of the street clean, did I have any hope of recovery. I had to swallow my pride and admit when I was wrong, and when I did that, miracles began to happen. Instead of feeling hard done by and bad about myself as I had thought I would, the exact opposite happened, and I started on a journey of growth and increasing self esteem that never ceases to surprise me. When I am able to admit that I'm wrong and apologize for my part in any conflict or misunderstanding, without expectation of anything back from the other person, I strengthen my recovery in this program.

One Day at a Time . . . .
I will admit my mistakes whether I believe that the fault is mine or not, because that is the way that I grow in my recovery.

~ *Sharon*

Meditation 44

SELF-PITY

*Sometimes I go about pitying myself and all the while I am
being carried across the sky by beautiful clouds.*
Ojibway Indian Saying

Before I came into the program, I never realized that I had succeeded in making myself a victim. Sure, I'd had my fair share of difficulties and yes, there had been physical problems in my life, but my reaction to all this in those days was to be angry at the unfairness of it all. I was so obsessed with self; it was always about me and my woes, so it was hardly surprising that I turned all those feelings inwards and became depressed. I ate, hoping to take away the pain of dealing with the uncomfortable feelings and the difficult circumstances. It was as if I had dug myself into this deep hole of despair and could not get out.

When I came into the program, I was given tools and Twelve Steps to help me to stop the compulsive eating; a way to get out of the abyss of despair and hopelessness that I had created for myself. When I had to look honestly at my life and the character defects that were keeping me stuck in destructive eating, I didn't want to own up to the character defect of self-pity because it made me feel less than. But what I have learned in this wonderful program is that I am still a child of God, no matter what imperfections I may have.

It has been a long and slow process of growth and change for me and not every day is wonderful. There are still days when the self-pity creeps back, but I try and not let myself wallow in it for too long. Unlike the past, where I would view everything from a totally negative perspective, I am now able to look past the difficulties at all the wonderful things in my life, and especially this life-saving program, with immense gratitude. Even when things seem to be really tough, I can still see beauty around me, and give thanks for wonderful, supportive friends and a loving family. What a gift that has been!

One Day at a Time . . . .
I will focus on what is positive and beautiful in my life rather than what is negative, and allow my Higher Power to relieve me of the character defect of self-pity.

~ *Sharon S.*

Meditation 45

SETTING EXAMPLES

"Don't worry that children never listen to you;
worry that they are always watching you."
Robert Fulgham

How many overweight people blame their size on genes? My whole family had weight problems. Everywhere I turn I see obese families. In my house we were taught that it is a sin to waste food. After all, there are starving people in the world. As if my cleaning my plate would really help a starving child. How many times was I rewarded with a sweet treat instead of a hug and a "Gee you did good - I'm really proud of you." A scraped knee always felt better if you put a candy on it. I could eat the treat after the pain was gone, so of course eating made you feel better fast. My parents didn't actually teach me that food would give me instant gratification in so many words, but I learned those lessons from observation. Food helped me get through some very difficult years. I never realized that there were tools that could help through them. Unfortunately, I only found OA after my children were grown up and had watched their COE mother make the same mistakes that her parents taught her. I am trying to set a better example now. I no longer have a pantry full of junk food and when I give my grandchildren treats, it's books, stickers, hairclips, toys, anything non-edible.

God, I realize that my parents unintentionally taught me bad eating habits and I forgive them. Please let my children forgive me for making the same mistakes. Help me to set a better example for the next generation. Please be with me when I buy groceries and let me bring only healthy food into my house. Help me to be satisfied with my abstinent meals so that I won't be tempted to binge and graze with little eyes upon me. I am so grateful for Your presence in my life, because I can't do this alone.

One Day at a Time . . . .
Please remind me that there are tools I can use instead of slipping into my old eating habits and let me be an example of the miracles that come with abstinence.

~ *Jeanette*

A TEENAGER'S PRAYER

"I felt as if angels were pushing."
Adolf Galland - on his first flight in a jet aircraft

Sometimes I feel I really can't take anymore, I really can't do it. I feel so alone. I feel no one cares. I just want to hide away and eat and eat until I am so sick I can't eat anymore.

A minute at a time I got through my day, and it was so hard. Didn't anyone understand how hard it is to get thru school with the teachers giving me a hard time. The other kids laughing at me in a corner, I know they are, I can feel them. They don't know what it's like to be me. And when I get home, I get even more of a hard time.

But sometimes I feel so bad and I come here on my computer and share or I go to an online meeting, and I know I'm not alone after all. Someone cares, they really do.

I feel heaps better and I suddenly realize that angels had pushed me through the day. And even though the day had been hard, I HAD got through it! I had a whole day of abstinence!

Suddenly I feel so much better about myself, about you and about the world in general.

One Day at a Time . . . .
I will remember tonight. An angel walked with me today, and if I close my eyes and sleep, maybe, just maybe an angel will walk with me in my dreams.

~ Marl

CHANGES

"They always say time changes things,
but you actually have to change them yourself."
Andy Warhol

Time changes things – but what things? Can I wait for time to change those ways of coping that don't serve me anymore? Can I wait for time to make me abstinent?

Yes, time will change things, but chances are that these will be the changes: my coping mechanisms will become even more entrenched and my eating even more destructive. I don't really want to wait for that kind of change. When I joined OA, I started a new trend. I asked for the wisdom to understand which things I can change and then, armed with the tools of the program, I set about following my new trend of eating healthy and living a life where I don't sit around waiting.

I will not wait idly for things to get better. I will ask my Higher Power to guide me to make necessary changes.

One Day at a Time . . . .
I will not wait idly for things to get better. I will ask my Higher Power to guide me to make necessary changes.

~ *Isabella M.*

Meditation 48

SERENITY

"God, grant me the serenity to accept the things I cannot change;
the courage to change the things I can;
and the wisdom to know the difference."
The Serenity Prayer

My life before abstinence was a fight in the dark to stabilize my world and protect myself from more pain. Too much suffering was endured by this child. She never understood that she could ever come back into the Light. But, the fog is lifting now ... there are days of clarity and joy. How could she have known? She was too little.

Circumstances change ... memories fade away ... I can be safe again ... I can allow myself to be me. I will work my program to secure the Light again in my world.

One Day at a Time . . . .
I pray to understand that the stream of life keeps moving ... I will live in darkness no longer.

~ Margaret

SELF KNOWLEDGE

"We're our own dragons as well as our own heroes
and we have to rescue ourselves from ourselves."
Tom Robbins

I always tried to do my best in everything I did. Studies, school, and managing my own family are some good examples. Being in control made it seem as though I always did as I was told, but I had a very difficult time being on my own and thinking for myself. The talent I was born with gave me a good start at being an artist, but I couldn't seem to make a successful career out of it. I was scared and shy and didn't dare be on the forefront of making this talent into what I wanted it to be.

When I started on my path to Recovery, I found that I was being too much of a perfectionist. I was always told to do things perfectly and I tried and tried but never seemed to satisfy my parents or the god of my childhood. So when I grew up I was so hard on myself that I lost the creativity I was born with. Creativity can't thrive in a hostile environment.

One day while reading an author I liked, I read that I had to "get out of my own way". I was a dragon trying to do something creative and it didn't work. I have to learn to "rescue myself from myself" so I can do my art with the talents that are God-given.

One Day at a Time . . . .
I realize that if I want to see myself as I really am, I cannot stand in my own shadow.

~ Myrlene

Meditation 50

SECRETS

"There were deep secrets hidden in my heart,
never said for fear others would scoff or sneer.
At last I can reveal my sufferings,
for the strength I once felt in silence has lost all its power."
Deidra Sarault

I have heard it said in program that we are only a sick as the secrets we keep. If that is the case, then I was very sick when desperation forced me through the doors of this wonderful fellowship.

Not one of my friends or family knew what I was doing around food, as most of it was done in secret, and I was always careful to remove all the evidence. I couldn't believe that anyone would love me if they knew what I was doing around food, and felt that I was either really bad or totally crazy, or both. But for the first time ever, I was able to come clean about what I was doing around food, and I wasn't judged or frowned upon. The love and acceptance I have received here has been totally overwhelming, but in addition I found out that others had done the same or similar things to what I had done, and so for the first time ever, I felt that I wasn't alone. Not only have I been able to talk freely about my food and what I had been doing, as well as what it was doing to me, but in the Fourth and Fifth Step, I was finally able to share with another person my darkest deepest secrets, that for years I'd thought had made me this terrible person. It was in fact in sharing all the things that I'd thought of as so bad, that I came to realize that it was only my magnifying mind that had made them appear so, and that in fact they really weren't bad at all. I would never have found that out, had I not been in this program, and I'm so grateful for the relief that sharing all these things has given me.

One Day at a Time . . . .
I will learn to get honest and share with my sponsor and others in this program, all the things that are bothering me, whether it be food or other issues, so I can be relieved of the pain that all my secrets are causing me.

~ *Sharon*

PROGRESS

*"... I was taught that the way of progress
is neither swift nor easy."*
Marie Curie

I have always been the queen of quick fix, so if I wanted something to happen, it had to happen today if not yesterday. So coming into the program was very hard for me, in that for the first time I have had to realize that recovery is not an overnight thing. For a perfectionist like me, that has been a very hard lesson to learn, in that I don't have to have perfect recovery. My journey in this program has been an up and down one, with many slips along the way, and every time I have slipped, I have had to remember that I may think I'm a failure, but I'm only a failure if I fail to pick myself up. In the past if I made a mistake, I was a total and utter failure, but I know now that all I have to do each time is to pick myself up, dust myself off and start over.

The other thing I've learned in the program is that I also always need to remember where I came from, and when I look back, I can see the progress I have made. My self esteem is growing, and even though I still seem to slip back into the old character defects from time to time, they are nowhere near as bad as in the past. I am able to forgive people whom I thought I would never be able to forgive, and I make amends whenever the need arises, and as a result my relationships with people have improved dramatically.

One Day at a Time . . . .
May I remember that in this program, it is always progress and not perfection that counts.

~ *Sharon*

Meditation 52

CHILDLIKE

"Anxiety is the rust of life,
destroying its brightness and weakening its power.
A childlike and abiding trust in Providence
is its best preventive and remedy."
Tyron Edwards

Like so many of us in OA, I grew up as a little adult. My parents didn't know better - treating me like an adult seemed a good way to them of both showing love to me and making their difficult post-war life easier. Providence was something that intervened once in a while, and in ways that were weighty and important. God was there - but God had to attend to serious matters.

There was little room in God's and my parents' life for the seemingly unimportant details of a child's world. I had no trouble internalizing that message. I learned very soon that no-one was going to take care of my "little" problems and anxieties, that I had to shove them out of the way, and that I could do that very well by daydreaming, by making sure I was the little adult my parents were so proud of - and by eating.

The trouble was that there were times when these coping mechanisms didn't work seamlessly and those anxieties would break through. Panic attacks were the result, and dogged attempts to do more of the insanity: more retreating from the world, more "adult" behavior, more eating.

One of the things I'm learning in recovery is that paradoxically, in order to really grow up, I need to risk the vulnerability of being more childlike. I need to learn that my Higher Power is not too busy worrying about world peace to listen and deeply care about my little booboos. I need to, I WANT to develop an abiding trust that I am safe with and cared for by my Higher Power, like a baby in a mother's arms.

One Day at a Time . . . .
I let go of the rust of anxiety so that like a child, I may marvel at and participate in the brightness and wonder of God's world.

~ *Isabella*

Meditation 53

HUMILITY

"To the humble man, and to the humble man alone,
the sun is really a sun;
to the humble man, and to the humble man alone,
the sea is really a sea."
G.K. Chesterton

Before I started recovery, lack of clarity was all around me and within me. There was too much fear. I was unable to acknowledge: This is who I am, and this is what's going on, no more, and no less. I was afraid to name my husband's abusive behavior. I was afraid to name my complicity in it. I was afraid to name who I was and what I wanted and needed, and I was afraid to name the behavior of those around me who wanted me to fit into their mould. My husband was scared silly that one day the world would find out that we weren't the perfect family.

So I was not humble. I kept nurturing the fog that covered what was really going on. And boy, was I good at it. I kind of had an inkling that something wasn't right, so, semi-consciously, I made sure that my denial was watertight. I knew that if we pretended that we were a 100% perfect family, there might be suspicions. So I made sure I'd slip in a little problem here and there.

At one point, luckily, I allowed the bubble to burst. I started naming things, loud and clear. I named them to the police, I named them to my friends and family, I named them in my poetry. I started playing with another Twelve Step program.

But it took me another twelve years to name that I was an overeater. In those years I gained another 70 pounds (with some yoyo dieting thrown in, of course). Humbly admitting that, yes, really, I was an overeater, was the best thing I've done since ridding my family of my abusive spouse. I humbly admitted that I had been abusing myself with my eating behaviors. Now I can see clearly. (I can also see more clearly how wounded my ex-spouse is, making it easier for me to work on forgiving him).

One Day at a Time . . . .
I accept the gift of humility. I am not afraid anymore to look reality in the eye - and what I see is as right as the sun and the sea.

~ J.M.

ANIMAL TEACHERS

"For perhaps if the truth were known, we're all a little blind, a little deaf, a little handicapped, a little lonely, a little less than perfect. And if we can learn to appreciate and utilize the dog's full potential, we will, together, make it in this life on earth."
Charlotte Schwartz

So many times it feels that what we are being asked is too great. We can barely care for ourselves so how can we possibly reach out our hand to another? How many times have we cried out for someone else to please "handle it" because we just weren't able?

There are so many lessons that come by working with animals. They know nothing of dishonesty. They can't lie. They force us to be honest with ourselves. They depend on us completely, even when we feel we have nothing to give. And our reward? Unconditional love. There is something extra special about a rescued animal. It is as though they know that their life was in darkest peril and they have been saved. The gratitude shows in their eyes, their kisses of devotion, their entire being. Any kindness shown is rewarded. I think this is no different than a member of OA, especially the new members. Any kindness, and the gratitude flows. These newbies know they too have been saved. So perhaps the next time you feel you have nothing to offer, and that what you have been asked is too great, take a moment to reflect on the moment you were 'saved'. How did you feel the first time someone reached out to you?

One Day at a Time . . . .
I can use the memory of my first encounters with OA to find the strength to reach out one more time. I know the rewards will be infinite.

~ *Mary W.*

Meditation 55

STARTING OVER

"Vitality shows not only in the ability to persist,
but in the ability to start over."
F. Scott Fitzgerald

Before coming into this program I was, and probably still am to a certain extent, a perfectionist, so one of the things I really struggled with is being able make mistakes without feeling bad about myself. So when I came into the program, I decided that I was going to do this program perfectly, and proceeded to do just that. I followed a meal plan, lost weight and worked the Steps, and I really thought I had it made. But I hadn't counted on the fact that this is a disease, and it is both cunning, baffling and powerful. So when I had my first slip, I was devastated and felt a real failure.

Fortunately for me, with the help of many loving sponsors over the years, I have realized that I am not a failure if I slip, but I am only one if I fail to get up. This program has enabled me to learn that when I make a mistake, I am not that mistake, and that all I need to do is to pick myself up and start over. In the old days if I failed at a diet, I would never have been able to pick myself up so soon, and it would always be an excuse to carry on eating and start the diet again on Monday. Now I know that my abstinence can even start at the end of the day, rather than waiting till tomorrow, next week or even next month. I am slowly starting to let go of the guilt I feel when I slip, and am also learning to love myself even when I do flounder, because with the love and support I am given in this program, I know I can always start over.

One Day at a Time . . . .
I will remember that I can start afresh any time I like, and don't need to feel as if I have failed.

~ Sharon

Meditation 56

MEMORIES

*"Some memories are realities...
and are better than anything that can ever
happen to one again."*
Willa Cather

When one is young, the world is large and the thought of exploring it is exciting. Each year that we live we add to our memory chest ... and by middle age those memories are substantial. I have found as I have grown older that I remember more of the good things that have happened in my life than the bad. The good things seem to become sharper as time goes by ... and the bad seem less so. It's almost as though the memory has turned into a "feeling" rather than a specific event.

When I work on the Fourth and the Eighth Steps, my life flashes before me and, like one of those calendars from an old movie, time whizzes by and people who have been part of my life hurtle through space ... each triggering a memory.

Memories aren't made more poignant by time. One might think that a decade of recurring events might be remembered with more clarity than a year ... but I have found in the case of my own memories that it is the quality and intensity of time that produces the kind of memories Willa Cather talks about. A year or two or three, given the right circumstances, can produce the feelings we love our memories to trigger, more than those experienced during a lifetime. And a lifetime of memories can be dwindled into just moments.

One Day at a Time . . . .
I will cherish my memories ~ because I may never experience the reality of some of them again.

~ Mari

Meditation 57

FIGHTING

"And we have ceased fighting anything or anyone ..."
The Big Book

When one goes through life at full speed ahead as I have done, it's hard to really step back and look at one's life. Everything is happening too fast and each day seems to blend into the next and, before you know it, the next segment of life seems to take over.

When I began my Twelve Step recovery program, I found myself slowing down ... examining my life ... observing those around me ... and reflecting on my past. I began to know who I was and I didn't like one of the things I discovered: I was a fighter. I didn't accept people, places or things unless and until they met my expectations of what they should be. I tried to control situations that I should have walked away from. I clung to people I should have distanced myself from. I tried to manipulate things that were toxic to me, and make them un-toxic ... and, in the process, did myself great harm.

When I first read those words from the AABB, "We have ceased fighting anything or anyone," I felt it didn't apply to me ... because at that point, I hadn't categorized myself as a fighter. It took living and working the Steps to realize that. And it took living and working the Steps to take the action necessary to stop being a fighter.

Life is calmer now. Relationships are smoother. I sometimes miss the excitement of going through like as though I were on a roller coaster ... but I won't go back there. Serenity means too much to me. Fighting is something I have put away forever.

One Day at a Time . . . .
I will direct my thinking and doing to those things in my life which will contribute to a meaningful and pleasant journey.

~ *Mari*

RECOVERY

*"The people who get on in the world are the people
who get up and look for the circumstances they want."*
George Bernard Shaw

There was a time, not so long ago, that my life was much different than it is right now. My weight was skyrocketing because my eating compulsion was out of control. I couldn't walk very far without huffing and puffing. My lower back hurt because my stomach pulled my spine out of alignment. My feet and ankles were swollen, my knees hurt, just standing was painful. I was hot all the time because my fat acted as insulation, keeping my body temperature high. My wife was hounding me about losing the weight, my doctor was taking her side, and even the kids at my son's daycare were asking me why I was so big.

I didn't start the recovery process (and it IS a process!) until I got to the point where I was so uncomfortable with myself that I had to do something. It wasn't just that I was physically uncomfortable. I had to get past the comfort zone I had mentally and emotionally set up for myself; I had to get uncomfortable. I had to jump into the unknown, which was the most frightening thing I'd ever done.

Sitting around, moaning about my circumstances and suffering the physical consequences of my weight, didn't get me anywhere. It was only when I became ready to see my life change, mentally, emotionally AND physically, that I began the footwork of this Program. That was the key to the beginning of my recovery, the getting up and actually doing something about it. When I took that first step, the miracle began.

One Day at a Time . . . .
I will take the necessary steps to maintain my recovery from compulsive eating.

~ *J.A.R.*

PATIENCE

"There is no fruit which is not bitter
before it is ripe."
Publilius Syrus

There are some things in life you simply cannot rush. In the early stages of my disease, I went through life like a steam roller ... impatiently starting one project after another. If there was something in my life that depended on the actions of another for resolution, it was excruciating while waiting on the decision. As a result, sometimes decisions were forced. I have made many bad decisions because of lack of patience.

I have learned that sometimes we have to turn decisions over to others ... we have to let go and let others take control. We must wait it out and hope that our decision to let go was a good one. Many times it is. Sometimes it isn't.

I have become a very patient person ... and sometimes that is to my detriment. It can be hard to find a middle ground in the decision making process. Snap decisions aren't good. Neither are those we sit on forever.

One Day at a Time . . . .
I will patiently wait on my Higher Power to direct me ... to guide me ... and to help me with the decisions I must make.

~ Mari

ANONYMITY

"Don't walk behind me, I may not lead.
Don't walk in front of me, I may not follow.
Just walk beside me and be my friend."
Albert Camus

When I first joined OA, the tool and tradition of Anonymity seemed a little strange to me. What's wrong with people knowing what members do for work? I'm not ashamed of my career, why should I not talk about it? What's with this cult-like behavior around initials for names? And what do they mean by Anonymity being the spiritual foundation of recovery?

And then, bit by bit, it dawned on me. When we don't talk about our jobs, when we don't care about our last names, three very important things happen. First, we don't get distracted. Second, it makes us all equal. Third, it starts us on the road of leaving judgment behind. An Elizabeth is just an Elizabeth, whether she's a queen, a unemployed single mother or an actress. The equality that comes with that means that I am not more or less, not better or worse than you. This equality strengthens our unity. We are all in the same boat. And with this equality we can row in unity towards recovery.

One Day at a Time . . . .
I will remember that my fellow OA members are my equals, that I can let go of judgment, and that the freedom that comes with this helps me concentrate on recovery.

~ *Isabella*

EXPERIENCE

"I'm not afraid of storms . . .
for I'm learning how to sail my ship."
Louisa May Alcott

We spend our youth living and experiencing life. At some point our experiences become lessons. We who are compulsive eaters weren't aware of that when we began to eat out of control. Deep down, however, we were living and experiencing food issues. These issues later would become our lessons.

I am so grateful that the Twelve Steps made it possible for me to look at my past experiences and see the reality they presented. If not, I may have continued life in denial.

One Day at a Time . . . .
I will use the lessons I have learned to make the quality of my life better.

~ *Mari*

Meditation 62

A DISEASE?

"Doc! What do you mean-nothing! What? An incurable disease?
Doc, you're kidding me! You're trying to scare me into stopping!
What's that you say? You wish you were?
What are those tears in your eyes Doc?"
The Big Book

For a very long time I scoffed at those who said my overweight was because I had a disease. Yes, my body had doubled in size ... but it was because I ate more calories than my body burned. My doctor said so ... he didn't say I had a disease. His "treatment" was to tell me to go on a diet and join a gym. The diet lasted for a few months and I believe I used the gym about six or seven times. I know now without a single doubt that I have a disease ... a serious one. I know that it is incurable and that I will have to live with this disease for the rest of my life. Dieting made me fat. Somewhere along the way I didn't "get it."

One Day at a Time . . . .
I will resist thinking that being a compulsive eater is not a disease. I will aggressively and tenaciously do the footwork necessarily to combat it.

~ *Mari*

Meditation 63

MARCH

"March is the month of expectation, The things we do not know,
The 'Persons of Prognostication' are coming now."
Emily Dickinson

I am not sure whether it's because I'm embroiled at the moment in working the Steps I love so much ... or whether the beginnings of Springtime are beginning to happen ... but there is a feeling that I have that "something" is beginning. The long winters of life have taken their toll on me and when I experience this awesome feeling of hope I am grateful.

If there were doubts of the promises coming true, March overshadows them. If the Spring and Summer times of program loomed large in the distance, they are no longer. Just the smell of a new Spring morning is enough to know that hope for spiritual, emotional and physical wellness abounds.

One Day at a Time . . . .
I must forget the winters of my life and hold on to the promises of March ... and of my Twelve Step program.

~ *Mari*

Meditation 64

IMPULSIVENESS

"It is especially important not to make major life changes
when you are guided by emotions. If you are emotionally excited
(either in the positive or negative), wait until you calm down
before taking action."
Rabbi Zelig Pliskin

When I first entered into recovery this was one of my main character defects. Since my life was out of control and spiraling downward, I acted impulsively and rarely did any thinking before acting. I wouldn't even admit that my actions were impulsive. I would get so mad at people if they said I was impulsive.

Thanks to the Steps I now have the tools that allow me to look at my actions in a new light - one of sanity and direction. Step One allowed me to admit that I was addicted to food and my life was unmanageable. Step Two allowed me to let others in to help with my problem. I was not in this alone. Step Three gave me a loving G-d to take care of growing me up and helping me with all my problems. Step Four brought things into perspective, Step Five brought healing from the shame of making those irreparable mistakes. Steps Six and Seven helped me look at what in me could be prayed about and improved. They taught me that this character defect was just a character asset being used improperly. Steps Eight and Nine brought me back into a right relationship with others. Step Ten keeps me focused in the now not the "what if's" or "you need to's" of the past. Sanity seemed to be coming from that awareness of living in today. Step Eleven gave me the gift of a G-d that is ever caring and always present to help me if I just do my side of the work. As a result I have a spirit of love today rather than a spirit of resentment and self-pity. Step Twelve might be the most important one because it is what keeps me in recovery and living a productive life.

Today I do not have to react immediately to everything that happens, I can even go to my sponsor and ask for guidance. If my sponsor doesn't have experience in that area I have a world full of people like me to go to who understand what I am experiencing. The tools give me a way to handle life on life's terms.

One Day at a Time . . . .
I will choose to live and recover in the Twelve Steps.

~ Judith

SCARS

"Dwelling on the negative
simply contributes to its power."
Shirley MacLaine

I have lived most of my life filled with bitterness towards people, God and myself. My mind, soul, and body were consumed by hatred, self-pity, pain, hopelessness, and a complete sense of powerlessness. I focused my energy on reviewing my scars. I counted them, checked them, nurtured them, and flaunted them. They were proof of all the wrongs I'd endured. They were my source of energy. They were my identity. They were my badge of sorrow.

As I work my recovery, I am beginning to see everything from a new perspective. Gradually my head is lifted and my eyes are turned away from my once-beloved scars. The more I allow myself to accept that my powerlessness is not a prison of doom, the more I discover that it is my doorway to faith, surrender, and serenity.

My scars are still here. There is no magic potion to remove them. What is magical, however, is that I see them so differently. I find that I have a choice to make every day: I can cherish my scars as proof of the pain I have suffered, or I can be thankful for them as evidence of things I have survived. Scar tissue forms and creates a stronger, thicker skin in its place. I can either pick at it and make it bleed, or I can welcome the lessons and endurance it has built into my life.

One Day at a Time . . . .
I will choose to see my scars as proof of the difficulties I have survived. I will choose to appreciate them as evidence that God has brought me through suffering and has used all things to strengthen my faith in Him, my hope for tomorrow, and my serenity for today.

~ *Lisa*

PERSEVERANCE

"To keep a lamp burning we have to keep putting oil on it."
Mother Teresa

As a child I can still remember being terribly stubborn, and would even have a temper tantrum if I didn't want to do something. As I grew up, the trait of stubbornness remained, and it would be hard to get me to budge if I had decided I didn't want to do something. After coming into the program, I realized that stubbornness is actually a character defect of mine, and whilst I am praying to be relieved of it in its negative form, I also know that that same character defect in its positive form has helped me tremendously in the program, especially seeing my journey has been one which has been characterized with many slips along the way. But one of the things that I've never stopped doing is coming back, and I know that it is this very character defect of stubbornness, turned into perseverance, that has made me keep working at the program, even when it would be easier to just give up. So I have kept coming to meetings, and working the Steps and the tools even when I was struggling, because I know that it is only when I do that, I have a chance of recovery.

It has been said that this is a program of action, and so I repeat on a daily basis the actions that have brought recovery to thousands. Some days it is harder than others, especially when the willingness is not there, and on those days my old pattern of wanting to block out the feelings with food resurfaces. But I also know that when I use the tools and work the Steps, I can deal with the feelings without resorting to food, because my Higher Power will help me to get through the daily struggles when I turn them over to Him. So what I need to do on a daily basis is to ask for help from my Higher Power with my unmanageable life, instead of turning to food, and even on days where I'm struggling, I just need to keep putting one foot in front of the other and persevering with working the program.

One Day at a Time . . . .
I will persevere with working the program, so that I can recover from this disease of compulsive overeating and be restored to sanity on a daily basis.

~ *Sharon*

Meditation 67

FEELINGS

*"We honor ourselves and our friends
when we can tell them how we feel."*
Theodore Isaac Rubin

I always felt that if I didn't rob a bank or tell a lie that I was being honest. But when I began working the Twelve Steps, I learned what honesty really meant. Expressing my negative thoughts and feelings in the fast-moving world I found myself caused problems ... or I imagined it would. Therefore, I tried to pretend everything was wonderful and right and perfect.

One of the great blessings of my life is to know that I can now "feel" my emotions, express them to others who understand and somehow always feel better for having done so. Of course, I am still selective in choosing to whom I express my deepest feelings, but I do not pretend anymore that things are right when they're wrong. I do not gloss over bad things and make them good.

One Day at a Time . . . .
I feel my feelings and express them honestly, knowing that they're neither right nor wrong ... and I rejoice at the feeling of freedom I experience when I allow my emotions to flow from me.

~ Mari

THE ITSY BITSY SPIDER

"I must not fear. Fear is the mind-killer. Fear is the little-death that brings total obliteration. I will face my fear. I will permit it to pass over me and through me. And when it has gone past I will turn the inner eye to see its path. Where the fear has gone there will be nothing. Only I will remain."
Frank Herbert, Bene Gesserit Litany Against Fear, Dune

Recently in our meeting room we had a new 'member'. He was HUGE – well, we thought so, but who are we to judge? He was hairy, well maybe we're not perfect...He strode into the room like he owned the place. Well certainly he had as much right to be there as we all did.

We shrieked. Maybe it was those 8 hairy legs, maybe it's because he ran towards us like a streak of lightening, who knows.

Whatever he must have thought watching us giants leaping around the room we can only guess. He certainly seemed far more scared of us than we of him. It got me thinking of the insanity of some fears. After all what could this fragile little hairy thing do to me? He didn't have 8 giant slippers to hit ME on the head. I was the one with the power, yet, through my fear I was giving HIM the power he really didn't have. Instead of using the Power to give myself more confidence and behave rationally, I was wasting it away, GIVING it away. So many times I seem to repeat this same pattern. Of course some fears are rational, but most aren't.

This program gives ME the freedom to ask my Higher Power to take away my shortcomings. To relax and step back and make a fresh start. I need never be afraid again of irrational things, not if I truly work the program.

Itsy Bitsy Spider scuttled out of the meeting in rather a hurry that night. Was he trying to avoid participating in the 7th Tradition? Or did he have a genuine rational fear?

Maybe he was quite simply restored to sanity.

One Day at a Time . . . .
I will not be afraid ... I will not empower anything to cause me to be fearful.

~ *Marlene*

THE WHOLE PICTURE

"It should be pointed out that physical treatment
is but a small part of the picture."
Big Book of Alcoholics Anonymous

Looking around a gallery recently my friend and I were looking at a mosaic picture. We pondered on what we thought of it, and each of us had our own ideas. Then as we chatted a thought popped into my head. Now this doesn't happen often, so make the most of it.

The mosaic, of course, is made up of lots of tiny tiles, each one seemingly insignificant on its own. In fact if you found one in the street, you probably wouldn't look at it twice, never mind pick it up. Yet together with all the other tiny tiles, pieced together it forms an unusual and beautiful work of art. I don't expect that all of the tiles are perfect, but together they are whole. Together they appear to be as one in unison with each other.

Then came the second thought (yes, two in one day). Some days for me are pretty awful. I feel sick, or saddened. I turn on the TV and the news is all depressing stuff, and I think, where is HP while all this is happening? A few years ago, I lost my baby and nearly my own life. Where was my HP then? Losing my nephew at age 8 a few years later, I really doubted that any God of anyone's understanding could help me with a weight problem.

But today I see the wonderful days, the glowing wonderful comforting days that make life worthwhile. Who am I to say that this life I'm living is good or bad? Only HP has the 'whole mosaic' picture of Life. Not just my life, but my life touching another life. The events happening in the world – again, only HP sees the whole picture. He has the lid of the jigsaw puzzle with the main picture on it; we only have one piece, just like the tile.

After I lost the baby, HP helped the surgeons to heal me. I certainly didn't feel worthy; in fact I felt at the time that I wasn't even good enough to die. Yet HP has stuck by me and has given me so much. I doubt I'll ever know whose life or lives I have touched as a result of being saved, but it doesn't matter. HP knows. HP cares.

One Day at a Time . . . .
I must remember that you and I are one in the eyes of our Creator. Not one of us is less than, or more than each other. Together we are one. Together we watch HP work miracles in our lives. Together, we are perfect as long as we are under HP's direction. Mind boggling isn't it?

~ Marlene

Meditation 70

INSANITY

*"Insanity: Doing the same thing over and
over again and expecting different results."*
Albert Einstein (1879-1955)

Every day I get up and fight the fight of 'I am not good enough.' Nevertheless, I know I am who I am and that's what counts. I may never be what others expect me to be and many times those expectations were so great that I used to beat myself up over my failures.

That is the insanity of the compulsion that I am being healed from. I now have a mirror in my bedroom! I now can go without cleaning my house compulsively for those who visit me and now I can stand up for myself. Why? Because I love ME!

Program has given me back who I am. The person I love. My welfare comes first! Above all I am grateful for my sponsor, my Higher Power and this program. I am also grateful to the many men and women who have inspired my life because if it were not for all of these, I would still be in that insanity.

One Day at a Time . . . .
I will not require everyone's approval; I will not continually beat myself up when I expect more of myself than I can give; I will continue to love ME and all the good things about me.

~ *Roschips*

OVERWHELMED

"If we don't see a failure as a challenge to modify our approach,
but rather as a problem with ourselves, as a personality defect,
we will immediately feel overwhelmed."
Anthony Robbins

For much of my life I have felt rootless, insecure, lost, ineffectual, and scattered by the seemingly-unforgiving winds of chaos, confusion, change, and pain in my life. I certainly do not feel the sense of strength, stability, and solidity that I imagine I'd feel as a "firmly planted tree." Many of my choices and behaviors add to the storms and fruitlessness of my life…yet I consider again the Tree. The Tree bears its fruit "in its season". The Tree participates in the work of its Creator by patiently standing strong through the winds, snow, and barrenness of winter…and the Tree knows that winter is only for a Season. The Tree does not rail against God, nor demand that it produce fruit in its season of barrenness; rather, the Tree patiently rests and knows that Spring will return, as it always does and always will.

Working our program calls us to trust God – to believe that which we might not yet see, feel, or experience. We can choose to accept with Serenity the seasons of our lives.

One Day at a Time . . . .
I will choose to believe that my Higher Power is at work in me through every season of my life. I will remember that He brings the Life of Spring after the "death" of winter. In trusting Him, I will be stable and fruitful, even when I feel overwhelmed by the winds of life.

~ Lisa

LOVE

*"Being deeply loved by someone gives you strength,
While loving someone deeply gives you courage."*
Lao Tzu

As we explore our Twelve Step program and peel away the onion that is us, we find many parts of our self that we had never known before. Those parts have always been there ... we just weren't aware of the importance of them. Suddenly, as though it were a light bulb flashing, it hits us full in the face and we find our self seeing what our deepest need in life is.

It took practically a lifetime to realize that my deepest need was to love and to be loved. How could I have lived so long and not realized that before? I am grateful that the Twelve Step program gave me the ability to feel love, perhaps for the very first time. I am also grateful that this beautiful way of living also gave me the ability to give love.

One Day at a Time . . . .
I will keep my heart open for opportunities to love ... and quietly but expectantly to be loved.

~ Mari

Meditation 73

CONTROL

"How beautiful it is to do nothing, and then to rest afterward."
Spanish Proverb

I can count on one hand the times in my life in which I've been able to feel truly relaxed. Our disease is often driven by our efforts to control our lives: we labor to control our emotions, our relationships, our image, and our "masks" which we wear in a valiant effort to control how other people see and respond to us.

This effort to control ourselves and our lives is a ruthless taskmaster and a double-edged sword. It cuts like a knife through our very souls and requires that we forsake who we are in a misguided – and fruitless – attempt to be who we believe we "should be." I have worked so hard at trying to mold myself into an Acceptable Person that I have lost who I truly Am. All of my ceaseless efforts to mold myself into who I thought I Should Be have cost me my very sense of Self, and has been a painful eroding of my own Identity – it is a tragic self-imposed suicide of my Soul.

Like many of us, in order to enter recovery I had to come to the End of Myself and lose any sense of Control I had over my life. This was terrifying for me – I believed that even without a false sense of control, my life would implode and leave only ruined remnants in its place.

But I have not imploded. I have not been destroyed. With the crumbling of my masks and my frantic efforts to control everything, I have found a surprising sense of peace and safety – even in the midst of the chaos in my life. I am convinced that had God not brought me to the end of my own efforts, I would not be in a place in which I can hear His Voice. My ears would have remained deaf to His promise to never forsake me. Had He not firmly – yet gently – gotten my attention, my unsettled Mind would have continued to shout warnings and commands into my withered soul. Hitting Bottom is the best thing that could have happened to me, for I landed not in destruction, but in His eternal loving arms.

One Day at a Time . . . .
I will choose to cease my own striving and efforts to control my life. I will practice being still and knowing that my Higher Power is with me at all times, in every circumstance of my life.

~ *Lisa*

LOYALTY

*"To state the facts frankly is not to despair the future
nor indict the past. The prudent heir takes careful inventory
of his legacies and gives a faithful accounting to those whom
he owes an obligation of trust."*
John F. Kennedy

As is often typical of a compulsive overeater, the more I struggled to be loyal in my relationships with others, God, and myself, the more I found myself to be capable of loyalty only to food, shame, hiding my secrets, and despairing of any hope for recovery.

It was my shame that drove me to ineffectual attempts at loyalty – and shame breeds loyalty only to shame.

My relationships were in chaos, my mind was my enemy, and my emotions were tumultuous. When my pain overcame my attempts to be loyal, and my addiction to shame led to broken relationships, I had to finally admit that my efforts to control my life were fruitless – and would remain fruitless – unless I sought help.

When I entered recovery I feared the honesty and transparency that loyalty to self, others, God, and the truth would require of me. Among others who struggled with the same disease, however, I found that there can be no loyalty without taking a fearless inventory of my life and making a faithful accounting of my legacy. I found that I must surrender my loyalty to my disease, and place my loyalty in the hands of my Higher Power and in the open sharing of my reality. Only then could I cultivate loyalty in my relationships.

One Day at a Time . . . .
I will choose loyalty to healthy relationships with others, God, and myself – and I will resist the temptation to be loyal to my disease.

~ *Lisa*

SERENITY

"Serenity is not freedom from the storm,
but peace amid the storm."
Anonymous

Why is serenity so important to our recovery? Because darkness cannot exist where there is light! If we can maintain a serene state of mind as established through our faith in HP and the BB Promises, negative emotions and behavior will have no power over us. Stress, fear, compulsiveness, obsessiveness, resentment, guilt, shame, willfulness, doubt, distrust, greed and envy, have no power over a mind that is kept in serene repose. Serenity allows us to see situations clearly and make wise decisions. Most importantly, by maintaining a serene mind, we keep the door to our High Power open.

One Day at a Time . . . .
I will face each challenge with grace and serenity.

~ Rob R.

PERSPECTIVE

"Nothing is lost upon a man who is bent upon growth;
nothing wasted on one who is always preparing for life.
By keeping eyes, mind, and heart open to nature, men,
books, experience, and what he gathers, serves
him at unexpected moments, is unforeseen."
Hamilton Wright Mabie

I love to walk in the woods. The silent serenity of shadowed sunlight; the soft bounce of scattered needles under my feet; and the cool, clear air breathe peace into my soul.

I've long been fascinated by "nurse logs" – those aged, fallen pines who serve as fertile sustenance for younger, healthy trees.

When I look back at my life I see so much death. I see wasted years of hiding, lying, pretending – years of wrapping myself in my sickness. I have held my disease close to me. At first it seemed to bring safety, but I came to find that it was actually a death shroud. I wondered how any good could ever come from my years of pain.

After entering Recovery and working the Program, I have come to see that Nothing Is Wasted. Every sorrow, every injury, and every failure have brought me to this fruitful forest of New Life. Had I never suffered, I would never have found the Serenity that comes from choosing Gratitude. Had my life been easy, I would not have the appreciation I have gained for each new day. No one values safety, peace, and growth quite so profoundly as do those who have lived without them for so very long.

As I keep my mind, heart, and perspective focused on God, growth, and life, I find that my pain has become a nurse log; rich with all that is needed to bring life where once was only death.

One Day at a Time . . . .
I will remember that nothing is wasted. I will choose to appreciate the pain and wisdom of the God-given nurse log which feeds me with hope and peace.

~ Lisa V

EXAMPLE

*"Setting an example is not the main means of
influencing another, it is the only means."*
Albert Einstein

Program's philosophy dictates that we gain new members by attraction rather than promotion. We should be striving to become living embodiments of Program principles in order that we might attract and inspire those in need whom we may encounter in our daily lives - just as we were fortunate enough to find our way here because of the amazing effort, inspiration and example of the Program founders. Because of their blood, sweat and tears, Program has grown in leaps and bounds over the years . Now - its future growth rests with us. Are you prepared for this responsibility?

One Day at a Time . . . .
I will diligently work the tools of my program and be a shining example of recovery to others.

~ Rob R.

Meditation 78

COMMITMENT

"Shallow men believe in luck ~
Strong men believe in cause and effect."
Ralph Waldo Emerson

Abstinence did not happen for me until I made a commitment to it. I realized that I would have abstinence until something was a bit too uncomfortable for me to face or feel. Then I would have a slip. So it became a game for me. Was this event or circumstance enough to justify another slip? Sure, why not? That's the nature of the disease. Everything and anything was an excuse to eat.

It wasn't until I made a commitment to abstinence that I was forced to find my solutions in the Twelve Steps and really let go of my addiction. I'm grateful to my Higher Power that I hit the bottom I did. By accepting the truth about myself and my food addiction, I am now free to live in the solution.

One Day at a Time . . . .
I will renew my commitment by receiving the gift of abstinence and practicing my program to the best of my ability.

~ Christine S.

MAINTENANCE

"Another flaw in the human character is
that everybody wants to build and nobody
wants to do maintenance."
Kurt Vonnegut Jr.

With the help of our Higher Power, sponsors, and fellow Program members we have, completed the Twelve Steps, studied the Big Book, hit regular meetings, worked the loops, given service, etc ....and finally were able to achieve abstinence and reach our recovery goals! Reaching our goals is one thing, but now we must maintain what we've struggled so hard to achieve. As COE's, we never truly lose our addiction for food. Relapse is only a heartbeat away. Therefore, we must diligently strive to continue working the Program tools to guard this precious gift that we have earned.

One Day at a Time . . . .
I will diligently maintain the recovery goals I have worked so long and hard to achieve.

~ Rob R.

Meditation 80

PATIENCE

"Patience is the companion of wisdom."
Saint Augustine

Patience is an area that I have had some REAL problems with in the past. I had a tendency to want - what I want - NOW! That included recovery. Gaining recovery, as I would eventually realize, is not the same as earning a university credit. It is a process not an end result. You have to be willing to learn to do things in HP's time and manner rather than your own. What began to happen was - the more impatient I became - the more life tended to resist my efforts. It took a long time for me to realize this. Instead of calming down, I would get even more impatient and struggle even harder. Eventually, I would have a big meltdown and feel like a fool afterwards.

The end result was absolutely no different for having done this. It took time for me to muster the willingness to do things in HP's time and manner. But when I did - life became much more peaceful and things had a tendency to work themselves out - without all the dramatics.

One Day at a Time . . . .
I will learn to patiently and willingly do things in HP's time and manner.

~ Rob R.

PATIENCE

"Adopt the pace of nature; her secret is Patience."
Ralph Waldo Emerson

Today's topic is Patience! When I first came to Program, I didn't really know what abstinence was. I thought it was a diet. It turned out to be far more than I ever imagined. since beginning, I've gained abstinence, I've lost weight and my physical, mental, emotional and spiritual well-being has changed more than I ever thought possible. I've come so far ... beyond my wildest dreams ... yet, sometimes it feels like it's still not enough. I'll get in a row with my 12 year old daughter over some minor issue. She has a way of pushing my buttons which sends me into "finger pointing" and "lecture" mode - good intentions gone totally awry! She'll ultimately tune me out - and I'll walk away feeling like a bad parent. The guilt will set in and I'll deride myself for lacking patience and having bad judgment! But once I've calmed down - I'll remind myself that my intentions were good and - as in my food plan - progress not perfection has to apply to my parenting just as it does to my any other aspect of my recovery. This requires me to be patient with MYSELF as well as with others.

One Day at a Time . . . .
I will learn to be patient with myself as well as with others.

~ Rob R.

Meditation 82

PROGRESS, NOT PERFECTION

"The maxim 'Nothing but perfection'
may be spelled 'Paralysis.'"
Winston Churchill

I can't count the number of times I've heard the expression, "progress not perfection" from my sponsor and used it with my sponsees. We take little steps - one day at a time - which gradually leads to greater steps. Small successes eventually will lead to bigger successes. Often though, we want it all and we want it NOW!

Recovery is a process - not an end result. It requires a kind of a balancing act - if we try to juggle more balls than what we're capable of comfortably balancing - we will crash and this can lead to relapse. So rather than juggling five balls and crashing - it's better to juggle three really well and gradually work in a fourth or a fifth.

One Day at a Time . . . .
I will focus on making progress rather than trying to be perfect.

~ Rob R.

POSITIVE THINKING

"It takes but one positive when given
a chance to survive and thrive to overpower
an entire army of negative thoughts."
Robert H. Schuller

A positive attitude is crucial for a successful recovery. This summer, I was laid up with two torn tendons in my left ankle. This happened right at the start of my summer vacation. When it first happened, I was VERY dejected. This had to happen NOW!!! Just when my holidays are starting? (not that ANY time is a good time to receive an injury!). However, upon reflection it WAS good timing. I didn't have get myself to and from work. My daughter was finished school for the summer and was able to be home to assist me with day to day stuff. Plus I had just taken on some new OA service responsibilities and being home allowed me the time to really focus and internalize my new roles. Instead of looking at this as a negative - I think HP gave me an opportunity here to rest up and do some service at the same time. My daughter and I did some wonderful bonding as well. It would have been very easy just to turn negative and feel sorry for myself . But I simply would have made myself (and everyone around me) miserable during my six weeks of recovery. Instead, it's turned out to be a wonderful learning experience (not to mention it provided a good idea for this meditation topic!). Life's too short for cheap wHine, n'est past?

One Day at a Time . . . .
I will look at life from a positive point of view.

~ Rob R.

PRESENT MOMENT

*"Do not dwell in the past, do not
dream of the future, concentrate on
the present moment."*
Buddha

Staying focused, serene and receptive requires that we keep our attention placed in the present moment. If we allow our minds to be overly focused in the future (ie, on outcomes such as "what if's" or "if only's") or in the past (ie, past resentments, past embarrassments, or "would've beens, "could've beens") we allow ourselves to be subject to the psychological and emotional roller coaster ride that can go with these states. These meanderings into the past or present, color our judgment and play a major role in contributing to our eating disorder. Therefore, it is imperative that we practice staying in the moment in order to maintain a healthy recovery.

One Day at a Time . . . .
I will choose to live in the serenity of the present moment.

~ Rob R.

STEP THREE

"Tis only God may be had for the asking."
James Russell Lowell

When I first came to the program and looked at the Steps on the walls, my ego told me that I had Step Three already made. Of course, I had skipped right over Steps One and Two! I thought because I had experienced a religious experience many years ago, I didn't need to take Step Three. What I was to discover in the next few months on my wonderful journey in recovery is that spirituality and religion were two different things. That my religion today is part of my spirituality, but my spirituality is so much more.

I finally in Step One "Came." I kept coming to meetings and admitted my powerless and unmanageability. Then I "Came to." Through Step Two a portion of my sanity was restored and continues to be restored on a daily basis. Then at the point of taking Step Three I "Came To Believe." I realized that I had not turned my will and my life over to the care of God in the area of my compulsive overeating. That was a task yet to be done. And I offered myself to my God to do with as He would. I said the Third Step prayer which can be found in Alcoholic Anonymous on page 63, "God, I offer myself to Thee – to build with me and to do with me as Thou wilt. Relieve me of the bondage of self, that I may better do Thy will. Take away my difficulties, that victory over them may bear witness to those I would help of Thy Power, Thy Love, and Thy Way of life. May I do Thy will always!" I had taken the Third Step. I was moved into a new dimension in my spiritual life.

One Day at a Time . . . .
I will take Step Three this day, turning my will and life over to the care of my God.

~ *Carolyn*

FORGIVENESS

"To err is human, to forgive is divine."
Alexander Pope

When most of us first came into Program, we carried around a great deal of shame, guilt, and resentment. This made it very difficult for us to forgive ourselves, or others, for various past transgressions. We usually must rely on the forgiveness and support of other Program members before we come to a point of being able to truly forgive ourselves.

Coming to the point of self-forgiveness is a crucial step because once we have achieved it for ourselves, we can finally come to the stage of maturity to begin to forgive others. By offering true forgiveness we can begin to release the plethora of harbored resentments that have poisoned our souls and hindered our recovery for so many years.

One Day at a Time . . . .
I will work towards learning to forgive myself so that I might eventually learn to forgive others.

~ *Rob R.*

GRATITUDE

*"Gratitude is a fruit of a great civilization
- you do not find it among gross people!"*
Samuel Johnson

Samuel Johnson quote from the TOUR OF THE HEBRIDES could easily been writing about the Recovery Program. The attitude of gratitude is an absolutely crucial tool to a successful recovery. Gratitude is the measure of our appreciation for what we've been given. We in Program have SO much for which we should be thankful. We stand on the shoulders of giants - we are indebted to those members who've proceeded us in Program and handed down the tools, wisdom and resources - the bedrock upon which our recovery is based. We are indebted to our HP, our sponsors, to those who do service in innumerable ways at the Recovery Group and - to each other - for mutual love and support - and for our precious gift of recovery. Be grateful for each day - each moment.

One Day at a Time . . . .
I will continue to practice the attitude of gratitude. learn to forgive others.

~ Rob R.

ISOLATION

"Isolation is the sum total of wretchedness to a man."
Thomas Carlyle

This past summer I was forced to play "catch-up" at work in order to compensate for time lost while recovering from a serious ankle injury. As a result of my increased responsibilities, I stopped touching base with my friends and family – Program family included – except via the occasional email or phone call.

Fortunately, my friends and my sponsor are not the "shrinking violet" types. They took me to task about my whereabouts and well being. Because COE is a disease of isolation, it's extremely important to make sure we're making contact with others. We do this by using the tools of the Program: sharing with our support group, meetings, and sponsor.

When we don't allow ourselves to have regular, daily social outflow and personal accountability – even with a good excuse – we are more likely to relapse.

One Day at a Time . . . .
I will make a determined effort to connect and share with others.

~ Rob R.

DISLOYALTY

"Health is the greatest gift,
contentment the greatest wealth,
faithfulness the best relationship."
Buddah

I have a history of chaotic relationships filled with destructive drama and a lack of loyalty. For many years, however, I believed that I was in fact a very loyal friend – and that it was my friends who were disloyal to me.

I was an avid – even rabid – people-pleaser. I drove myself crazy trying to figure out what people wanted and how I could best provide that for them. Because I thought I knew what was best for everybody, I failed to truly listen to the people in my life. Instead, I tried to impose my will upon them…then I wondered why they didn't appreciate all of my efforts on "their" behalf. When they inevitably became frustrated with me, I was wounded by what I perceived to be their lack of loyalty to me.

Only recently in my recovery program have I come to learn that my efforts at people-pleasing were actually symptoms of my own disloyalty. I was failing to relate with people as they are – rather I was relating to them as I thought they "should be". That is perhaps the most egregious form of disloyalty…insisting that others be loyal to my concept of them and myself.

Now I am taking steps to honestly listen to people and to relate with them as they are – and as I truly am. I am no longer hiding behind food. In order to be loyal in my relationships, I must be loyal to the 'Truth of Reality.' Only then can we share the joy of faithful relationships.

One Day at a Time . . . .
I will practice listening to the people in my life and I will honor them as they are.
Each day I can choose to be loyal, rather than critical or people-pleasing.

~ *Lisa*

WORDS

"Handle them carefully ...
for words have more power than atom bombs."
Pearl Strachan Hurd

A friend wrote to me tonight about the "healing power of words" I began to think about that and she was right. Words can truly heal. I thought back to times in my life when the right word at the right time by the right person made an enormous difference in my life. I also thought of the times when words devastated me.

Many times I get busy and don't think about what I'm going to say and words come out and in my "busyness" of the moment, I don't realize they could have a double meaning. It is afterwards ... many times days afterwards .... that I realize my choice of words were inappropriate. We speak and listen to tens of millions of words in our lifetime and, perhaps, we need to weigh the words we use more carefully. I hope, however, that I don't ever find myself saying words to others I don't mean or out of fear restrict words that need to be said.

Although this British politician of the 1930s, Pearl Strachan Hurd, said that words have more power than atom bombs, there is something that I find even more powerful. Silence. Silence when there should be words can hurt. Silence when someone should have the courage to speak harms. I tend to think of silence as the ultimate insult. And yet some of the most beautiful words ever spoken to me were the silent ones.

One Day at a Time . . . .
Let me choose my words carefully but not so carefully that I become callous. Let me use words to heal and not hurt; to make things better and not worse; to express feelings, even negative feelings to and about others, kindly ... courageously ... carefully.

~ Mari

HAPPINESS

"Happiness is an achievement brought about by inner productiveness.
People succeed at being happy by building a liking for themselves."
Erich Fromm

It has been said that if one of us ever treated another human being the way we treated ourselves, we would be liable for criminal charges. I did not treat myself as a friend, someone I loved; I constantly fed into my unhappiness.

Alcoholics Anonymous co-founder Bill W. was asked, shortly before he died, to sum up the program in the lowest common denominator. He replied, "Get right with yourself, with God, then with your neighbor." Therefore, it stands to reason that I must start making friends with myself. I must treat myself with love and dignity, and the result will be happiness. To be happy, joyous, and free is the by-product of obedience to the program.

One Day at a Time . . . .
Am I going to try being happy?
Am I going to make friends with myself?
If not today, when?

~ Jeremiah

Meditation 92

LOVE

"There is only one happiness in life ... to love and be loved."
George Sand

It took me many, many years to really and truly discover what turned out to be something that I have yearned for all of my life. That "something" was love ~ both the ability to love and to accept love.

As a child, I felt I had to achieve to be loved and, in the process of achieving, lost a great deal of my childhood. This carried over to adulthood and thus began the years of doing what was expected of me (or so I thought) in order to be loved, valued and respected.

Recovery has taught me so much about myself and about love. One of the greatest truths I have learned about myself and my ability to love is that for me to love someone, it is not necessary that they love me back. My loving someone else never depends on their loving me ... but how wonderful it is when they do.

One Day at a Time . . . .
Let me realize that love is something that just happens ... I can't make it happen ... and I can't stop it from happening.

~ Mari

THE FUTURE

"When I look into the future, it's so bright it burns my eyes."
Oprah Winfrey

I receive the gift of abstinence one day at a time. I am relieved from the obsession to eat one day at a time. With the help of my Higher Power, I can live life on life's terms... one day at a time.

As my recovery builds and builds, I start to imagine all the possibilities for my life. Things I never had the confidence or emotional stability to pursue are options for me. Now that I am free from the despair and self-destruction of overeating, there is space to actualize new adventures. But before I become overwhelmed or grandiose in my thinking, the Program gently reminds me that it is STILL just one day a time.

One Day at a Time . . . .
I will work my program so that I have a future.

~ *Christine S.*

COMMITMENT

"Shallow men believe in luck ~
Strong men believe in cause and effect."
Ralph Waldo Emerson

Abstinence did not happen for me until I made a commitment to it. I realized that I would have abstinence until something was a bit too uncomfortable for me to face or feel. Then I would have a slip. So it became a game for me. Was this event or circumstance enough to justify another slip? Sure, why not? That's the nature of the disease. Everything and anything was an excuse to eat.

It wasn't until I made a commitment to abstinence that I was forced to find my solutions in the Twelve Steps and really let go of my addiction. I'm grateful to my Higher Power that I hit the bottom I did. By accepting the truth about myself and my food addiction, I am now free to live in the solution.

One Day at a Time . . . .
I will renew my commitment by receiving the gift of abstinence and practicing my program to the best of my ability.

~ Christine S.

ACCEPTANCE

"Until you make peace with who you are,
you will never be content with what you have."
Doris Mortman

Through abstinence and recovery, I can begin to accept myself. I can pay attention to my likes and my dislikes as I continue to grow and learn about me. Learning about myself is a new adventure. There are so many layers that have been hidden under years of food abuse and weight obsession. Exploring and discovering the new me requires a lot of acceptance. There are parts of me that I do not like, and there are also wonderful surprises. By accepting all parts of myself, I am honoring my Higher Power and demonstrating spiritual recovery.

One Day at a Time . . . .
I will accept myself. By learning to accept myself, I will find myself growing in my acceptance of others.

~ *Christine S.*

Meditation 96

COURAGE

*"It takes a lot of courage
to show your dreams to someone else."*
Erma Bombeck

I remember first starting my Twelve Step program. I had lots of expectations and dreams, but I couldn't talk to anyone about them. I thought my dreams were stupid and that nobody there really cared about who I was or what I wanted to achieve.

This is a big problem with all of us compulsive overeaters. We all have hopes and dreams of losing our impulse to eat all the time, and of losing our excess weight. Thinking we're not worth anyone's time keeps us strong in our addiction.

As we work through the Steps and learn to trust our new family of choice, we get the courage to begin to open up and share our dreams and hopes. We all find our hidden courage by praying and trusting our Higher Power. We find the courage to tell people about ourselves and trust that nobody will put us down for our past or for the future we dream of achieving. Our dreams have no time limit; they don't have to happen immediately. They may happen immediately, or it may take a long time of struggling, but as long as we have hope and courage, they will become a reality in Higher Power's time.

One Day at a Time . . . .
I remember that we learn that, together, things become much easier. As we share our experience, strength and dreams with others, they will help us learn how we can work with a special program and plan. With Higher Power and our recovery friends, our courage grows stronger, and we find we can and will succeed.

~ *Jeanette*

HIGHER POWER

"If you spend all your time looking for Him,
you might miss Her when She shows up."
Neale Donald Walsch

Our program of recovery teaches us that we each must lean on a Higher Power. This Higher Power is also known as "the God of my understanding." There is nothing in this Twelve Step program of ours that says that my Higher Power must be the same as your Higher Power. For some, the Higher Power in their life is a deity. The program itself, or a weekly meeting, might be the Higher Power for someone else. It doesn't matter what or who each person has for a Higher Power.

Recovery is possible for everyone. Those who believe in one God can come together with those who believe in many Gods, or maybe no God at all. The atheist has just as much chance of recovery as a very religious person. The beauty of this program is that it works for everybody, regardless of their approach to the spiritual aspect. That is why it is imperative that we accept each other's ideas of a Higher Power. What works for one individual might not work for another. But one thing is sure ... the program that works if you work it, regardless of which Higher Power you decide on.

One Day at a Time . . . .
I will work my program with my Higher Power, the God of my understanding, and allow others to work their program with the God of their understanding.

~ Jeff

WILLINGNESS

"I cannot change what I am unwilling to face."
James Baldwin

Before I found this program I was locked in a battle with myself. I knew I was eating too much, and I couldn't help myself. I tried to control my eating, and for a while, I was able to keep the upper hand. Then something would happen in my life, and I'd lose that control.

I couldn't face the fact that I was a compulsive eater. I couldn't bear to think that I had a disease that kept me in bondage to food. So during the time I was in denial about my eating, I continued sinking deeper into my disease of compulsion. I sought comfort in food, and did some serious damage to my body, to my self-esteem, and to my relationships.

It was only after I hit bottom that I realized that I had to face the facts. I had a disease that had me in a death grip, and there wasn't one thing I could do about it. When I found this program, I found hope. I discovered a Higher Power who could help me do what I'd never been able to do before. I slowly began to see the changes I'd tried all my life to effect on my own. But it didn't happen until I became willing to face the truth, until I became willing to ask God for help.

One Day at a Time . . . .
I am willing to face my disease
and let my Higher Power help me overcome it.

~ *Jeff*

FEELINGS

"Few are those who see with their own eyes
and feel with their own hearts."
Albert Einstein

Before working the Twelve Step program, one reason I used to overeat was that I couldn't manage my feelings. My feelings were overwhelming and incapacitating to me. I would also overreact to feelings and this would make them truly more than I could handle. So I would then overeat to make the feelings stop. I would stuff myself, to stuff them down!

In working the Twelve Step program, I got a chance to work through past hurts and resentments that intensified my feelings. I learned to feel my feelings, just as they are, and how to stop overreacting to them. I learned to sort through messages my family gave me about feelings, that it's not okay to have or feel or express them. I learned to decide what is true for me, today, about feelings. I also worked through my codependency issues and learned how to communicate feelings in an appropriate, effective and loving way.

Now feelings are a part of my life and not something overwhelming and incapacitating. In fact, they have become something beautiful that enrich my life and give it color and texture and even pleasure.

One Day at a Time . . . .
I honor the blessing of having my feelings returned to me. I enjoy them, and I respect my feelings and those of others. I thank my Higher Power for this wonderful gift.

~ *Lynne*

Meditation 100

AGING

"Those who love deeply never grow old;
they may die of old age, but they die young."
Benjamin Franklin

I used to be afraid of getting older. I was also afraid to become friends with older people, because I would come to love them and then they would die. I could not handle unpleasant feelings (other than if I overate to stop feeling them) because the feeling of unpleasantness would totally devastate me.

In working the Twelve Step program, my Higher Power has brought me great recovery in this area ... I am now able to handle the grief and sorrow that come up when I allow myself to get to know and love older people and then they die. I am now free in this area! I get to enjoy the wisdom and beauty that they have to share, from all their life experiences, and from the beautiful people they are!

Another beautiful gift from my Higher Power came when I started relating to older people again. When the first one died, it really threw me, and I was very sad. But I got up the next day and had a great spiritual awakening: this person was missing and that was sad, but I looked around and saw all the other wonderful people still there in my life, with whom I got to share another day! Life suddenly became much more precious to me ... to have one more day to be with and share with someone who touches my soul!

One Day at a Time . . . .
I enjoy myself as I become older. I allow myself to enjoy friendships with those who are older than me. I thank my Higher Power for every day and every moment of precious life!

~ *Lynne*

Meditation 101

MEDITATION

"When you are with others, be with them wholeheartedly.
But when you are by yourself, be alone with God."
Paramahansa Yogananda

When I pray to the God of my understanding, I am able to share my thoughts, to vent my feelings, to express my gratitude. But it isn't enough for me to speak to God. I also need to listen. That's where meditation comes in.

Sometimes I select a passage from program literature to meditate on. I read the passage, and then sit quietly and allow my Higher Power to help me make connections between what I've read and the life I'm leading.

Other times, I will pick a word or phrase, like "love" or "peace" and repeat it, over and over, in my mind. I allow myself to align with the feeling of that word.

I may picture a serene place, and mentally go there, to rest and regroup from the pressures of the day.

I also will sometimes sit quietly, "in the silence," as the Quakers say. I listen to my breath moving in and out of my body, and I allow my Higher Power to speak to my heart.

No matter which meditation practice I select, the important thing for me is to do it faithfully, every day, and to totally give myself to it. I figure, if God can give to me, then I can give a little of myself back to the One who has blessed me with this program.

One Day at a Time . . . .
I will spend some quiet time alone with my Higher Power, and listen to that still, small voice within.

~ *Jeff*

RECOVERY

"I'm sick and tired of being sick and tired."
Fannie Lou Hamer

I used to get so disgusted with myself. I was sick and tired of trying to lose weight because I always failed. I had lost weight several times but I would still feel ugly, fat and unacceptable to everybody else. The sickness and tiredness remained because I had not changed anything inside my head, just my body size! My past was still there and it continued to haunt me, and I was filled with the guilt and shame of the past.

A friend told me about this great program where I could discover what was really making me sick and how I could recover. She said, "You will have someone with you to help continually 24 hours a day, seven days a week."

"How can this be?" I asked.

She said, "Well, this wonderful program helps you recover by teaching you what really has been bothering you. Maybe it's things you are sorry you did or didn't do in the past, people you've hurt or who have hurt you."

"Do I need to leave home or pay a lot of money?" I asked.

She said, "No. You work it at home, at work and everywhere you go. The cost is nothing, except a desire to stop eating compulsively. Your continual help is your Higher Power and he never goes to sleep, he listens and helps you when you ask for his help."

"Wow, you mean I don't have to be sick and tired anymore?"

"That's right and all it takes is Twelve small but important Steps, a lot of love, hugs, acceptance, trust and sincere honesty. It's easy and works as long as you work it."

One Day at a Time . . . .
I don't need to be sick and tired of myself any more. I have a wonderful program with a lot of tools, friends and my Higher Power to help me. I can achieve recovery one day at a time ... it's a matter of progress, not perfection.

~ *Jeanette*

Meditation 103

NORMALITY

"Normality is in the eye of the beholder."
Anonymous

I don't always know what "normal" is. I'm learning that my disease keeps me from having a normal relationship with food, but I also know that there are times when my feelings and thoughts are due to normal circumstances. I might not feel well physically, I could be fatigued from a demanding task, or I might simply be having an off day. There are normal reactions to these situations and I can feel them. Not everything is caused by my disease!

However, the way I handle these kinds of experiences can very much be affected by my disease. On those bad days, I don't have to make important decisions and I don't have to filter experiences through these thoughts and feelings. I can postpone things until I'm on a more even keel and, just for today, take care of myself and do the next right thing.

One Day at a Time . . . .
I am grateful for the ways I am "normal" and thank God for the knowledge that I don't have to let my disease make me think everything about me is "sick." Let me simply be still on those uneven days and know that God is God and He is there.

~ *Sandee S.*

FEARLESS

"As we felt new power flow in, as we enjoyed peace of mind,
as we discovered we could face life successfully,
as we became conscious of His presence,
we began to lose our fear of today, tomorrow or the hereafter."
The Big Book

I refuse to be frightened to the point of missing the opportunities my Higher Power has provided for me. I will no longer hurt myself by avoiding being hurt. When I avoid risks because I'm afraid the outcome will be painful, I am stuck – not safe.

By working my program I have discovered that many times when I'm engulfed in fear, I am not trusting my Higher Power. The more I practice the Serenity Prayer, the more serene I become. From my new perspective I can see numerous occasions in which my Higher Power did things for me which I could not do by myself. Possibly a doomed relationship I couldn't end, and my Higher Power ended for me by having the other person walk away. Maybe a financial crisis that was suddenly alleviated from an unexpected source. How about the ability to detach from a loved one's issues without feeling responsible for "fixing" everything or taking their struggles personally. In order to surrender my control over these things, I choose to be fearless in trusting my Higher Power.

Today I will be grateful even for the painful times because sometimes they are the lesser of two hurts: the easiest being when God steps in to protect me, and the hardest being when my will prevents me from letting go of something that isn't good for me.

One Day at a Time . . . .
I will trust my Higher Power and know that where I am today is right where I need to be. I don't have to have all the answers.

~ *Sandee S.*

SUCCESS

"I have begun everything with the idea that I could succeed,
and I never had much patience with the multitudes
of people who are always ready to explain why one
cannot succeed. I have always had a high regard
for the man who could tell me how to succeed."
Booker T. Washington

The Big Book of Alcoholics Anonymous is my main source of inspiration when it comes to recovery issues. It's proven to be a valuable asset to my program.

I've learned from the Big Book that recovery from any compulsive disease is possible. We are given Twelve Steps to follow, and told that if we do what our predecessors did, then we WILL recover. We have to be willing to go to any length to succeed. We have to do the footwork. The people who don't succeed in this program are the ones who don't avail themselves of all the help that's available to them. They don't read the literature, they don't go to meetings, they don't do service ... they don't do what those who have gone before have done. So they wallow in their disease instead of recovering.

There's a reason why we're told, "Rarely have we seen a person fail who has thoroughly followed our path." That means the program works IF you work it. Those who don't work the program don't recover. That's a pretty powerful statement, but it's true, and for some reason, a lot of compulsive people just don't get it. They keep doing the same old things and getting the same old results. In the process, they remain fully in the grip of their disease. Sure, recovery is a miracle, but it won't fall into your lap. You need to work for it, and by the grace of the God of your understanding, you'll receive the miracle.

One Day at a Time . . . .
I remember that it's not enough to talk the talk; I need to walk the walk if I want to recover.

~ Jeff

PAIN

*"Your pain is the breaking of the shell
that encloses your understanding."*
Kahlil Gibran

How many of us in recovery thought we were in pain before seeking help, only to find that recovery itself was even more painful? I know that is how my progress in Twelve Step recovery from compulsive eating has been. Fortunately, pain in recovery doesn't break my spirit the way pain did before I started working the Twelve Steps. As I work my recovery, the walls that I had built for protection around my inner-spirit are being slowly broken down and moved away.

This changing and renewing of my inner-self is extremely painful at times. If I didn't have the tools of the program, (such as sponsorship, a food plan, working the Steps, and conscious contact with my Higher Power) there would be no understanding born out of my pain. Before recovery, the pain would start to fill my inner-shell with self-pity, self-disgust and despair. Now when the pain comes to me, I've slowly learned to embrace it and hold it close to my heart. This new pain means that I will be shown by my Higher Power the insight and understanding needed for me to continue this daily recovery process. Does this mean I am filled with joy as I see the pain coming? Absolutely not! This means that I now have a power greater than myself to shield me from the pain that would break me. After feeling the pain needed to give me understanding, I am given healing to continue my journey.

One Day at a Time . . . .
I will seek to feel and face the pain on this journey, knowing that understanding and healing will follow through my Higher Power's hand.

~ *Ohitika*

FORGIVENESS

"Forgiving is not forgetting; it's letting go of the hurt."
Mary McCleod Bethune

When I first came into the program, I was so fired up with anger and resentment that I had no space for any other emotions. After all, I had the food which would anesthetize me against any emotions I didn't want to feel. I was angry with God for all the trauma and losses that had happened to me in my life. I blamed my mother for not being the kind of mother I wanted, which was, of course, why I ate. But the person towards whom I felt the most anger and resentment was my ex-husband, who never financially supported my children, making my financial burden and my present husband's very heavy. What made it worse was that he was good to the children and they thought he was great because they would have fun with him on a weekend, while we had all the financial responsibility and resulting worry.

But when I came to Step Eight, my sponsor gently reminded me that I needed to forgive the people towards whom I felt the most anger, namely my mother and my ex-husband. My mother had passed away and so I had to write a long letter to her, forgiving her for not being the person I wanted her to be and also making amends to her for my part in it all. I realize now that she did the best she knew how, just as I have done with my children, and I have been able to forgive her with love. When it came to forgiving my ex-husband, I knew that I wasn't able forgive him in person, but I was able to write a letter to him which I never sent. In it, I forgave him for being the irresponsible person that he is. It was like a weight had been lifted from my shoulders. When my younger daughter had her 21st birthday, I could be there for her and not spoil it as I had done before, and in fact, I could be almost friendly to her father. As a result, the relationship with all my children has improved a hundredfold, but more importantly, I'm a much better person for it.

One Day at a Time . . . .
I will forgive the people who have harmed me, let them go with love, and entrust them to their Higher Power.

~ *Sharon*

UNCONDITIONAL LOVE

"The ultimate lesson all of us have to learn is unconditional love,
which includes not only others but ourselves as well."
Elisabeth Kubler-Ross

I don't think I knew what unconditional love was before I came into the program. After all, I had always felt that my mother had only loved and accepted me conditionally, and that in order for me to receive approval and love from her, I had to be the best at everything I did. I had to be at the top of the class, win prizes for ballet and in general be a credit to her, so that she could bask in the reflected limelight. Perhaps that was only my perception. But as a result, I wrote a script for myself that, in order to be loved, accepted and loveable, I had to excel at everything. I became an overachiever academically, I had to be the best wife, best mother, best cook, in short, the best everything. No wonder I had to eat to cope with all this self-inflicted pressure.

The unconditional love and acceptance I received when I first came into these program rooms was something I had never experienced before. "Let us love you until you can learn to love yourself," they said. This was something totally foreign to me. How could I be loveable when I was fat and bloated? How could they love me when I hated myself for all the secret eating that caused me to feel totally miserable? But love me they did, and that was the beginning of my healing. At one stage fairly early in my recovery, one of my daughters accused me of being so busy going to meetings and doing courses and learning to love myself, that I was too busy to love them. How wrong she was! It was only when I had learned enough self- love and approval of myself, exactly as I was, that I was able to love all my children fully and unconditionally.

I am now able to love and accept all my children exactly as they are. None of them are perfect, as I am not, but they are special in their own right, and I love them for who they are and not for anything they do or don't do.

One Day at a Time . . . .
I practice being warm and accepting of all those I love,
as I accept and love myself for being who I am today - a child of God.

~ *Sharon*

Meditation 109

HAPPINESS

"The greatest happiness you can have
is knowing that you do not necessarily require happiness."
William Saroyan

How many times during my life have I said that all I want is "just to be happy." We are told early on that our legacy is "life, liberty and the pursuit of happiness." Did you notice that our forefathers used the word "pursuit?" How very wise they were.

Happiness is not automatic. Life is difficult and it's supposed to be that way. If we expect happiness and we expect life to be easy, at some point in time we are going to be very disappointed. I thought eating food made me happy and it did ... for a short time. There were other temporary compulsions in my life that made me think I was happy ~ but again for only a short time.

As I began to work the Steps, I began to desire something other than happiness. I found myself yearning for serenity ... and I found it. The way I found it was by not expecting the world and everyone in it to make me happy. I learned that life was more of an adventure than a bowl of cherries. I learned that the more I expected from people, places and things, the more disappointed I was ... and the more disappointed I became, the less happy I was.

One Day at a Time . . . .
I will not require happiness. But when I least expect it .... happiness will find me.

~ Mari

THE PRESENT MOMENT

*"How simple it is to see that we can only be happy now,
and there will never be a time when it is not now."*
Gerald Jampolsky

During my many years of life as an compulsive eater, I thought happiness was something that was the privilege of other people. I could not imagine that happiness would be a part of my life. All I really wanted was to lose weight.

My issues with food and weight colored everything else. I always thought the biggest weight I carried was physical in nature. When I accepted the fact that I have a disease, and the weight I carried was physical, emotional and spiritual, my life began to change immeasurably. As I took the Steps to recovery, I began to experience healing on all three levels. I began to see life differently, and to live life in a whole new way.

Before recovery, I could not see the precious moment of the present. My eyes were focused on regret of the past, and fear of the future. I totally missed the complete joy of each present moment. Recovery has helped me to clear up weight I carried from my past, and to eliminate my fear of the future; replacing fear with faith. As I live in recovery, I can choose to be present in each moment, and enjoy the wonder and delight that is the gift of life.

One Day at a Time . . . .
I choose to live in the present moment ... and to embrace the happiness found there.

~ Cate

RELIGION

Religion is for people who don't want to go to hell.
Program is for people who have already been there.
Unknown

I was religious when I came into program and I was ready and willing to tell everyone what the "true" faith was. I went to church every Sunday. I was a religion teacher. I knew it all.

The truth is I didn't know ANYTHING. It didn't take long for me to begin to question my own religiosity. In fact, it began at Steps Two and Three. Before long, I wondered if there was a God at all. If there was, is God a He, a She or an It? Then I decided, yes there was a God, but did He/She/It care about me?

The real truth is God is who God needs to be to work through me. There's no right or wrong answer to my questions. What I DO know is that God loves me just the way I am.

The greatest gift my Higher Power gave me came on the day I looked up to "heaven" and told God, "I don't believe in You!" And that still, quiet voice inside of me asked, "Then to Whom are you speaking?"

One Day at a Time . . . .
I don't have to have theological "proof" that there is a Power greater than myself. I just need to believe.

~ *Debbie*

COMPULSIONS

*"Compulsive urges to overeat, gorge or purge
are inadequate coping mechanisms.
Compulsion is loss of control
and continuation of the behavior
despite the consequences."*
Gloria Arenson

Compulsive overeating is not a moral dilemma. It is not about "right" or "wrong." It is not a black-and-white situation. I learned at a pre-verbal stage that compulsive overeating is a coping mechanism. When I cried to be held, I was fed. When I cried because I was wet, I was fed. When I cried because I was in pain, I was fed. When life was good, I was fed. Is it any wonder I came to reach for food when life was happening around me?

This program teaches me better ways to cope with life. Instead of reacting to life, I have learned through the Steps how to take action. I did not choose this disease, but I do choose recovery. Through the help of my Higher Power, the program, and other program members I can recover. I can live in the solution one day at a time and one meal at a time.

One Day at a Time . . . .
I will have a program. I choose recovery, health, love and life.

~ Sarah H.

Meditation 113

BIRTHRIGHT

*"I've continued to recognize the power individuals
have to change virtually anything and everything in their lives in an instant. I've
learned that the resources we need to turn our dreams into reality are within us,
merely waiting for the day when we decide to wake up and claim our birthright."*
Anthony Robbins

I have divine origins because I am part of my Higher Power. Whether I see my Higher Power as a male, female or neither; no matter if I experience my Higher Power as a Heavenly Parent, a Divine Friend, or a Great Spirit; whether I find my Higher Power in a temple, in the mountains, or in my child's eyes ... I am connected to something greater than myself, my problems, and my fears. The who, what, where, when, and how of my Higher Power are not important. I don't have to completely understand HP because my HP understands me.

I have been endowed with all the things I need to be successful in recovery and in life. All I have to do is step up and claim them. I have intellect, I have emotion, and I have a spirit. All of those things have a direct line to my Higher Power. What I can't yet access is given to me as a gift when I claim my divine birthright by simply saying, "I can't. You can. I think I'll let You." What greater power is there than to give our power to our Higher Power? Knowing when I can't do it alone is a gift!

One Day at a Time . . . .
*I will remember I come from royalty. I will remember my divine birthright and step
up to claim it. Today I will not sell my divine birthright for a mess of pottage.*

~ Sandee

LONELINESS

"Feeling our loneliness magnifies it.
Understanding our loneliness can open doors into our self-awareness,
which we long for and need."
Anthony Robbins

Before I found my Twelve Step program, I felt so lonely. I was stuck in total isolation and the feeling of loneliness felt one hundred times worse. The isolation and loneliness caused me to continually eat ... and so I'd isolate more. What a vicious cycle!

When I found my recovery program, I still wanted to isolate. When going to meetings, I wanted the seat with nobody around it. I didn't want to open my mouth to share or talk, even after the meeting. I kept coming back even though I felt alone, because I heard familiar things that really interested me. I eventually saw that most of the people in the room felt the same loneliness I did. I began to understand why I felt so lonely.

When I understood that my compulsive eating was causing me to isolate and be more lonely, a big burden was lifted off my shoulders. I finally felt some hope! Then I found that there were many other doors in the past that I should open and become more aware of. These past happenings were what started and fueled this disease of compulsive eating. I wanted to know but I was also afraid to find out.

The similarities, kindness and love I found in the rooms made it easier to look at my past. Understanding that I was not the total reason for my loneliness, I began making amends. I needed to forgive others who had harmed me and those I had harmed. I felt lighter and more self aware, and confidence began to emerge.

One Day at a Time . . . .
I will remember that it's okay and good to feel my feelings but they don't have to rule my life. I don't have to let loneliness magnify, causing me to eat uncontrollably to solve the problem. I've learned to turn things over to my Higher Power and to let them go. Looking back is the key to my self-awareness and my recovery.

~ *Jeanette*

UNDERSTANDING

"If you would understand him, listen not to what he says,
but rather what he does not say."
Kahlil Gibran

Early on in my recovery I became aware that understanding myself and my disease was going to be a tool of success. For many years I lived day after day in my addiction, bemoaning it, suffering in it, struggling against it, and adopting the world view of my condition. I came to believe that losing weight was the answer to all my problems ... if I could stick to a diet. Because I couldn't, the thoughts of worthlessness, ignorance, shame and guilt were repeatedly reinforced.

In working the Steps, the idea of recovery through understanding myself was born. Through knowledge of my Higher Power, and by His guidance, the understanding of my past and my present have given me keys to freedom from compulsive overeating. I welcome working the Steps because they have opened doors of my heart to mend the past and receive hope for the future. Understanding who I am and why I'm like I am, allows me to be abstinent and to develop new ways of coping with the stresses of life. Understanding the disease frees me from guilt and shame and releases self-acceptance.

One Day at a Time . . . .
I continue to seek knowledge and understanding as a way to recovery.

~ *Diane*

FORGIVENESS

"You keep carryin' that anger, it'll eat you up inside."
Don Henley

I have been carrying around so much anger in my life that it has fanned the flames of my addiction. I wouldn't allow myself to feel the anger because I was afraid it would overwhelm me. I used food and other substances to stuff it down and the anger became rage and turned inward as depression. My compulsive eating spiraled out of control.

Many things have happened to me to justify the anger I've been carrying. Healthy anger indicates that someone has violated my boundaries or placed me in an untenable position. Anger that is felt and then released is a healthy emotion. But anger that is stuffed is toxic and will surely corrode my spirit and trap me even further in the cycle of addiction.

I have learned through the Twelve Steps that forgiveness is the only path to letting go of toxic anger. Forgiveness does not mean excusing others' abusive behavior nor accepting my abusers back into my life. Forgiveness happens when I allow myself to feel and work through my anger, and then release it to my Higher Power. Forgiveness is self-love.

One Day at a Time . . . .
I will feel and express my healthy anger and strive for forgiveness.

~ *Suzanne*

Meditation 117

RELATIONSHIPS

"And let there be no purpose in friendship
save the deepening of Spirit."
Kahlil Gibran

My initial experience of relationships in recovery was one of wonder and relief. I was so amazed to find that there actually were other people who understood life as I lived it! Until I walked into the rooms of recovery, I felt so alone and different from other people. Finding people who had also lived the nightmare of compulsive eating, helped my isolation fade away. Seeing that they had found a new way of living gave me hope!!

As I began to share more deeply with my sponsor and other people in recovery, I discovered a deeper gift of friendship in recovery. I received unconditional love and focused guidance toward the Steps of recovery which would transform me completely. This was the greatest gift of relationship that I had ever known. This was the beginning of the transformation that invited me to share the Spirit of recovery with others.

As I carry the principles of recovery into all aspects of my life, I find my relationships with all people are transformed. My character defects no longer stand in the way of my honesty, and fear no longer holds me prisoner. The Spirit of recovery which has been so generously shared with me, continues to be shared joyously through me.

One Day at a Time . . . .
I will be carried by the Spirit of recovery into all of my relationships.

~ *Cate*

UNITY

"Separate needs are weak and easily broken;
but bound together they are strong and hard to tear apart."
The Midrash, Judaic Text

For most of my life before coming into the program, I was a bit of a loner. I never had a lot of friends, perhaps because of my feelings of inadequacy, and was never good at sports, especially team sports. So I buried myself a lot in books, in academic achievements at which I excelled, mainly because I could do that on my own. I lived in a fantasy world where a knight in shining armor would come and rescue me, and my life would then be perfect. I had never even had a serious long-term relationship until I met my first husband, so it was hardly surprising that I made a bad choice and after having three children and much heartache, got divorced.

When I first came into program, it was the first time I had ever felt part of a big group, and most importantly they all spoke my language. Their experiences were my experiences. These wonderful people became my family. There was, and still is, for me an incredible sense of belonging in the fellowship. No longer do I have to brave it on my own as there will always be someone on the other end of the line or in a meeting who can identify and share with me what I am going through. The strength that I feel when I come into the meeting rooms or speak to a fellow member on the phone is a powerful sustaining force for me that has helped me through countless difficult situations and continues to do so.

One Day at a Time . . . .
I only need to reach out and join hands with others in the fellowship to gain the strength to do things I could never do before. It is only with their help, support and love that I am fully able to recover.

~ *Sharon*

GOODNESS

"Above all, let us never forget that an act of goodness
is in itself an act of happiness."
Count Maurice Maeterlinck

While in the disease, most of the goodness I tried to do was for ulterior motives. It was only in recovery that I learned to give unselfishly and without strings to help another. In doing so, I have found happiness beyond measure. I can create my own happiness in the service of my Higher Power and other compulsive overeaters. I can make the promise of a "new happiness and a new freedom" come true.

One Day at a Time . . . .
I will do acts of goodness.

~ Judy N.

SPIRITUAL RECOVERY

*"There is a time to let things happen
and a time to make things happen."*
Hugh Prather

One of the many facets of the disease of compulsive overeating, in my experience, has been the inability to make a positive change in my choice of foods without using the spiritual Steps of recovery. Prior to coming into program, I would plan, pray, and write down what I wanted to do, but change never happened permanently. Looking back, it seems that I was really trying to make things happen, but I was trying to do it without the spiritual guidance and strength of this program through my Higher Power. I didn't have all the spiritual pieces needed to make the almost impossible changes inside myself before the physical changes could happen.

There are many tools of the program, such as sponsorship, a food plan, food abstinence, and practicing the spiritual program through actively working the Twelve Steps. I have learned through failure that I must actively work the Steps of the program. I can't just let things happen in my recovery in regard to Step work, because then the disease will win. When I daily commit to working the Steps to the best of my ability, this brings me the spiritual recovery that allows physical and emotional recovery as well. I cannot make the spiritual recovery happen, since that action belongs only to my Higher Power. What I can do is to take the action by doing the Step work, and from there leave the outcome in my Higher Power's hands.

One Day at a Time . . . .
I will strive to work the Twelve Steps to the best of my ability, and let things happen in my Higher Power's time.

~ *Ohitika*

SHARING OUR STORIES

"You leave home to seek your fortune and, when you get it,
you go home and share it with your family."
Anita Baker

For much of my life I tried to be "Strong." I kept silent about my own suffering and focused instead on others people's needs and how I could help them. Though I could listen and offer advice, I lacked empathy and understanding.

When my stoic, stubborn, and silent avoidance of my own struggles finally made my life unmanageable, I entered recovery. By listening to stories shared by others, I have been blessed. I have found that none of us walk this path alone. We learn from each other and from the strength of traditions. I have found empathy.

I came to see that my silence was born from weakness, not from strength. It was shame, fear, and pride, which kept me hiding. Now I find great joy and freedom in sharing my story with others. I am particularly grateful to God for the way He used my story with my Dad.

My crisis not only drove me to seek help, but it freed my Dad to get help too. If I had remained silent, not only would I have been destroyed, but I would have robbed my Dad of the acceptance and freedom to admit and seek the help he needed ~ and that has so profoundly changed his life.

One Day at a Time . . . .
I will recognize that my history and my current experiences are not to be hidden in silence. I will share my story with others.

~ Lisa V.

HELPING OTHERS

"If I can stop one heart from breaking,
I shall not live in vain
If I can ease one life the aching or cool one pain
or help one fainting Robin unto his nest again
I shall not live in vain"
Emily Dickinson

Somewhere along the way I found myself to be a caretaker. Injustices, pain, discrimination, bullying; all these things affected me deeply. I carried it too far. It reached a point where I truly believe I began taking better care of others than I did myself. Was this ego? Codependency? Altruism? Or was this a guiltless way I found to deflect my own problems, pain, injustices and needs?

When I was doing my first Fourth Step inventory, I learned something very important. As my sponsor read over one "bad thing" I had done after another she cautioned me to take a broader look at myself. Finally, she made me do my entire inventory over and for every 5th character defect or offense to someone, I was required to write something good about myself. She explained that an inventory is never meant to be focused on just the bad ... but the good also. After all, when a store takes inventory on its products, it counts bent cans of beans as well as the perfect cans of beans and crushed boxes of cereal as well as the perfect ones.

This helped me to see that my life's purpose was not just to help others but also to nurture me when my heart was breaking, to make my own life good and to have a nest for myself that was safe and serene. After working the Steps, I know that I'm not living my life in vain and I still want to help others as much as I possibly can, but not to the detriment of myself ... and certainly not to keep me from looking at my own life and my own problems realistically.

One Day at a Time . . . .
May I help others who are less fortunate than I find their way. And let me also make my own nest as comfortable as it can be.

~ *Mari*

Meditation 123

STEP ONE

"The cause is hidden, but the result is known."
Ovid

When I went to my first meeting and was told about Step One, that I was to admit my powerlessness, it was somewhat of a mystery to me. I thought powerlessness was weakness. It was obvious that the result of my compulsive overeating could be seen by everyone, but to me, I was not sure that powerlessness was the answer to the problem. As I kept going to meetings and listening to people share about powerlessness, read the literature, and talked to my sponsor, I learned that powerlessness was not weakness. In fact, to admit my powerlessness, was to connect me to a power that was greater than I had ever experienced before in my life.

The paradoxes of the program, such as we "lose to win" and "give to receive" are true of admitting my powerlessness to find a greater power. In The Twelve Steps and Twelve Traditions of Overeaters Anonymous on p. 5 it reads, "Later we discovered that, far from being a negative factor, the admission of our powerlessness over food opened the door to an amazing newfound power." What a blessing it is to now know that I am powerless, and have opened the door of a newfound power through the Steps, the tools and my Higher Power.

One Day at a Time . . . .
I will freely admit my powerlessness and gladly open the door to the newfound power in my life.

~ *Carolyn*

Meditation 124

LIGHT

*"It's better to light a candle
then to curse the darkness."*
Old Chinese Proverb

I have been living with this disease of compulsive eating for as long as I can remember. I remember stealing money out of my mother's purse to buy sugar-filled soft drinks and candy, and sneaking food out of the cupboard and trying to make it look like nothing was missing. I hid food and ate in isolation, pretending on the outside that nothing was wrong. But I carried this terrible secret – I lived to eat.

As my disease progressed, I acted out in other compulsive ways, and surrounded myself with people who cared nothing for my welfare. I kept running faster and faster, and eating more and more, as my disease sucked all of the energy from my spirit. I sank deeper into the darkness of despair and depression, cursing all those I blamed for my unhappiness.

Through the grace of my Higher Power, my life became so painful that I had to seek help outside of myself. I found this program, and a candle was lit. While my recovery has been rocky over the last 10 years, that candle of progress and hope continues to light my way. No matter how bad things get now, I know that I have my Higher Power and my program friends to lean on. The wonderful people I have met through the program have saved my life, and have shown me the path to peace and abstinence. While I don't always choose to follow that path perfectly, I continue to recover, and to find everyday joys that make life worth living.

One Day at a Time . . . .
I will keep the light of recovery burning.

~ *Suzanne*

Meditation 125

CHOOSE HAPPINESS

"Some cause happiness wherever they go;
others whenever they go."
Oscar Wilde

If happiness were to be found on a coin, anger and frustration would be on the other side of that coin, for they are all the children of expectation. As adults, we try to recapture those special moments and feelings of our childhood by recreating them. We use them as a model for happiness, only this time we are the adults and operating the controls. Unfortunately, our expectations are not grounded in reality. Reaching that level of childhood bliss is usually either impossible or fleeting. How can you as an adult compete with the happiness of being a child?

My experience is that we usually have a set-point for happiness. And though we can feel joy and sadness, we return to that same level of happiness afterward. There are things, however, that can help change that set-point. We can come to believe that a power greater than ourselves can feed our spirit, help keep us living in the moment, and enjoying the kind of peace and wisdom that only our Higher Power can provide. It helps ground us in the truth and gets rid of unrealistic expectations. It helps to relax us as opposed to letting our mind bounce back and forth from past to future and pain to fantasy. We learn to accept our life - just as it is. Today. Now

What choices have I been making to choose happiness? I choose to go to meetings and give shares. I choose to abstain from compulsive overeating. I choose to set time for myself every day where I can organize my affairs, and help ward off stressful situations. I also try to spend time with myself in ways that will feed my soul and spirit, not just keep myself entertained until I go to bed. I give to service to others, but remember that I need to take care of myself, for when I am not strong; I have no strength to give.

One Day at a Time . . . .
Today I will choose happiness.

~ Marilyn S.

EXPECTATIONS

*"The best thing about the future
is that it only comes one day at a time."*
Abraham Lincoln

Being a rational, logical person I have always worked from the premise that If I did something then the following would be the outcome and maybe in the scientific world that may have been true. But in the real world of relationships and people it certainly doesn't work like that as I have discovered since coming into program. As it says in the Big Book "serenity is inversely proportional to one's expectations" and I know now how true this is.

Just recently after having set a boundary with my son I was expecting all sorts of repercussions and imagined him trying to talk me out of my decision and the result was that I lost my serenity and became really anxious. Of course the truth was nowhere like I had imagined and the situation ended very differently from what I had expected. This was a lesson to me once again that things don't turn out the way we expect them to but the way they are meant to.

One Day at a Time . . . .
When I let go of any expectations I have of how a situation is going to turn out, I get to keep my serenity and the situation turns out the way it's supposed to.

~ *Sharon S.*

Meditation 127

SUBLIMATION

*"People who are happy don't use food to
sublimate. Food is supposed to be good for
you - not make you feel good!"*
Gary Null

All compulsive overeaters use food to sublimate. Sublimation in layman's terms is any habit or technique we use to alter or change our reality - for better or worse! Sublimation methods of choice are a great gauge to measure mental and physical health. Poor choices are using food, gambling, television, alcohol, drugs, shopping, excessive sleep or too many passive activities. Healthy choices are meditation, visual imagery, prayer, journaling, yoga, physical exercise, relaxation exercises, deep breathing, etc. Anything from lawn mowing to vacuuming could be an act of sublimation - IF done with high level of awareness and concentration. A person who's high up the ladder spiritually sees Higher Power in all things at all times. Since we sublimate regardless, the trick is to make it a consciously controlled positive sublimation rather than subconscious negative sublimation.

One Day at a Time . . . .
I will consciously incorporate positive, healthy methods of sublimation.

~ Rob R.

POSITIVE THOUGHTS

*"I've always believed that you can think positive
just as well as you can think negative."*
James Arthur Baldwin

What did I think about before I was in recovery? I worried about what others thought of me. I thought of what and when I could eat next. I picked apart the way others' bodies looked, while being jealous of them. I didn't know that thinking of negative things brought my energy level down. I thought self-discipline meant disciplining myself – which meant mentally beating myself up.

My Higher Power has shown me a way of thinking that was new to me, but is age old – positive thoughts. Thinking positive brings me to a level of serenity. When my mind wanders, I can bring it back. When I find myself obsessing over something negative, I can work the first three Steps with it. I am powerless over negativity. I have a HP who can remove it from me. I choose to let my HP direct my thoughts. And then let myself to think of something else.

One Day at a Time . . . .
I choose to think positively. The result is serenity.

~ *Nancy F.*

OPEN MINDEDNESS

*"Let go of your attachment to being right,
and suddenly your mind is more open.
You're able to benefit from the unique viewpoints of others,
without being crippled by your own judgment."*
Ralph Marston

Before joining this program much of my life was taken up with defending myself against those who would hurl abuse. I kept everything and everybody at arm's length in a bid to protect my increasingly fragile and sensitive self-assurance. As time marched on, and my disease became parasitical, the walls around me grew higher and isolation drew me inwards.

Ironically, the fortress I was building didn't protect me from myself and I soon became my own worst enemy. My self-loathing and my unceasing search for perfection led me deeper into a self-induced state of depression. Keeping everybody out and locking myself in became an exhausting exercise.

On entering the Twelve Step program I soon realized that the fortress I had so carefully built to protect myself against the outside world was also preventing any kind of light, warmth and love from entering in.

As my journey of recovery progressed, brick by brick the walls came down and afforded me the nourishment I needed to blossom and grow. In learning to accept myself, I found that what others thought of me paled into insignificance. I learned that there was a wealth of experience, strength and hope which would help me along the journey. I learned that I could take what I needed and put down the remainder, without the resentment, anger, fear or pain, which previously would have sent me running for cover.

One Day at a Time . . . .
I aim to be willing to keep my mind open, to accept what I need to continue my journey, and to leave the rest.

~ Sue G

Meditation 130

GOOD DAYS ~ BAD DAYS

"Most of the shadows of this life are caused by
standing in one's own sunshine."
Ralph Waldo Emerson

Thank You, God, for always loving and accepting me right where I am, and working with me, even when I am not willing to give You much to work with. It is so comforting to know that wherever I am, whether I am willing and open, or have once again shut myself off from the Light of Your Spirit, You will meet me there and provide whatever is necessary for me to keep on.

Thank You for forgiving me those times when I am not willing enough to put forth any effort–some days I just want to skate, God–some days I just want to wallow in it. Why else would I resist changing into what You would have me be? Some days I am lazy and comfortable just where I am.

One Day at a Time . . . .
God, Help me to be willing to reach out to You, good day or bad. Keep me mindful that my conscious contact with You makes even the best day better, and the worst day tolerable.

~ Jeanine

COURAGE

"The courage of life is often less a dramatic spectacle
than the courage of the final moment;
but it is no less than a magnificent mixture
of triumph and tragedy."
John F. Kennedy

As a little girl, I often daydreamed of a knight in shining armor who would ride bravely into my life and rescue me from my fears and insecurities. This knight would be fearless; un-fazed by fire-breathing dragons, deep dark caves, or howling winds. He would have courage where I had only fear.

The knight never came. I began to look for other rescuers in my friends, role models, teachers, and church. Still I could not find what I sought. My fears continued to scream in my soul ... and I felt so weak. I turned to food in an attempt to silence the monsters in my belly.

Sometimes my fear and hopelessness were so desperate that I almost ended my life – yet something inside of myself stopped me from doing so. Something inside of me clung to life and eventually brought me to The Recovery Group.

In this group of amazing people I immediately noticed the courage they exhibited in confronting the challenges in their lives and in choosing to learn and grow from every failure and every success. I marvel at the courage with which they keep moving towards more and more healing, in spite of their fears.

They have courage in spite of their fears.

The open, honest sharing of dear friends in recovery has taught me that even I had courage all along. Courage is not the absence of fear; if there were no fear, there'd be no need for courage.

Courage means making the choice to move forward in spite of our fears.

One Day at a Time . . . .
I will honor the courage I have. I will thank God for giving me the strength to move forward in spite of fear. I will celebrate the courage I see in my friends and I will encourage them on their journey.

~ *Lisa V.*

Meditation 132

WORRY

*"Don't worry about the world coming to an end today.
It's already tomorrow in Australia."*
Charles Schultz

Worry...that's a topic I'm really good at! Since working the Twelve Steps, however, I am beginning to see some things about worry that, hopefully, will soon make it a thing of the past in my life. After all, why should I worry? What has worry ever done for me, except mess up my life?

I am seeing that when I am worrying about something, I have not turned it over to my Higher Power, and I am continuing to act from my own self-will. Or, I did turn it over to my Higher Power, but didn't really trust Him to take care of it, and so I took it back!

I had a breakthrough, just a couple of days ago, concerning worry. I was concerned about a decision my husband and I had to make and it was so far beyond my ability to see into the future that I gave up and prayed for help. Somehow I let go and let God. Suddenly a beautiful stillness and peace came over me. I felt calmer than I had in years ... very calm and still and at peace. I felt completely reassured that God was handling my "decision" and that God was completely competent to do so.

One Day at a Time . . . .
I abandon worry. I let go and let God, and enjoy the serenity and peace of trust in God.

~ Lynne T.

SERENITY

*"The final wisdom of life requires not the annulment of incongruity
but the achievement of serenity with and above it."*
Reinhold Niebuhr

When I started coming to Recovery Group meetings, I heard the word "serenity" used frequently. I waited for someone to turn the serenity light switch on for me. I thought if I kept coming, the guy in charge of lights would turn mine on, and then I would possess and understand serenity! But the people in the meetings kept telling me, "You need to work the Steps." I began to work them with a vengeance, the way a compulsive person – such as I am – tends to function.

With each passing day I have begun to feel more comfortable living in my own skin. My fears, worries about the future, and anxieties have all decreased. I have made a more personal connection with my Higher Power. I have begun to develop friendships with other people in Recovery Group. The loving friendships here have had a huge impact on how I feel about myself. They have caused me to experience more self-love and self-acceptance. I have come to the point where I now know that no matter what happens, things will eventually work out for the best for me.

One Day at a Time . . . .
I will continue to attend meetings to experience serenity.

~ Karen A.

Meditation 134

PERFECTIONISM

"Shooting stars come out of the darkness."
Unknown Author

Today I am wading through guilt and shame as I try to step into the Light. My ankles are mired in unfulfilled visions and lost dreams. Childhood voices scream at me of my Potential. What are you doing? You're smart, talented, and beautiful. What are you doing with your life? You have the capacity for a great job, why do you loll in mediocrity? You're close to thinness, why can't you eat less? You could be beautiful, why don't you take more time with your hair, makeup, have manicures or plastic surgery? Why do you hover around "good enough"?

I remember when I had all these things, I wanted different things. The voices remind me I am not perfect, only a perfectionist. My goals remind me of what I lack. My tears remind me I am not what I preach. My Higher Power reminds me I am still on the easel, and grateful for my journey. My darkness reminds me I live in the Light.

One Day at a Time . . . .
I seek the light of recovery that is seeking me.

~ *Dodee*

Meditation 135

POSITIVE THOUGHTS

"The pessimist sees the difficulty in every opportunity.
The optimist sees the opportunity in every difficulty."
Winston Churchill

What did I think about before I was in recovery? I worried about what others thought of me. I thought of what and when I could eat next. I picked apart the way others' bodies looked, while being jealous of them. I didn't know that thinking of negative things brought my energy level down. I thought self-discipline meant disciplining myself – which meant mentally beating myself up.

My Higher Power has shown me a way of thinking that was new to me, but is age old – positive thoughts. Just reading this quotation brings me to a level of serenity. When my mind wanders, I can bring it back. When I find myself obsessing over something negative, I can work the first three Steps with it. I am powerless over negativity. I have a HP who can remove it from me. I choose to let my HP direct my thoughts. And then let myself to think of something else.

One Day at a Time . . . .
I choose to think of truth, honesty, beauty, praise, gratitude. The result: is serenity.

~ *Nancy F.*

LOOKING AT THE STARS

"We are all in the gutter, but some of us are looking at the stars."
Oscar Wilde

Before I made the Twelve Steps part of my life, I considered myself to have been in the gutter. My weight had doubled, I was in a major depression, and I was going through the motions of life. Those looking at me from afar saw only a perfect marriage, a perfect career, a perfect home, and perfect children. Although I was blessed, the disease I suffered from day in and day out made it quite obvious to anyone who truly knew me that I was not "looking at the stars." It took my first sponsor to start the healing process for me.

As I began to work Steps One, Two and Three, I felt "different." Nothing had changed . . . everything had changed. It's hard to describe because outwardly I looked the same ... but my entire being opened up. Weight began to come off because I was able to focus on a plan of eating. I found my feelings returned ... the ability to love and accept love came back. My spirituality blossomed once again. I truly felt alive.

One Day at a Time . . . .
I want to remember each time I find myself in the gutter and giving up hope ... to look at the stars ... and remember that my program works if I will just work it.

~ *Mari*

THE HUMAN SPIRIT

"The human spirit is stronger than anything that can happen to it."
Unknown

I spent most years of my life feeling like a damaged person, one who was permanently and irreparably defective. I am the survivor of abuse, and had been a practicing compulsive overeater since early childhood. The only way I knew myself was broken, hopeless, and damaged beyond repair. On the days when I could manage to have a goal, my goal was to make the best of it ... and to simply survive the remainder of my days on this earth.

Recovery has transformed my view of myself and my experience of life. In receiving the love, support and guidance of my friends on this journey I began to see a glimmer of hope. With the loving care of my sponsors I began to take the Steps, and I learned to live them out ... one day at a time.

In taking the Steps and living them out, I found my buried spirit, and I found that it was alive and well! In recovery I became reacquainted with the spiritual part of myself that I thought was lost forever. In this connection, I learned to live, laugh, and hope again. My spiritual connection is stronger than anything that can happen to me. This is the truth in my life today, and it transforms me to peace, joy, and love greater than I had ever dreamed.

One Day at a Time . . . .
I will practice Step Eleven, and improve my conscious contact with God. I will choose to live in connection with my inner spirit.

~ *Cate*

STEP ELEVEN

"Be like the bird that, passing on her flight
awhile on boughs too slight,
feels them give way beneath her,
and yet sings, knowing that she hath wings."
Victor Hugo

Step Eleven tells us to seek "through prayer and meditation to improve our conscious contact with God as we understand Him, praying only for knowledge of His will for us and the power to carry that out." For me, that is a daily, sometimes, minute by minute task. As a food addict and compulsive overeater I face temptation daily and need to be in fit spiritual condition to resist. I do this by making a daily conscious contact with the God of my understanding. Then I am connected when I need the fox hole prayers like, "Help me!" or "I'm in trouble!"

Step Eleven for me is a spiritual discipline to be practiced daily. I do not do that perfectly, but I aspire to connect daily with my God. As I connect I pray for His will for my life and the power to carry that out. It is easy to get selfish with my prayers and Step Eleven helps me with this. There are certain things that I know are His will, such as attending meetings, talking to my sponsor, using the tools and staying connected to my God. If I am unsure, I pray for God's will and leave the rest to Him.

One Day at a Time . . . .
I will maintain a fit spiritual condition by connecting with the God of my understanding.

~ *Carolyn*

DENIAL

"The ability to delude yourself
may be an important survival tool."
Jane Wagner

I had many delusions when I entered the Twelve Step program. One by one they have shattered, but only when I was able to handle the truth.

Still, I have looked back at the things I was in denial about during my sickness, and I blamed myself for not seeing the truth sooner, for not seeking recovery sooner. On the good days, which are becoming more and more common for me, I see that my denial was indeed a survival tool.

I spent 33 years with eating disorders without ever consciously knowing about them. Subconsciously, I was very interested in books and movies about anorexia and bulimia, and was fascinated to learn about compulsive overeating. I can only believe I was unknowingly preparing myself for the day when I would be able to face my addiction and still survive.

One Day at a Time . . . .
I will remind myself that many things are in our lives for a reason, even denial.

~ *Rhonda H.*

Meditation 140

AVOIDANCE

"Facts do not cease to exist because they are ignored…"
Aldous Huxley

Step 1 has a basic principle behind it which is truth. For me that truth is, just as I use tools for recovery, there are tools that my willful mind uses to keep me rooted in my disease. One of the strongest is avoidance.

Recovery can bring up a lot of painful issues and have me recall situations in which I feel uncomfortable. Sometimes I find that these old feelings have a way of creeping into my psyche. Suddenly some old behavior comes rushing back and I find myself using avoidance as a means to protect myself. Other times, I find myself acting very willfully by deliberately putting things off like going to the gym even when I know that it is good for me, I enjoy myself and am always happy for having gone..

My avoidance can take the form of rebellion against a person, chore, or situation.

Recovery has taught me to face situations. Once the situation has been faced, I often feel a sense of immediate relief. I know that the deed is done, my fears whether they be realistic or not, usually fall away, and sometimes I even feel a little silly for having avoided the situation in the first place.

One Day at a Time . . . .
I will fact the situations that I encounter today with action.

~ Marilyn S.

Meditation 141

THOUGHTS

"The universe is transformation;
our lives are what our thoughts make it."
Marcus Aurelius Antoninus

The power of our thoughts is astounding, and my negative thoughts kept me in chains for many years. I was constantly thinking of what was not right, what I didn't do right, what needs of mine went unmet. My life was miserable by my own making. My own thoughts kept me in a prison of negativity. The only person who had the key was me. For many years I stayed locked in, not knowing the key was in my possession.

When I came to the program I learned that I had responsibility for my "side of the street." I finally came to understand that I was able to change my thinking, one day at a time. It was a slow process. It took a life-time to learn negative thinking patterns, and it took years to learn positive thinking patterns. Using the tools of the program was the key to re-educating my mind. At meetings I heard positive statements that others made about themselves and me. Reading program literature was always a positive experience. As I chose nurturing, loving sponsors, they affirmed me and my baby steps toward wholeness and healing. All of these, and other tools, worked slowly to bring about an awareness that I held the key to my own prison door and gave me the courage to take the key and free myself from negativity.

One Day at a Time . . . .
I will choose positive thoughts and actions that bring me freedom.

~ *Carolyn H.*

FAITH

*"The inability of the materialistic mind to grasp
the idea of the Life Eternal is no proof of the
non-existence of that life."*
'Abdu'l-Baha

I grew up in a family where there was no belief in the existence of God, although we were told that it was up to us to decide where to put our faith.

I struggled through various addictions and disorders, but never forgot that one special time as a child, where I spontaneously went down on my knees one night to pray to God, who for a few moments had suddenly become very real.

As an adult, my belief in a Higher Power came and went like the breeze, so that some days I was an atheist, others an agnostic, and at other times filled with an awareness that God is in all things.

I am grateful that my addiction to overeating has brought me to this Twelve Step program. Every day I come to believe that a Power greater than myself can restore my sense of balance, and I make sure that I put in effort to maintain my conscious connection with God.

One Day at a Time . . . .
I pray that my spiritual faculties and aspirations will daily increase, and that I will never allow the material senses to veil my eyes from the light of my Higher Power.

~ *John M.*

Meditation 143

OPPORTUNITY

"In the middle of difficulty, lies opportunity."
Albert Einstein

Pain, struggle, and difficulty can be catalysts for changes in me. If I am having so much difficulty living the way I do, then surely my current means of coping and survival are not working. The insanity of it all was that in spite of all the proof I saw that those methods did not work, I continued to live the same way – and suffer the same difficulties and struggles – for many years. Then opportunity for change knocked on my door. I found TRG online.

The Recovery Group program has shown me that there are much better ways to deal with life than to stuff myself with food, fear, resentments, and anger. The methods and tools I have been given here work. My defects still rear their ugly heads, but I no longer live focused on – or living in – those defects. Now I direct my thinking to program material, prayer and program works. What a gift that has been! Joy is mine for today ~ for the taking!

When I find that what I am doing today is not working, what do I need to do? As a COE with no recovery I would have kept doing what wasn't working. That made no sense, but that's what I did. Now when I struggle with the food, I look at my thinking, 'cause thinking affects how I feel and feelings impact my compulsions. When the thinking starts to spiral downward I know I need to act. I need to read program material, contact a program person, pray and meditate, and/or do program service. I need to use the tools to get me focused back on recovery.

One Day at a Time . . . .
I will be mindful of my thinking, and when negative or self-pitying thoughts arise, I will remember that I have the opportunity now to redirect and refocus anew on recovery.

~ *Karen A.*

Meditation 144

PERFECTION

"The thing that is really hard, and really amazing,
is giving up on being perfect and
beginning the work of becoming yourself."
Anna Quindlen

Perfect...to me that word sounds like: "Do it again. You didn't do it right." That's the message I get from the voices in my head. The messages of perfectionism tell me over and over that I did it wrong. It's a powerful weapon when you use it as a whip against yourself, just like negative messages when you look in a mirror. I have a choice every single moment of every single day to either pick up that whip and hurt myself, or to "get out of my own way" and be kind. I can choose to look in the mirror and be thankful, and to look at myself and feel love. It takes a lot of practice, but it is worth it.

If you love yourself more than you love anyone else, you can feel happiness again. You can create again. You can look at your shadow and say good things about it too! It's another beautiful you ~ unique and wonderfully made.

One Day at a Time . . . .
I will celebrate the beauty of myself today and every day.

~ *Karen*

Meditation 145

SHARING

"What most of us want is to be heard, to communicate."
Dory Previn

When I am privileged to be involved in a meeting, hear sharing and have the opportunity to share, magic happens. For me, it is the end of isolation, the times of being alone with my mind and my thoughts that run away with me as long as they are stewing inside without me allowing myself to give them expression. That is why sharing is so important. If I receive constantly without giving, I stagnate. If I give consistently without taking the time to take in and be helped, I go bankrupt.

I need to share and listen for the God of my understanding in others' voices. I often refer to others who share as "God with skin on." I also need to share with others. For me, sharing is a type of prayer, talking to my Higher Power from my heart with others listening in on our conversation! That way I am heard by my HP and those at the meeting I am attending. That is the true magic of the program.

One Day at a Time . . . .
I will reach out to others by sharing in meetings and allowing others to bless me with their sharing.

~ Carolyn H.

Meditation 146

SERVING OTHERS

"It is one of the most beautiful compensations of life,
that no man can sincerely try to help another without helping himself."
Ralph Waldo Emerson

I am not sure when I learned about giving service to others ... it seems like a long time ago. There's a feeling one gets deep inside when we do something to help others that makes us know we want to keep that feeling coming forever.

I believe our Higher Powers give us certain gifts. Maybe they're all put in a large bag and when we're born, HP distributes them ... sort of like one reaches in a grab bag at parties. I do know that everyone I have ever met has some sort of gift ... something that they do that comes easily and becomes something they get very good at doing. When they start giving others this gift, they get even better at doing what they do ... and that "feeling" inside begins to grow.

I was given three gifts: music, listening to others and writing. Music was the first gift I was aware of and I spent my life sharing it. In adulthood I learned I had another gift ~ the gift of being able to listen. I realized that a lot of people don't feel "heard." When I spent my time listening to others, I realized I was giving them a gift. Now I get that same special feeling I had when I performed in front of many people as I quietly sit and listen to someone pour out their heart to me. Finally, there came a time when I began to write ... and that same feeling emerged when someone would tell me that what I wrote made a difference to them.

I belong to an organization where hundreds of people give their gifts to others each day and I finally learned that there were reasons why so many people devote so much of their lives to service. It doesn't take a rocket scientist to figure that out ... we serve because we experience that feeling. We serve because it makes us feel good. We serve others because in doing so we serve ourselves.

One Day at a Time . . . .
Let me continue to serve.

~ *Mari*

BALANCE

"I've learned that you can't have everything ...
and do everything ...
at the same time."
Oprah Winfrey

Learning about balance has been a struggle throughout my life; both as an addict and as a mother, friend, lover, sister... and woman. I'm not sure if it is my addiction that causes me to be over-zealous when it comes to giving too much to too many, or if my desire for love has manifested my addiction out of a need to feel full and satisfied. For me, finding that spot where a relationship is comfortable and not one-sided, where work is just 'work' and not all that nourishes my life... where school is an enhancement and not a crutch for hiding and isolating, is a hard place to for me to find. I see patterns within my life where I consistently struggle for harmony and balance. Why isn't one of anything enough? No matter what it is that is in my life; relationships, work, eating, shopping, I have to work at managing balance so that things flow at the right pace, otherwise, my entire life is off kilter.

But today, I don't need to struggle. I don't need to overdo my relationships or my work. I can do just one thing and know that the rest will be there tomorrow. Today I have the gifts that have been given to me to manage my life.

One Day at a Time . . . .
I pray that God will help me to manage and balance my life so that I can do a good job with all things, especially living.

~ *Pamela*

Meditation 148

VICTIMS

*"People are always blaming their circumstances
for being what they are. The people who get on
in this world are the people who get up and look
for the circumstances they want, and if they
can't find them, make them."*
George Bernard Shaw

My life began with an unfortunate start in a dysfunctional family with an alcoholic father and mentally ill mother. It is easy to reach back there for the "victim mode" and blame others for what I am today. I have reached a point in my life today that I realize others bear responsibility for their part in how I am ~ but if I stay that way, I bear the responsibility. I can make choices today to use the program and its many tools to bring about health and freedom in my life.

The Twelve Steps give me the framework to take the responsibility and begin to mold my life into something functional and good. The things I longed for and did not have in the past, are in the past ~ and I choose to leave the past behind me. I have a great new future in the program, one day at a time, in which I can create a new life. I can say "Goodbye" to the victim role and greet the person with the responsibility for my life – a joyful and free life.

One Day at a Time . . . .
*I will take responsibility for my life and make circumstances that are healthy for me.
It is my choice.*

~ Carolyn H.

Meditation 149

HIGHER POWER

"Think not because no man sees,
such things will remain unseen."
Henry Wadsworth Longfellow

Recently at a meeting I heard a person share that they weren't sure that the program would work for them because they did not believe in God. They were very distressed. I wanted to get out the Big Book and quote to them from page 47, "When, therefore, we speak to you of God, we mean your own conception of God. This applies too, to other spiritual expressions which you find in this book. Do not let any prejudice you may have against spiritual terms deter you from honestly asking yourself what they mean to you. At the start this was all we needed to commence spiritual growth, to effect our first conscious relation with God as we understood Him."

Many of us have a problem with God in the beginning of our program. We may be atheists, agnostics, or simply have had bad experiences regarding God or His/Her people. We can choose the group, or the Higher Power of another, to be our Higher Power until we are able to begin, bit-by-bit, to define and establish a relationship with our own Higher Power. I know that when I came into the program I was very angry with God. I used the group as my Higher Power at first. Then I used my sponsor's God of her understanding as my Higher Power because He was so loving and full of grace. We had many talks about her God. This helped me greatly until I was able to reconnect to my relationship with the God of my understanding. Today I have a full, rich and intimate relationship with my God.

One Day at a Time . . . .
I will be tolerant of others' conception of their Higher Power and will continue to grow in my relationship with the God of my understanding.

~ Carolyn H.

Meditation 150

HOME

"A person can run for years but sooner or later
he has to take a stand in the place which, for better or worse,
he calls home, do what he can to change things there."
Paule Marshall

I have been running for most of my life. I was in a hurry to grow up. As a kid, all I wanted was to grow up and move out. I was so sick of everything and everyone in my life. I didn't want to be told what to do. I wanted to be able to call the shots. Then, when I grew up, I wanted to be a kid again. I wanted people to tell me what to do and to take care of me. When I was calling the shots, I found myself in bars and eating out all the time because I didn't want to go to the grocery store or cook. The only foods I kept in my studio apartment were binge foods. I lived in a very urban area and could very easily walk to fast food or to convenience stores. I didn't know what home meant. When I'm running, I get out of breath, my body hurts, my soul hurts, and I have no space for my Higher Power to guide me. I run laps in the same place, expecting to feel better, but never feeling better.

As a relative newcomer to program, I have made a conscious choice to stop. I turned it over to my Higher Power and asked for guidance in finding home and staying there. Now, as I am standing in place, I find that my home is my Higher Power. Standing in place, I've found that the world isn't as adverse as I'd perceived it to be. I can actually see the beauty in the world around me and feel nurtured by the feeling of home.

One Day at a Time . . . .
Today I can stand in place and look around. I can be aware of the ever-loving presence of my Higher Power and the comfort of the home that have both been with me all along.

~ AJ

THE TITANIC

"Men at some time are masters of their fates."
William Shakespeare

Our early days in OA can be compared to being a passenger on the Titanic. As we took our beloved and wonderfully-powerful first three Steps, we were taking a voyage. In Step One we realized we were on the Titanic and that we were doomed. In Step Two we spotted a lifeboat. And in Step Three we took our seats in the lifeboat.

My voyage began with Step One when I realized the connection between the weight I was carrying and some health issues I had last year. I had developed "pitting edema" in both ankles. That was a sign of congestive heart failure. I was on the Titanic! In addition to my physical health condition, I discovered that my inner-health was also challenged. I had lived my life filled with resentments and negative thinking which ate at my very being. I had lost much of my spiritual strength and was in need of spiritual renewal. I was indeed a passenger on my own personal Titanic.

My voyage continued with Step Two. I can't even remember how I found The Recovery Group online, but I know that my Higher Power must have brought me here. Though I didn't believe at that time what the fellowship said in the meetings, I "acted as if" I believed my Higher Power could relieve me of these horrible compulsions to overeat and to live in resentment and negativity. That was all it took. I had spotted the lifeboat and was "acting as if" I believed it had come for me.

I was being changed. My early days of abstinence were difficult, but achievable. I had gotten into the lifeboat. I will always remember where I was when I suddenly realized that God had relieved me of the compulsion to eat between meals and at night. That realization had a huge impact on me. That day I took my seat on the lifeboat. I have been blessed with so much recovery. The ride I am on in this lifeboat isn't a free ride; it requires that I work this program on a daily basis. But when I consider the alternative, I love the ride I am on and I truly cherish the passengers with whom I am sharing this boat!

One Day at a Time . . . .
I will cherish the lifeboat that this program has given me.

~ *Karen A.*

Meditation 152

PERFECTION

*"My imperfections and failures are as much a blessing from God
as my successes and my talents, and I lay them both at His feet."*
Mahatma Gandhi

I don't know why I used to think that if something wasn't done perfectly, it wasn't worth doing. I was an all-time overachiever and to fail at anything was totally unacceptable. Since I set such impossibly high standards, it was hardly surprising that I couldn't love – or even like – myself. I was constantly pushing to excel at those things I was good at, and I would beat myself up if I failed to meet my high expectations. I was especially critical of my body. I thought that if I had the perfect body, my life would be perfect.

When I came into the program I had to learn to not be so hard on myself. For the first time I began to realize that I was human and could still be loveable and worthy ~ even with all my imperfections and character defects. I am lovingly reminded by my sponsor and my friends in the fellowship to be gentler with myself. They remind me that I don't even have to do the program perfectly. I just need to do the best I know how for that day; then I can see progress one day at a time. I don't have to push myself to be perfect all the time in order to win approval or gain love. What a relief that is!

One Day at a Time . . . .
I don't have to be perfect all the time. I just need to be the best me that I can be for today...and that's the way God intended me to be.

~ Sharon S.

Meditation 153

STEP ONE

"Well begun is half done."
Aristotle

The first time I took Step One I knew that I was beat. Because I knew that I was beat, I knew I had to have help to survive. I sought and accepted that help in OA. I put the program into action. I completed the Twelve Steps and tasted recovery.

Over the years I have had to renew my Step One, and each time I was convinced that I was not going to make it without the help in program. That spurred me on to complete the Twelve Steps many times. Step One is essentially what made me complete all Twelve Steps and go on to a fuller and fuller life in recovery. Without step one, there really was no need or motivation for Steps Two through Twelve.

Recently I realized that Step One is particularly necessary to do Step Twelve. I cannot help anyone without my Higher Power. I cannot control another's program. I cannot carry the message on my own, nor can I practice the principles in all my affairs by myself. Step One – my powerlessness and my inability to manage – is a great blessing. It is what spurs me on to turn to my Higher Power in all tasks great and small; it is what helps me to gain more and more ground in recovery.

One Day at a Time . . . .
I will admit my powerlessness and my inability to manage, then I will turn to God Who will take me through my program and my life - with His power and His ability to manage.

~ *Q*

EXPERIENCE, STRENGTH AND HOPE

"Experience is not what happens to you.
It is what you do with what happens to you."
Aldous Huxley

Every day is filled with experiences. I can choose to let them pass me by, or I can allow myself to learn lessons from them. It is easy to let the day pass by quickly and virtually unlived. If I refuse to stay in the present moment and choose rather to be filled with resentment, stuck in the past, filled with fear, or stuck in the future, life truly does pass me by. My experience truly has no value. But if I choose to learn lessons, stay in the present moment, and remain connected to my Higher Power, my day becomes experience, strength and hope.

Since coming to the program I have learned that I can share my experience, strength and hope in so many ways. A call to or from an OA friend gives me an opportunity to give and receive experience, strength and hope. I hear experience, strength and hope shared daily as I attend meetings. People share not only what has happened to them, but the great lessons that they have allowed their Higher Power to teach them. This is such an honor to be part of, an honor that I would not want to miss. I give and receive my experience, strength and hope on the loops where I share – and receive shares – on a daily basis. I am blessed to be a part of strong loops with great recovery and sharing. My sponsors frequently share their experience, strength and hope with me. I am privileged to have two sponsors with quality recovery who are members of The Recovery Group. I am so grateful for their input in my life and recovery. They have been such an important part of my life lessons. Every source of experience, strength and hope in my life gives me more encouragement to learn new lessons with every experience I have every day.

One Day at a Time . . . .
I will find every opportunity to share my experience, strength and hope.

~ *Carolyn H.*

Meditation 155

FOURTH STEP SECRETS

"These are weighty secrets and we must whisper them."
Sarah Chauncey Woolsey (Susan Coolidge)

When I came to the Recovery Group, I was wearing the pain of a lifetime of well-kept secrets - secrets about a childhood of poverty and secrets about a difficult marriage. No one ever saw my secret pain; I never shared it with anyone. But all could see the effects of the food I used as a coping mechanism.

Because of my willingness "to do whatever it takes," I shared these secrets with the person who took my Fifth Step. I later shared it with my sponsor and some of them later with a sponsee during her Fifth Step. Sharing this pain the first two times was like the bursting of a painful abscess, with poison being released. The poison that kept me living in resentful, negative thinking has been gradually replaced with gratitude for what I had and now have, and with the ability to experience joy in my many, many blessings.

One Day at a Time . . . .
I will experience gratitude for the gifts I was given in my Fourth and Fifth Steps and for the gifts of this program.

~ Karen A.

HONESTY

"Only God can fully know what absolute honesty is.
Therefore each of us has to conceive what this great ideal
might be to the best of our ability."
Bill W.

Honesty has its opposite of dishonesty. In my experience, when trying to deal with my own level of dishonesty, I find that it comes off in layers. I'm not always ready to deal with something that I've been in denial in of. In some cases I'm so focused on what I can see that I'm completely unaware of the other things I'm doing. In these cases, my dishonesty is actually an honest one at that moment. I'm only able to see the dishonesty with the top layer in focus. It's usually those dishonest items that I am most embarrassed about. This other lower level is currently in the dark or sometimes called a blind spot.

To be relieved of my obsession for food, I needed to be a thorough as I could be. When I held something back and was practicing my dishonesty, I was the one who hurt in the end. My hanging onto my dishonesty was preventing me from the freedom of the things I really wanted freedom from. But God would only let me have a reprieve for so long. My dishonesty eventually broke my spiritual connection and my relief from food obsession dissipated. Working the Twelve Steps always restores my connection.

One Day at a Time . . . .
I will let go of the embarrassment and pain of being wrong. It's hard to feel good about myself when I'm clinging onto my negative feelings towards myself. I will practice forgiving myself and letting it go. I will choose to focus on seeing myself as a slightly imperfect human doing my best, instead of clinging to the fantasy of being perfect.

~ *Pam*

HUMAN EMOTION

"Character cannot be developed in ease and quiet.
Only through experiences of trial and suffering
can the soul be strengthened, vision cleared,
ambition inspired and success achieved."
Helen Keller

While traveling through life, I have made choices that have injured myself and others. Others have made choices that have hurt me. Remembering and writing about my past has proved to bring up a plethora of negative emotions. At this moment I feel pain, remorse, anger, frustration, and am overwhelmed.

Every human on earth experiences these same feelings at one time or another. This is part of what I am here for. How could I ever comprehend bliss without experiencing misery? How could I enjoy inspiration without suffering depression? How could I appreciate peace without encountering turmoil? I am grateful for the problems life gives me – partnered with the emotions they bring – because without the bad I could not understand the good. Everything has its opposite. Things will always change. Things will always get better, just like the sun shines after each storm. The good news is that even though I may be experiencing negative feelings, I am learning empathy and I am gaining wisdom. And how much more will I value the rays of sunshine that break through the gray clouds?

One Day at a Time . . . .
I will allow myself the honor of feeling human emotion. I will ask my Higher Power to give me comfort in my hardships and to help me remember why I am here. I will ask my Higher Power to open my heart to the lessons I am learning. For today, with hope and faith, I will look for the sunbeams shining through the haze.

~ *Susanne*

COMPASSION

"How far you go in life depends on your being tender with the young,
compassionate with the aged, sympathetic with the striving,
and tolerant of the weak and the strong.
Because sometime in your life you will have been all of these."
George Washington Carver

This Twelve Step program works wonders on many levels. But one of the most noticeable changes I've seen in my life has been in the area of compassion.

Eating disorders can really mess a person up. All of us who have the disease of compulsive eating, in no matter what form, have been laughed at, discriminated against, or generally overlooked by those who don't suffer from our disease. So, one would think that compulsive eaters would be more loving and understanding to their fellows. For the most part this is true. But I have seen compulsive eaters be just as cruel as our more normal-weight counterparts.

If we can mistreat each other, how can we ever expect others to treat us differently? We need to remember where we were in our disease, for there are others in that same situation. We need to see ourselves in the newcomers to our program, because we run the risk of returning to where they are now. "There but for the grace of God go I" takes on a whole new meaning when we apply that phrase to our situation.

Sometimes we see varying degrees of success in this program of recovery. We must each work our program, and allow our fellows to work their program. It's not up to us to take someone else's inventory concerning the success or failure of their program. We need only to keep our own side of the street clean, and to show compassion to those of our fellows who are struggling. After all, compassion was what prompted the founding of our fellowship in the first place.

One Day at a Time . . . .
I will consciously practice compassion toward those who still suffer, because I remember where I came from on this path, and realize I could return there.

~ JAR

TOGETHERNESS

"The Praying Hands – let them be your reminder,
if you need one, that no one ever makes it alone."
Anonymous

I don't need a sponsor; God and I walk alone."

"Why do I need to go to a meeting tonight? I'll be OK; I've got other things I need to be doing."

"I can't sponsor, I haven't worked enough of the Steps yet, and besides, I haven't got time; it takes all my time to do MY program."

When my thoughts drift in these directions, I am reminded of an old picture my grandfather had of "The Praying Hands" and of the story of two brothers, Albrecht and Albert Durer, both gifted in art.

The Durer family was poor and only one brother could go to art school, so they tossed a coin; Albrecht went to art school while Albert worked hard to pay his brother's tuition at the Academy in Nuremburg.

After a few years, the artist, Albrecht, said to his brother Albert, "I can afford for you to go to art school now, so I will finance YOUR education." But Albert, who had worked so hard in the dangerous mines, looked down at his work-worn, arthritic hands which had been smashed numerous times, and knew it was too late for him. He would never be an artist. So Albrecht painted his brother's hands and they are the hands we now see in copies of the painting ... two hands lifted up towards a Power Greater.

I know that I, too, have my Higher Power waiting to help me if only I seek the help I need. I am reminded of the friends I have found in the fellowship. I remember how it feels to hold the hand of a shaky newcomer at the end of their first meeting, or the hand of my sponsor who reaches out to give me comfort when I share a personal hurt.

One Day at a Time . . . .
Alone I have proved again and again that I am defenseless over my disease, but together – TOGETHER - with my Higher Power and all of my fellows, I have a Power and Strength I never believed possible.

~ Marlene

PROMISES

"Experience is simply the name we give our mistakes."
Oscar Wilde

Before program, I would dwell in my mistakes. Experience, feh! I was all about self-abuse and feeling rotten about mistakes. My mistakes would certainly lead to overeating, since there was no other option in my mind. Even with years of therapy – with the same therapist – I still used eating as a soothing tool for those times when the mistake was enough to send me into a tailspin. Time and time again people would tell me I was too hard on myself, or that I should just relax and smile. Another mistake for me to internalize – I couldn't even make a mistake right. I wonder now if I sometimes looked for things to call mistakes so I'd have a reason to feel as rotten as I did most of the time. Having been abused as a child wasn't enough, blaming other people for my pain never satiated me.

In my first OA meeting, I heard the promises and I started to feel something melt away. Some of the shame and self-pity evaporated into the room of men and women who also felt this lack of satisfaction. A room of men and women loved me because I struggled with the same addictive behaviors. I don't think I'd ever been loved for my weakness, and there is something powerful in that. When I make a mistake, I can think about my friends in OA who tell me that there is no wrong way, just another way.

One Day at a Time . . . .
I can know that there are people who love me because I share in their weakness, and
I can read the promises to realize that recovery is possible.

GROWTH

"You will either step forward into growth,
or you will step back into safety."
Abraham Maslow

In my early years in program, one of my sponsors told me, "You're in a very well-decorated rut. You even have wall-to-wall carpeting and curtains in it." As I continued trudging my road to happy destiny, her words would crop up in my head any time I got "stuck." I could see how far I had come each time, so I persevered and kept turning my fear into faith. As I continued to work the Steps, I was led to new levels of recovery.

One Day at a Time . . . .
I put one foot in front of the other, keep taking the next right action and continue working the Steps. I live the promises of the program. Safety or growth? My choice is clear.

~ Rory

PAIN

Iron left in the rain and fog and dew,
With rust is covered.—Pain rusts into beauty too.
Mary Carolyn Davies

When the emotional pain of compulsive overeating finally brought me to my knees and I found this wonderful program, I really thought I had got it all right. I had physical recovery and weight loss and I thought that for the most part, I was slowly letting go of my character defects. There were times that I would go back to my old behaviors and have, what I would call, an emotional binge, but I reckoned that recovery was a process and that I was certainly making progress.

I have heard it said that recovery is like peeling away the layers of an onion, and that there will always be another one to peel away. It was only when months of physical pain, again brought me to my knees, that I once more became open and willing to look at the deeper meaning of my pain. I am so grateful that through my sponsor and what I have learned in the program, I have been willing to look beyond the physical pain at the underlying causes. I have realized that this pain, like the emotional pain of the eating, was my body's way of getting my attention that my life was out of balance.

I have had to face many issues in my life and again face many character defects that were stopping me from having a life that is happy, joyous and free. The worst of these was that I have spent most my life being there for everyone else at my own expense, and am now having to learn to put myself first. If I am not well and cannot love myself, I have nothing to give to all the people in my life. Just like my early phase in the program, when I first worked the Steps and achieved what I had thought was a fair measure of recovery, so too now am I having to peel away more of those layers and working at becoming the best person my Higher Power intended me to be.

One Day at a Time . . . .
I will continue working at my own recovery so that I am able to be of any use to others, both my family and my wonderful friends in the fellowship. As hard as it is, I know that I have to grow through this pain and learn the lessons that I will learn in the process, as I have heard it said that the flip side of pain is joy.

~ Sharon

EXPECTATIONS

"It's astonishing in this world how things don't
turn out at all the way you expect them to."
Agatha Christie

My life has been strangled by expectations ~ expectations I've held for myself; expectations others had of me; expectations I had of others; expectations I had for my life; and expectations I had of the God of my understanding. Again and again, my expectations were not met ~ and I was angry. I felt grossly let down and I was filled with resentment and shame. Eventually I became consumed by a toxic sense of angry and depressing apathy. If nothing turned out as I expected, why bother? I'd held so tightly to my expectations that they choked the life out of my soul. They condemned me to an existence of futility, frustration, selfishness, and despair. I thought that my expectations were realistic and "right"; therefore each variance from my expectations seemed a violation of the natural order of things.

Since beginning my Recovery work, I've come to recognize that I virtually believed that I was God. I thought I knew what was "best", what was "right", and what was "supposed" to happen. Though I am sometimes resistant, I am learning to let go of my expectations. I am learning to change my focus from my finite understanding to the mysterious and omniscient plan held safely and sanely in the hands of God. As I work my Steps and learn from others, I find that I am relieved that my earlier expectations did not come to fruition.

One Day at a Time . . . .
I surrender my former expectations and now expect only one thing: that as I work my
Steps, God will bring me increasing depths of sanity.

~ *Sharon*

Meditation 164

LONERS

*"I never found a companion
that was so companionable as solitude."
Henry David Thoreau*

When I am physically, emotionally or spiritually unfit, I find myself isolating. On the other hand, I also find there are differences between solitude and isolation. Granted, sometimes those differences are subtle; nevertheless, they are different. It only takes abstinence to clearly see the difference and unless one has experienced that state, I doubt if this can really be understood.

Isolation shuts us off, not only from other people, but from God Himself. We tuck in our tails and busy ourselves with whatever comes to mind and our sole purpose is to avoid human contact. Isolation is not good. When I am isolating, I feel shame and I risk overeating. While I may not do this consciously, I run a risk of depression. I also feel guilty and the negative thoughts run amok.

Solitude is not hiding from others as isolation can be. On the contrary, I can nourish myself by being in solitude. Because I have a creative nature, solitude allows me the freedom to explore and be as creative as God intends for me to be. If I don't allow myself solitude on occasion, I am in essence damming up the gifts God has given me. These gifts need the freedom of solitude to make them materialize and be all they can be. Because I have experienced the disease of compulsive eating and all the manifestations of this disease, I can clearly see the differences between solitude and isolation. I learned that I can be in a crowd of people and still be isolating. I can also be in a crowd of people and be in solitude. If I have spiritually and emotionally shut down, I would be going through the motions but deep down in my soul I would know that I'm isolating. When my spirit is free and I am working the program, one might glance at me and see me drifting off to a room where there is a piano and recapturing a moment of music ... or staring out a window at a view so beautiful that it takes my breath away ... or sipping a cup of coffee and observing those around me but not actively participating in their small talk but wondering who they really are.

One Day at a Time . . . .
Let me remove myself from the pain of the seclusion of isolation and substitute the wonderful state of solitude that brings me such great joy and peace of mind.

~ *Mari*

Meditation 165

PEACE

"If you do not find peace in yourself,
you will never find it anywhere else."
Paula A. Bendry

No outside reality can bring me peace. In the past, I tried to find it in many things, including relationships, ownership, and my vocation. But none of these externals brought me real peace. I had the opportunity of having all of them stripped away by a crisis in my life. I had surgery and got an infection that required a long period of recovery and resulted in disability. Many of my relationships ended, my income was reduced drastically, my capacity for ownership was decreased greatly, and I could no longer work. Although it was a painful lesson, it has been good for my spiritual condition.

I have been forced to look inside myself and realize that true peace and joy are found within. It is not about externals. Once I realized that, I found a relationship with my Higher Power that was deeper and more intimate than before, and the peace in my life settled inside of me in even greater measure.

One Day at a Time . . . .
I will look inwardly for the peace that I long for.

~ *Carolyn H.*

Meditation 166

PERFECTIONISM

"The wise man, the true friend the finished character
we seek everywhere and only find in fragments."
Ralph Waldo Emerson

Like a spider, perfectionism builds its web through every fiber of my life. My perfectionism leads me to a host of other character defects. When I expect people to be perfect, I can be plagued with self-absorption. When I think of myself as "better than them," I practice being judgmental towards others ~ especially when I see behaviors that I'd never do. It also leads to my defects of self-criticism and self-loathing. I begin to hate myself for all the things that I can't do perfectly. I'm afraid to try things for fear of not doing them perfectly and looking like a failure.

Perfectionism leads me to procrastination and sometimes paralysis. This obsession for my wanting something to be just right – or put in just the right place – causes all sorts of feelings that can overwhelm me. Mostly it's a fear of what another might think of me if I owned this thing or put it in that illogical place. I learned as a child that being perfect meant that I was validated as a human; therefore my perfectionism is hard for me to be willing to let God remove.

One Day at a Time . . . .
I will become willing to let God remove my defect of perfectionism. I will forgive myself and others for not being perfect. I will focus on a person's best moment instead of zeroing in on a person's defects.

~ *Pam*

Meditation 167

MIRROR, MIRROR

"Beauty is eternity gazing at itself in a mirror."
Kahlil Gibran

As a child, I often looked in the mirror and wished I were a boy. I thought I was ugly, had a deep voice, and was a disappointment as a girl. Even as a young woman I could never enjoy my appearance. I never saw the truth in the mirror. I would always focus on my "problem areas" and feel devastated that this had happened to my body. I felt totally helpless and wanted to cry; but I didn't cry ~ I ate instead. Compulsive overeating stripped me of my true self. It made me incapable of seeing the truth, feeling the truth, and perceiving the truth.

Since coming to OA the scales have fallen from my eyes. By reading the Big Book, going to meetings, interacting with my sponsor, and working the Steps, I have been able to see things as they are. Now I see my true self in the mirror and I can deal with life as it is. I can feel my feelings and know that they are neither right nor wrong and they will pass and change with the wind. This healing has cleared space in my mind and spirit for me to connect with my Higher Power. It has made room for me to grow, to love and care for myself, and to appreciate the body God gave me. When I doubt my perceptions, my feelings, or what I'm seeing in the mirror, I just surrender and remind myself that God has given me new eyes and new tools for living my life. The Twelve Steps of OA shine a light into my soul and show me the truth in all areas of my life and recovery.

One Day at a Time . . . .
I will look at myself ~ in all areas of my recovery ~ and know that what I am seeing is the truth because the light of OA and the Twelve Steps are guiding my life today.

~ *Karen*

Meditation 168

VICES AND VIRTUES

*"It has been my experience that folks who
have no vices have very few virtues."*
Abraham Lincoln

In doing a Tenth Step daily, I am faced with my character defects – and yes, even vices. While I may not be compulsively eating, I may over-indulge in any number of other things like talking, whining, or frenetic busy-ness. I have been told that in life I must learn to "take my foot off the gas." I have also been told that I am "too intense" or just "too much." I guess this means I am not moderate in all things (by a mile.)

This thought comforts me in all of this: at least I am in the game. If someone asks for my opinion, he or she will get it ~ straight from the heart or the hip, as they say. If someone needs a favor, I am apt to be excessive in performing it. If someone needs a friend, he or she often gets much more than a casual acquaintance in me. In essence, my being "too much in general" has its good side – at least I am not asleep at the wheel. I am fully engaged in life.

One Day at a Time . . . .
I will not forget that my zest for overindulging and overdoing-it-in-general has its counterpart in my zest for goodness and service. I am alive and kicking. I will not hate myself for being fully alive.

~ *Q*

Meditation 169

GUILT

"The worst guilt is to accept an unearned guilt."
Ayn Rand

I think that I was fed on guilt from the minute I was knee-high to a grasshopper. My mother's favorite saying was, "After all I've done for you..." I'd immediately feel guilty because of all that I perceived my mother had given up for me. As a result, I was given the message that love had to be earned and that as far as my mother was concerned, I had to do something to be worthy of her love. I felt like I had to be the perfect daughter my mother wanted. No matter what I did, it never seemed to be good enough. My guilt grew even more.

Of course I know now that I didn't deserve that guilt and that I chose to take it on ~ but as a child I didn't know that. Thank goodness for the program which is enabling me to see what I deserve – and what doesn't belong to me. I am realizing that most of the time it's other people's stuff and that I don't have to take that on.

One Day at a Time . . . .
I will remember to only take on what is rightfully mine and I don't need to feel guilty if I don't deserve to.

~ *Sharon*

KIND WORDS

"Kind words can be short and easy to speak,
but their echoes are truly endless."
Mother Teresa

How many times are we gifted with newcomers to our meetings? They are so easy to see as they huddle in the back of the room – usually as close to the exit as possible. Their oversized coat is a good giveaway, especially in July. Their eyes show the fear and anxiety that we all felt. Sure, we made it, and so can they.

I remember the elder who first said those magical words to me – those two simple words – "Welcome Home." The warmth and safety those words held were immense. I felt that my body was huge, and I was embarrassed in a room full of people who looked very similar to me…but my eyes could not see that. They were filled with tears because of those two words. Welcome home. Whoever that person was, I have two words for you, "Thank you."

What can you do to make a newcomer feel welcome to your meeting? Let us not forget that all-important first hug. I remember mine; do you remember yours? It felt good, I'll bet. So welcome the newcomer and let them know they are home.

One Day at a Time . . . .
I will do my part to welcome the newcomer into our fellowship.

~ Danny

STRUGGLE

*"Our way is not soft grass,
it's a mountain path with lots of rocks.
But it goes upward, forward, toward the sun."*
Ruth Westheimer

I have been in a Twelve Step program for a while now. When I look back, I sometimes think how easy the journey has been to find the peace, serenity and love I've been given – thanks to the program. I brought a lot of denial with me when I joined the program, and apparently I'm still in some denial. I'm so grateful to be where I am today that I have forgotten the struggles I've faced to get here.

No wonder some newcomers look at longtimers and think they'll never be able to get there! When I stretch my memory, I remember running headlong into the Fourth Step and thinking it the scariest thing I'd ever faced in my life. I know that first one was traumatic–holding my pencil to do it, getting the first page down, and admitting so many things that had been shaming me for decades. I usually don't think about that today. Now I know firsthand the cleansing of a good Fourth Step and I look forward to them as I peel the onion and find more defects.

When I look back over my journey, I can remember sitting in an emergency room using the slogan "One Day at a Time" for the first time. I changed "one day" to "five minutes" because it was all I could handle. But it got me through that day and the next two days. A few years ago I read that the slogans are the handrails to the Steps. I wish I'd known that before. For me to use that slogan when I did was an act of faith ~ and at the time my faith was shaky. After having proved to my satisfaction that there is a Higher Power out there who wants the best for me, I have faith now. Maybe this is why I look back on my journey and have a hard time finding the struggles. Maybe it's my new attitude of gratitude that keeps me looking to the positive rather than the negative. Whatever the reason, I'd like to say that I struggled in the program, but it was worth it.

One Day at a Time . . . .
I will remember to turn to the program to help maintain my peace and serenity, especially through the bad times.

~ *Rhonda*

A PERSON OF WORTH

"It is funny about life:
if you refuse to accept anything but the very best
you will very often get it."
W. Somerset Maugham

Upon entering recovery, I found it ironic, even strange, that I was so very good at taking care of others and helping them secure the help that they needed, yet often in my life I have not done this for myself. I would grow depressed and very frozen in anger, grief, and fear. Why wasn't I ever able to care properly for myself? At what point did I begin to expect the worst as my own allotment in life?

It is possible that I dreamed of a "rescue" or an intervention of some kind that would "save me." It is likely that my Higher Power knew of my tendencies for magical thinking. He caught my attention by the introduction of someone who knew of a program that would point me in a realistic direction. In this program, I would be taught to take small actions – "One day at a time" – that would encourage and re-build my shattered self-esteem. I now am in possession of a wonderful program that has given me tools for recovery and change so that I can learn to treat myself as well as I treat others.

One Day at a Time . . . .
I no longer accept anything but the best, as it will indirectly affect my recovery. This is my new mindset: that I am a person of worth.

~ January K.

Meditation 173

SUNLIGHT OF THE SPIRIT

"Trust God and buy broccoli."
Author Unknown

I heard that quotation in an OA meeting years ago. "What an odd thing," I thought. "Why does God care what I buy?" But as years have gone by and my abstinence continues one day at a time, I see the meaning of that phrase and have deep respect for its principle.

I can trust God 'til the cows come home, but there is work to be done. A more familiar quote is: "Trust God but continue to row toward shore."

Abstinence for me is not only refraining from compulsive overeating, but abstaining from what I call my "alcoholic foods." They block that beautiful contact between me and the Sunlight of the Spirit. It is my responsibility to purchase, prepare, weigh and measure the best foods for my peace of mind ~ and to open the channel to a Power Greater than Myself. Now I live this way, with thanks to the Twelve Steps.

One Day at a Time . . . .
I will be grateful that food does not have power today.

~ Gerri

MIRACLES

"Miracles are instantaneous,
they cannot be summoned but come of themselves,
usually at unlikely moments and to those who least expect them."
Katherine Ann Porter

I never believed that we live in an age of miracles. As far as I was concerned, those happened only in the days of the Bible – with burning bushes and the Red Sea opening up. When I first came into the program and heard people talking about miracles, I was skeptical. As I became more open to the possibility, things began to happen which I can only consider to be miracles. They may not have seemed large to my old closed mind, but being able to give up certain trigger foods – or having a fellow member in the program call me when I most needed a call – have become miracles in my life today.

Being able to maintain my weight, rather than losing and gaining weight every few months, is a miracle. Most importantly, my transformed relationships with my children and other loved ones are miracles.

One Day at a Time . . . .
I will open my mind to the possibility of miracles occurring in my life…and they will come.

~ *Sharon*

ACCEPTANCE

*"Because you're not what I would have you be,
I blind myself to who in truth, you are."*
Madeleine L'Engle

The Big Book of AA says, "Acceptance is the answer to all my problems." I am finding this to be true for me. Living in a household with several family members, I need to not focus on others' faults. I can choose to practice acceptance by looking past what others do that I think they shouldn't do, and instead I can love them for who they are.

In order to show unconditional love I must look past their shortcomings. I need to stop dwelling on the fact that they sometimes don't do things the way I want them to. If I don't do that, anger and resentments follow and I find myself trying to control things and play God. We all know that doesn't work. It just causes misery and takes away my joy, peace and serenity.

As I work my program of recovery, I am better off to "let go and let God" and just accept others as they are. Putting others in God's hands and resisting the temptation to try to make things turn out the way I want them to is the definition of acceptance for me. When I love others unconditionally I experience peace and serenity beyond my wildest dreams.

One Day at a Time . . . .
I will practice the miracle of acceptance and unconditional love.

~ Bluerose

STEP TWELVE

"One must really have suffered oneself to help others."
Mother Teresa

Before coming into the program, I always worked in some sort of caring profession and was always either helping or "fixing" someone else ~ mostly in areas in which I had no personal experience. I was a people-pleaser and I would be there for someone else. If anything needed to be done, I was the one to offer to do it. But ultimately that backfired because I would feel used and resentful, and I would land up in the food as my way of compensating.

Since coming into program I have changed the way I help others. Instead of doing for others so they would like me – or so I would get a pat on the back – I share my experience, strength and hope with other compulsive overeaters. I have been where they have been, and I can share with them my struggles and how I've overcome them. Not only do I help others in the program with what I have learned, but, as they say, I can only keep what I have if I give it away. I get as much – if not more – from sharing with another in the program. How different this is from the way it was before I began the program, and I'm so grateful for that!

One Day at a Time . . . .
I will share my experience, strength and hope with another compulsive overeater. By doing so, I get to keep what I have so generously been given in this program.

~ Sharon

TOOLS

"We shall neither fail nor falter; we shall not weaken or tire...
give us the tools and we will finish the job."
Winston Churchill

We use tools everyday to complete a task at hand. To cook, we need tools such as pots, pans, knives, and silverware; to tend to our laundry, we need soap and water; to clean our home, we use a vacuum, dust rags, and cleaners.

Our journey of recovery is handled in the same way. The tools we use to help us throughout each day include: Step Work, Sponsorship, Meetings, Prayer, Meditation, Writing, Literature, Meal Plan, Service and Abstinence. These tools assist us in keeping our days balanced and they allow for a meaningful, productive day, each day of our recovery.

We hold strong to our recovery with the assistance of these tools, building our endurance each day. Like soldiers marching across the field, we are on the frontline day-to-day. By using these tools and keeping them close to us, we are ready to take on anything that might come our way.

One Day at a Time . . . .
Give us the tools, and I will keep them close to me.

~ Kimber

EFFICIENCY AND FUNCTION

"In God's economy, nothing is wasted.
Through failure, we learn a lesson in humility
which is probably needed, painful though it is."
Bill W., Letter of 1942

I have spent a lot of time cultivating perfectionism in the vain attempt to make up for being a "failure" – or what I have now come to understand is compulsive eating and an illness. I was trying to make up with efficiency for that feeling of not being good enough ~ and that feeling seems to be a hallmark of our illness.

By my past behaviors, I wanted you to notice how efficient and functional I was despite my obese body that belied I had a problem. If I could somehow convince you that I was "normal" and "ok," I would not have to admit my powerlessness. This is the single greatest obsession of every compulsive eater: that we are "normal" eaters. But we are not!

I built a lifetime around efficiency and function trying to show you how normal I was. Thank God I was brought to my compulsive eating knees time and time again until I could finally make that admission of failure as a normal eater and admit that I was powerless. The humility brought about by that admission afforded me an open-mindedness and willingness I had hitherto not known. I became teachable.

One Day at a Time . . . .
I pray to remain teachable.

~ *Lanaya*

Meditation 179

ISOLATION

"Solitude vivifies; isolation kills."
Joseph Roux

As an introvert and an agoraphobic I relate to both sides of this quote. From an introverted point of view, I need solitude to regroup, renew, and refresh. It's part of my process in life to have quiet time alone in order to "get it together". When I'm alone and I read my OA literature and meditate on what I'm reading and learning, I'm able to gain new insight and a renewed sense of direction in my program.

From an agoraphobic point of view, isolation kills my ability to stick to my program. When my social anxiety cycles and it becomes difficult to get to meetings or make phone calls, I hide from the world ~ and from my friends and other OA members who can help me maintain my abstinence.

Solitude and Isolation are both active decisions. Both require some forethought. If solitude is what I need to in order to regroup, I have to make time for it. I have to take a walk, read a book, putter around my house. On the flip side, if I'm having a hard time with Program and my social anxiety is becoming unmanageable, I can either isolate and spiral down, or I can choose to take action and get to a meeting, make a phone call, or ask my sponsor to meet me for coffee. I don't have to be alone in this program.

One Day at a Time . . . .
I remember that I have control over my actions. Although I need solitude to heal, I don't have to be alone in my disease.

~ *Deb B.*

RESENTMENT

*"When you hold resentment toward another, you are bound
to that person or condition by an emotional link that is
stronger than steel. Forgiveness is the only way to
dissolve that link and get free."*
Catherine Ponder

I once had a situation in which someone I was acquainted with said unkind things about my weight and verbally attacked my spouse in front of my daughter. I worried and revisited the situation over and over for many years until the anger turned to resentment and became a major, entrenched grudge. Because so many of my eating issues stem from emotional ones, this would drive me to eat in an effort to dull, numb and forget my anger. That didn't work ~ the eating didn't stop that anger from turning into resentment.

When I would complain about this situation to a friend, she told me that I had to stop allowing that person to "rent space in my mind." I came to realize that I had allowed – and even nurtured – a negative energetic link to that person and situation. I couldn't let go of resentment until I was willing to take the needed steps in program and to forgive. Forgiving doesn't mean I didn't learn anything from the situation, and I haven't forgotten the unkind words. But I learned that I needed to be more cautious in my dealings with this type of individual. I learned I can't surround myself with people who are overly-negative and say poisonous things without accepting any accountability for their actions. I have learned that I can be accountable for mine, and that I no longer have to allow myself to be bound by an emotional link to the situation.

One Day at a Time . . . .
I will ask my Higher Power to help me to learn to forgive and forget. With the help of my Higher Power, I will let go of unnecessary baggage that causes resentment.

~ *Deb B.*

PROCRASTINATION

"How does a project get to be a year behind schedule?
One day at a time."
Fred Brooks

I have been given many talents, and I count them as gifts from my Maker. Throughout life I have discovered that there was virtually nothing that I could not make, bake, say or do with the help of my Higher Power. At the age of three years I learned to crochet and read. I learned to draw, paint, write poetry and quilt. The fact that I was not afraid of failing had a great influence on my ability to tackle any task.

Surprisingly, when I felt that I was "grown" and needed to leave home and start a life of my own, I found that finishing anything was almost impossible. I could start anything – but I seemed to complete nothing. Much to my dismay I had developed the art of procrastination. Just waiting to finish anything tomorrow puts me one day behind. Day by day, the project gets put on the back burner and forgotten. One day at a time I eventually find that I am years into finishing some things.

Thanks to this program and its wonderful Steps and tools, I have found that by working "one day at a time" I can be – and am – a person who starts and finishes things. This is who God created me to be...not the person who continually puts things off. It took a lot of reading and prayer and meditating on God's Word for me to get where I am today...a person who takes action on the tasks before me. I am far from perfect, but I am making progress.

One Day at a Time . . . .
Just for today I will take action and not put off until tomorrow what I can do today.

~ Annie K.

THE BOTTOM

"Those who cannot remember the past
are condemned to repeat it."
George Santayana

Sometimes we have to go to the absolute bottom. If we're extremely lucky, the absolute bottom is where we find our inspiration. Sometimes I think that people who don't hit absolute bottom are missing a valuable experience. Then again, living life on the edge of that precipice is no fun at all. The greatest gift is to be able to step away from the edge and live life without the fear of falling.

If we aren't extremely lucky, what we find at the absolute bottom is a trapdoor that opens to a vast, empty space. The door opens and the empty space gratefully accepts the body and the soul given to it.

One Day at a Time . . . .
I will stop living on the edge;
I will stop regretting my past;
I will avoid the trapdoor.

~ *Richard H.*

Meditation 183

COMMITMENT

"One small step for a man ~
One giant leap for mankind."
Neil Armstrong

When I came into program, I was very overwhelmed by the idea of commitment. The thought of committing to a food plan or exercise regime was more than I could comprehend; in fact, I would feel panic rising in me at the thought of it. I would have dreams of being a mouse caught in a corner with nowhere to run. I would throw in the proverbial monkey wrench after a short time, and soon be on my own turf ... the desperation and depression which were my "old friends" would reappear, and I would be back into my "safe" and always-waiting disease.

This recovery program taught me "one day at a time;" it taught me to put one foot in front of the other; that for one day I could do what I couldn't do, or even fathom doing, for a lifetime. This is how I found abstinence. Breaking up my days, weeks, months and years into 24-hour periods allows me to live in the now, and not feel swallowed up in thinking that I have to do this for the rest of my life.

One Day at a Time . . . .
The steps may seem small, it may even look as though I'm not moving at all, but with God's help I make giant leaps toward wellness and peace of mind.

~ *Shana*

HOPE

"Hope is the thing with feathers
That perches in the soul
And sings the tune without the words
And never stops at all."
Emily Dickinson

I wanted desperately to lose weight, be happy, be spiritually and emotionally fulfilled, and feel serenity in my soul. How long must one wait in a single lifetime to achieve these things? How long must one function day-to-day at a fairly high level, only to close the door at night to a world of emptiness? How long must one go without hope?

My compulsion for food had come close to destroying my life. I was in a constant state of denial that the simple act of eating food could account for a life run amok and totally unmanageable. But the truth of the matter is that it could ... and it did.

I found Twelve Steps that empowered me to do things I'd never dreamed of doing. These Twelve Steps enabled me to see the simple reality that compulsive eating could destroy my life. They showed me that life was beautiful and that my disease could turn out to be my greatest blessing. The Twelve Steps gave me something so precious that I am in awe of their power .... something so empowering that I had to admit powerlessness in order to become powerful. The Twelve Steps gave me the most beautiful gift I have ever received ... a gift that no one can ever take away from me ... a gift that I treasure above all gifts: hope. They gave me the gift of hope.

One Day at a Time . . . .
One day at a time ... I will hold onto my hope.
One day at a time ... I will treasure my hope.
One day at a time ... hope perches in my soul.
One day at a time ... hope sings its song.

~ Mari

YES AND NO

"Yes and No are very short words to say,
but we should think for some length of time
before saying them."
Anonymous

he disease of compulsive eating really warps a person's life. Many compulsive overeaters become people-pleasers and do not know how to set boundaries. We end up not being able to say "No." However, we also end up saying "Yes" to our disease. In the depths of our disease we lose complete control in our lives.

This program of recovery helps us to set our lives back in order. When we give our disease over to our Higher Power, work the Twelve Steps and practice the principles of our program, we see that our lives can be turned around ~ and daily we have victory over our disease.

One Day at a Time . . . .
I will say "No" to my disease and "Yes" to recovery by working the Twelve Steps,
surrendering to my Higher Power, and living the principles of my program.

~ Jeff

OVERCOMING RELAPSE

"Come, whoever you are! Wanderer, worshipper,
Lover of Leaving. Come, this is not a caravan of despair.
It doesn't matter if you've broken your vow a thousand times.
Still, and yet again, come, come."
Rumi

Perhaps the best thing my recovery plan has given me is finding the gift of inspiration almost anywhere. The above quote is such an example. Mevlana Jelalu'ddin Rumi was a Persian poet and theologian who lived from 1207 to 1273. Rumi also seemed to understand recovery quite well, judging from this quote.

I have fallen so many times on my recovery path. Once down, the disease really starts talking to me. "You're already down; you may as well stay down," it will say. Or, "You screwed up your food plan, so you might as well eat this, too." On and on, it never fails.

That's why this quote from Rumi means so much to me. My Higher Power sent it as an invitation to begin again, however many times I need. Even if I slip over and over and over, I can always begin again. My Higher Power and this program of recovery are very forgiving, and I can pick up and move on. I needn't fear failure, because I only fail if I don't get up and forge ahead.

One Day at a Time . . . .
I will remember that I may fall, but I can get up again. I can begin anew, and know that I will overcome relapse when I make a fresh start.

- Jeff

Meditation 187

SUFFERING

"The desire to stop suffering
is not the same thing as the desire to stop the behavior
we are doing which causes us to suffer."
Dr. James Golden

Our disease of addiction causes tremendous suffering to ourselves and to those around us. It consumes our lives and often leads to painful losses. No matter how profoundly we long to be rid of our disease, recovery is not something that falls into our laps just because we want it. We don't magically stop being compulsive eaters just because that's our desire. It would be great if recovery happened magically and all we'd have to do is say, "I don't want this disease anymore; I don't want to suffer any longer." If it were that easy, we'd immediately find ourselves in a place of complete and total recovery. Unfortunately, it doesn't work that way.

In the depths of my disease I cried out to the God of my understanding to help me achieve abstinence and an alleviation of my suffering. What was the answer to my prayers? This wonderful Twelve Step program.

One of the first things I learned was that I could wish and hope and pray, but until I put feet to my prayers and actually started working the Steps, I wouldn't recover from my disease. God will only do for us what He can do through us. If I'm not willing to do even a little bit of the work, I shouldn't expect recovery. If I won't take the first step on this journey, I can't expect to reach my final destination. I can do some things for myself – like putting the Steps into practice – but what about the things I can't do for myself? I'll let God handle those.

One Day at a Time . . . .
I'll remember that it's not enough
to want to stop suffering from my disease;
I also need to do some footwork to make it happen.

~ *Jeff*

FEAR

"Few persons live up to the faith which they really have.
Unreasoned fear is a master intellectual fraud
practiced upon the evolving mortal soul."
The Urantia Book

Unreasoned fear was my main problem for most of my life. I lived with a myriad of fears which seemed to be too awesome and terrible to face. I love the fact that since finding this recovery program, I no longer have to live in fear. What wondrous freedom I found in the realization that unreasoned fear is "intellectual fraud!"

One slogan I recall about fear says: "Future Events Appear Real." That is the first one that really helped me to realize that most of my fears were not based on what was real. By working the Steps of this program I have managed to stop attempting to live in a future filled with fear. When I focus on just being here now – living in this moment only – I don't have to run from fear.

One Day at a Time . . . .
I will stay in this moment. I will look at the people and things that are here right now and enjoy what my Higher Power has given me.

~ Steph

ACTION

"He does not believe who does not live his belief."
Thomas Fuller

It is an old axiom that actions speak louder than words. Our Twelve Step program is one of action, no matter how much we want to avoid working the Steps. The Big Book states that IF you want what we have, you will do what we did. That also means the opposite ... if you don't want what we have, don't do it. The insanity of this disease is expecting a different result by continually doing the same old thing. Sanity is giving up what didn't work and daring to try something new.

One Day at a Time . . . .
I am going to trust that obedience to the program will, in time, restore me to sanity.

~ Jeremiah

CONTROL

"I offer you this prayer for all the difficult relationships in our lives:
God, grant me the serenity to accept the people I cannot change,
The courage to change the person I can,
And the wisdom to know that person is me."
Rev. Mary Manin Morrissey

My disease tells me that my life would be so much better if people would only do what I tell them to do. If they would listen to me, I could solve all their problems, fix their lives, and everybody would be happy. Why can't they see that our relationships would be better if they'd just do what I say, and not what I do? Don't they realize that I know more than they do about how to run their lives?

Well, luckily for the people in my life, this disease lies. I DON'T know what's best for them. Because I have a disease of compulsion, I don't even know what's best for me. If I had known what was best for me, my life would not have been in shambles like it was before I found the Twelve Steps of recovery.

I had to come to the realization that my life had become unmanageable. Only then could I find a Higher Power to restore sanity to the crazy drama that had become my life ~ and to grant me the serenity which accompanies sanity. Now I realize the only person I can control is myself. I can't make other people change into what I want them to be, nor can I make them do what I think is best for them. Since I've begun letting my Higher Power restore me to sanity, I no longer want to be a control freak. I can't even fathom trying to run another person's life. I have enough on my hands just living my own life; I don't have the strength, knowledge or wisdom to live someone else's. I will always be grateful to my Higher Power for helping me to realize that.

One Day at a Time . . . .
I will live my own life and allow others to live theirs.

~ Jeff

SANITY

"Came to believe ...
That a power greater than ourselves ...
Could restore us to sanity."
Step Two

What a powerful statement! There's a power greater than me. At first glance it seemed so frightening. As I looked at my situation, it seemed impossible ... who or what could be greater than I am? To be "restored" to sanity meant I must be crazy. After all, that is what insanity means. My Higher Power happened to be my sponsor and she was determined enough to be that power, if only until I opened the door to another.

One day when my ears were open and my mouth shut, these words came from another sufferer: "God can." I thought to myself, "What?! What does 'God can' mean?" Later – when my body was clean and my mind receptive – those words came to mean a great deal to me. "God can" if I let Him. God can take away my compulsion to overeat. God can remove my desire for nicotine. God can take away my desire for booze. Yes, God can.

I no longer worry about what I can't accomplish because I know that "God can." So now when my day begins I think of what I can do right, and do it for today. That which I cannot do right – I just let God handle that. We make a pretty good team, God and me.

One Day at a Time . . . .
I let my Higher Power restore me to sanity.

~ Danny

Meditation 192

HONESTY

"Our lives improve only when we take chances ~
and the first and most difficult risk we can take
is to be honest with ourselves."
Walter Anderson

After the initial shock and realization that I am a compulsive overeater, it transpired that in order to recover, I had to get honest. This was – and still is – a painful process for me, yet it is an essential step towards my recovery.

First I had to admit that I wasn't in control of my life and that recovery couldn't be achieved unaided. As with most revelations, this was an uncomfortable truth to behold. I was also prompted through honesty to stop blaming everyone else for my unwillingness to help myself. I had to find conviction in my actions and not just emptiness in my words.

I conceded that I am not as perfect as I would like to think. I make mistakes and sometimes slip from the path of recovery, but with honesty comes acceptance that I am only human. This disease would deceive me into thinking that I am a failure when in fact it's my actions that have failed me. Like a magician who performs illusions for the crowd, this disease would have me think I have committed unforgivable sins. Honesty is the key to my recovery; it unlocks the chains that have imprisoned me for so long. It allows me to recognize my weaknesses and turn them into strengths. It turns simple existence into life ~ and inner-conflicts into outward serenity.

One Day at a Time . . . .
I will be honest with myself.

~ Sue G.

Meditation 193

APATHY

"The world is a dangerous place to live;
not because of the people who are evil,
but because of the people who don't do anything about it."
Albert Einstein

In my life as an addict, I found myself deteriorating in every way possible. I was spiritually hungry, emotionally bereft, and physically a mess. I stopped caring about people, places or things. I was apathetic to such a degree that I no longer cared about anything.

That gradually changed when I embraced the Twelve Steps. I began to open my eyes to the world around me ~ the world I had shut out. The more I worked the Steps, the more I saw the reality of things. I became less selfish and began to try to make a difference – not only in my own life, but also in the lives of those I cared about. I found myself loving more. I found I was once again capable of having compassion.

I am no longer afraid to speak out when I see misdeeds. I don't cower before those who would do harm to others. I embrace the good and the bad in this world I call home.

One Day at a Time . . . .
I will do my part in making the world a better place. I will listen and hear what my Higher Power has in mind for me.

~ Mari

Meditation 194

SERVICE

"I do not know what path in life you will take,
but I do know this:
If, on that path, you do not find a way to serve,
you will never be happy."
Albert Schweitzer

Working the Twelfth Step means carrying the message of recovery to those who still suffer from our disease. To be a messenger of hope has to be the highest form of service we can provide to our fellow compulsive eaters.

Giving service means more than volunteering to set chairs up at a meeting, tidying up afterwards, or giving another person a ride to the meeting. Giving service means living a triumphant program every single day. It's taking a telephone call from someone who's having a rough day … and it's making an outreach call even when I don't feel like it. It's not hiding my slips in abstinence, and it sure isn't wallowing in my misery. It's getting up and moving on. It's presenting a positive view of the program.

We don't recruit members to recovery; we attract them by our example. If I don't put a positive face on my program, I can't expect a fellow-sufferer to consider the Twelve Steps as a way to recover from the disease of compulsive overeating. I know this program works – and others won't know it unless I show them that it does.

One Day at a Time . . . .
I will serve by living a triumphant program.

~ JAR

ETERNITY

"Every action of our lives
touches on some chord that will vibrate in eternity."
Edwin Hubbel Chapin

When I first read this quote two thoughts came to mind. The first thought was that I owed it – to myself and to every compulsive overeater in the world – to recover from my disease. If I can recover from compulsive eating with the help of my Higher Power, then others will know that recovery is possible for them as well.

My second thought had to do with Bill W., Dr. Bob and all the other Twelve Step trailblazers. Did they realize that what they did in 1935 would have such a far-reaching impact on the world? Did they know that they would set in motion a program that would bring hope to addicted people everywhere? My guess is that they did not know, and that they probably would have scoffed at the very idea that they were starting a global recovery program that would empower millions.

I have written Edwin Chapin's quote in my Big Book to remind me of those who went before me and of those who will come after. It is my tribute to the eternal value of the Twelve Step program.

One Day at a Time . . . .
I will remember that the things I do today will have a lasting impact on the future.

~ Jeff

SELF-TRUTH

"You cannot be true to God or to anyone else
until you are true to yourself."
Sr. Jeanne Koma, H.M.

I have spent much of my life role-playing. As spouse, parent, employee, addict, I have often lost myself. Who am I? Why am I here? If I played none of those roles, would I still exist?

It wasn't until I took the time to discover the 'real' me, the person God created, that I was able to be a better spouse, parent, and employee. And it was through this discovery that the addict in me began taking a back seat to the child of God that I truly am.

I cannot do God's will or be supportive of others if I am dishonest about who I am.

When Moses asked God who He was, God replied, "I am who I am." I am also who I am. I have nothing of which to be ashamed.

One Day at a Time . . . .
I must be true to myself if I wish to be of service to anyone else.

~ *Debbie*

SELF-RESPECT

"In his private heart ...
no man much respects himself."
Mark Twain

I had no confidence or satisfaction in myself. I covered my lack of self-respect with absurd and harmful behaviors. I shielded myself from the respect and love of others by using these behaviors. I wanted to hide from the truth I knew - that I was behaving badly and dishonestly.

Having begun this program which restores us to sanity, we have stepped into a new realm of learning to love and respect ourselves. We have come to realize that we gain self-respect by working the Steps, surrendering ego, doing service for others, and relying on a Higher Power. Our lives become useful, our hearts are healed, and we are filled with respect for who we have become.

One Day at a Time . . . .
May I come to realize I am worthy of self-respect because I am doing the right things for the right reasons ... and giving credit to my Higher Power.

~ Judy N.

LIVING RIGHT

"Life is not a matter of having good cards ...
but of playing a poor hand well."
Robert Louis Stevenson

There are many things in this world we have no control over, such as: our gender, our stature, our race, or physical abnormalities. But we always have the power to choose how we deal with events and circumstances. We can always take the right action ~ if it is not predicated on achieving a favorable outcome.

The Big Book tells us that it is a "well-understood fact that in God's sight all human beings are important, the proof that love freely given surely brings a full return."

I must ask myself ~

One Day at a Time . . . .
Am I living properly?
Am I living properly today?
Am I really trying at all?

~ Jeremiah

Meditation 199

ACTION

"I have always thought the actions of men
the best interpreters of their thoughts."
John Locke

I was in therapy many years ago and I remember something my therapist said that I have since followed: "People can say anything that they want but it is their actions that speak the truth." For years I wanted to be thin and food was all that I thought about. Even though I wanted to be thin, I never had the motivation to do the work necessary to lose weight and keep it off.

It wasn't until I came to OA that I began to take the actions required to change my life. The Twelve Step Program is one of action ~ and action requires commitment, energy and time. I am willing to take action by using the 8 Tools of OA and by incorporating the Twelve Steps into my daily life. My program of recovery is a priority for me now. If I am to keep the abstinence and strong recovery that I have attained, I must take daily action to work this wonderful program.

One Day at a Time . . . .
I will take daily action to keep my recovery.

~ *Cindi L.*

HONORING MYSELF

"And how shall you punish those whose remorse
is already greater than their misdeeds?"
Kahlil Gibran

We are not bad people trying to become good; rather, we are sick people trying to get well. It takes a long time for some of us to believe this truth. We have been programmed to believe the worst about ourselves ... or ironically, to believe ourselves to be much better than others. This appears to be a common denominator in our disease.

We despise the person we perceive ourselves to be. Virtually every event in our lives drives us deeper into the abyss of remorse, self-abuse, self-hate, and self-serving. We must stop believing lies about ourselves. The fact that we are here on Earth is proof that we belong and that we have the right – even the obligation – to be what we can be.

One Day at a Time . . . .
I will honor and respect myself.

~ Jeremiah

BEFORE AND AFTER

"The Light of God surrounds me.
The Love of God enfolds me.
The Power of God protects me.
The Presence of God watches over me.
Wherever I am, God is ... and all is well."
James Dillet Freeman

Before I found the Twelve Steps, I was walking in darkness.
Now God's Light is all around me.

Before I found the Twelve Steps, I was lonely and felt no one cared.
Now I'm enveloped in God's love.

Before I found the Twelve Steps, my life was out of control.
Now God is the Higher Power in my life.

Before I found the Twelve Steps, I was lost in my disease of compulsion.
Now God looks out for me.

Before I found the Twelve Steps, I was isolated and alone.
Now anywhere I go, I know I don't go there by myself ...
for God is with me.

One Day at a Time . . . .
I remember that wherever I am,
God is ...
And all is well.

~ Jeff

GROWING OLDER

"I think, therefore I am."
Rene Descartes

Before beginning my recovery process with our online groups, I used to look in the mirror and want to cry. I'm not a young, lovely creature anymore. I'm showing my age. Inside I'm still a young girl, but now I have a grandma's face.

The Twelve Steps to recovery have opened up a whole new world to me ~ and it is a world that is ageless. Its principles are timeless: honesty, hope, faith, courage, integrity, willingness, humility, love, forgiveness, self-discipline, perseverance, spiritual awareness and service. Maturing without benefit of these principles would be choosing to simply get old.

Through my program of recovery, I have been inspired to keep my body strong and well – the way my Higher Power made it. I am encouraged to stay as attractive as possible for as long as possible, out of concern for myself and for others. By the time I reached the Ninth Step, the worry lines in my face began to soften … now they look like smile lines. It seems that participating in our program of recovery has reversed my age.

One Day at a Time . . . .
I will grow older, but also much wiser.

~ *SAG*

FALSE BELIEFS

"There is only one cause of unhappiness;
the false beliefs you have in your head,
beliefs so widespread, so commonly held,
that it never occurs to you to question them."
Anthony de Mello

As a child of poverty, neglect, and a family that moved frequently, I was always an "outsider." I was looked on as "unacceptable." As an adult I moved away, married, and lived in the same community all the rest of my years. I've had the same friends and lived a very respected life. Yet internally I was still "unacceptable" ~ always feeling "less than" others. I never even told my husband or children about those aspects of my childhood. There were parts of me I never shared with anyone. I did not question the idea that I was still an "unacceptable" person, though there was lots of evidence to discount that idea.

Since joining The Recovery Group program and sharing that pain with my sponsor and others, that pain-filled inner child has been freed and has integrated with the person that I am today. This freeing process has enabled me to finally see and feel the love, the acceptance, and the respect that has always been there for me.

One Day at a Time . . . .
I will reach out to others at meetings and within our Recovery Group ~ especially those who have had a childhood similar to mine. It has been a tremendous gift to be able to go back, take that neglected little girl by the hand, and bring her into my world to live with me.

~ Karen H.

CHOICES

"Destiny is not a matter of chance;
it is a matter of choice.
It is not a thing to be waited for;
it is a thing to be achieved."
William Jennings Bryan

I have often wished that my life were easier. I have resented the fact that others seemed to have been given a free ride, whereas I have had to walk the distance. I often prayed that on waking one morning, I would find that the shadow I cast the day before had been vastly reduced overnight.

Wallowing in self-pity has taken me nowhere. It has wasted time that I could have spent reaching my recovery. I could choose to waste my days wishing for something that I obviously don't have – and will never have – unless I actively do the legwork to obtain it. I could sit back and expect the world to come to my door, but I would find that it passes me by.

Often I find myself slipping down the emotional slide into the depths of depression. In those dark times, walking through life is as easy as walking waist-deep through wet tar. It's a place where the sun never shines, thus its warm rays don't land on my skin.

Recovery comes only when I make the choice and do the work needed to attain it.

One Day at a Time . . . .
I choose to use the wisdom, strength and shelter of God; my Higher Power. I choose to follow the Twelve Steps and use the tools provided in the recovery program. I choose to be guided by the Big Book. In essence ... I choose life.

~ *Sue G*

Meditation 205

IDENTITY

"Resolve to be thyself:
And know that he who finds himself loses his misery."
Matthew Arnold

Life before recovery was a theatrical production in which I played all parts to all audiences. I gave a performance which aimed to satisfy everyone's requirements but my own. I proffered whatever I felt others wanted, giving no thought to my own needs. Some may say that's a worthy attitude, but it was influenced by a desire to be accepted – not for who I am – but for whom I thought everyone wanted me to be. I used my performance to control situations and to avoid any nasty surprises. I furnished more than I could afford, often lavishing what wasn't mine to give. Frequently I didn't feel that I had gained the acceptance I so fervently sought, and this yielded feelings of incompetence.

To be everything to all people took time and sapped considerable quantities of energy physically, spiritually and emotionally. Often I found I couldn't keep up with this self-inflicted regimen of people-pleasing. I began to resent the performance and gained no satisfaction from the results.

Through my recovery I realized that I had never been happy with the results of my role-playing. It had been a compulsion to seek the approval from others because I couldn't grant myself the authorization to be me. The only person I can be is me. The only person I have a right to be is me.

One Day at a Time . . . .
I give myself permission to be who I truly am: ME!

~ Sue G.

OPPORTUNITIES

"A wise man will make more opportunities than he finds."
Francis Bacon

There is a promise that more will be revealed as we trudge the road of happy destiny. We all start by building on the basics, the foundation that must be in place. In grade school I learned to read and write; in high school, how to research and train myself to acquire information. In college, I gained specific advanced information that allowed me to build upon, and advance my interests. When I applied the same principles to the program, I got similar results, but even more so. When my mind was opened to spiritual principles, I received much more than that I was seeking. My thoughts were lifted to a much higher plane of ethics.

In searching for an answer to compulsive overeating, I was exposed to additional opportunities to grow by doing. Often I tried them. These exercises sent my thoughts to other areas, which I again explored. I am amazed at what I have learned while looking for something else.

We can all learn truth if we will open our hearts and minds. We will then be without excuse not to exercise every opportunity to practice it.

One Day at a Time . . . .
Am I taking advantage of every opportunity to grow?
Some opportunities?
Any opportunities?

~ *Jeremiah*

SURRENDER

"Most folks are as happy
as they make up their minds to be."
Abraham Lincoln

More than seven years ago I weighed over 320 pounds and was living the painful life of a compulsive eater. Nothing I tried helped me to make lasting changes … until I began my recovery program. This healing process included Twelve Step recovery, therapy, and changing my life completely. I ended a long-term relationship and moved 2,300 miles away from all of my family and friends. I had no idea as to the extent of this journey I was beginning.

I've learned how ignorant I can be ~ and how wise I am. I've learned that humility is not humiliation ~ it is found by maintaining a willingness to learn. I've been taught how to walk through my fears. I've been shown that my HP and God are in all things ~ and that Spirit follows and supports me with each and every step I take. Some of those steps go forwards, some backwards … yet with each there is progress.

I've never forgotten the pain. Some days it's very severe because I don't have the food to numb it or to hide behind. Thanks to my program, I can always see hope and joy all around me now, even in the midst of pain.

I now weigh 220 pounds. Somehow I've lost 100 pounds of my old self and am beginning to see the new me. The new me is still losing weight. The new me is also incredibly beautiful, deserving, loving, and worthy ... all things I thought I wasn't. I'm slowly, gently, learning that with each day I live well ... I AM WELL! I am only as happy as I am choosing to be.

One Day at a Time . . . .
I pray for complete surrender. I ask for patience, abstinence and peace. I reflect on where I've come from, and remember to embrace the deepest gratitude for where I am now. Today I am well.

~ Melanie S.

Meditation 208

FOOTWORK

"I've lost so much weight
that I should be hanging from a charm bracelet."
Erma Bombeck

I have lost and gained the same weight so many times I've lost count. Lack of willpower was never an issue with me. I've whipped myself into shape many times. There was nothing I didn't do in order to lose weight. I just couldn't keep it off.

The tide finally turned for me when I quit relying on my own power, turned my focus away from my weight problem and toward "trusting in God and cleaning house," as the Big Book states.

I did Step work under the guidance of my sponsor. I passed along to others the lessons I'd learned. I did service work. I kept practicing a conscious contact with the God of my understanding. I went to meetings and talked to others. I kept a journal. Then one day I looked up from the tasks at hand to discover I was abstinent. God did for me what I couldn't do for myself.

One Day at a Time . . . .
I will do the footwork and leave the results up to God.

~ Shirley G.

EXAMPLES

"Preach always ... use words if necessary."
St. Francis of Assisi

I have heard it said many times that the Twelve Step way of life is a way of attraction, not promotion. I can project an image of serenity and recovery by the way I conduct my life. By using the Twelve Steps to work on my inventory, by promptly making amends when needed, by striving daily to use the tools of recovery, I am assuring compulsive eaters who are living in chaos and confusion that there is a better way. When they ask my "secret," I can then share the words of recovery.

One Day at a Time . . . .
I will preach recovery by the examples of serenity and peace.

~ *Hopeful*

TRADITION TWELVE

"If you cannot mould yourself to such as you would wish,
how can you expect others to be entirely to your liking?"
Thomas à Kempis

Compulsive overeaters come from every age group, socioeconomic group, race, color, creed, sexual orientation, and so on. No two of us are alike. The Twelfth Tradition teaches us to place principles before personalities. This is one of the traditions by which our program either lives or dies. Because we are so very different, we are going to have varying opinions – sometimes almost explosively different opinions – on issues affecting our fellowship as a whole. When those times arise, it is essential that we remember to place principles before personalities.

When I served on my first Group Conscience Committee, our home group called it "serving our one-year sentence." It was a hard year and it was difficult to get much business done because it was difficult to get people to agree on much business. But it was just the experience I needed in practicing the Twelfth Tradition in my life. Always remembering that Tradition, I did my best to not allow personalities to clutter my decision-making process in the committee.

The principles of the program are set forth in the Steps. They are principles such as: honesty, faith, forgiveness, trust, hope, courage, willingness and humility. As we work to embody these principles by working the Steps in our lives, we reduce the chance that issues affecting our fellowship will divide us. It will be easier to look beyond the perceived faults of others and to see the needs of the fellowship and the good of the whole.

One Day at a Time . . . .
I will look past my OA members' perceived faults and see the needs of the fellowship.

~ *Carolyn H.*

FORGIVENESS

Forgiveness for ourselves
is the journey from guilt
over what we have done or not done
to the celebration of what we have become."
Dr. Joan Borysenko

Steps 8 and 9 are very important to our recovery from compulsive eating. The Eighth Step says that we need to make a list of those people we have harmed because of our disease, and to be willing to make amends to them.

The Ninth Step says that we need to make direct amends to those people, if possible.

I would never condemn a sick person for being sick, yet I was ready to level blame at myself for being a compulsive overeater. I was mentally cruel to myself.

I abused my physical body with food and excess weight. While working Step Eight, I needed to realize that I didn't hurt just my family or friends when I was deep in my disease. I had to understand that I hurt myself as well. I said and did things that I'm not proud of because I didn't know that I had a disease of compulsion. I had to place myself at the top of my amends list.

Some of the ways I can work Step Nine include remembering that I am a good person who just happens to be sick with a potentially fatal disease of compulsion. If I can remember that I am sick, then I won't add more pain to what the disease already heaps on me. I can remember that a slip in abstinence is just that...a slip. It doesn't reflect on my worth as a human being. I can be gentle with myself whenever times are rough. I can lean more on my Higher Power, so that I don't have to depend upon my own unsteady willpower. I can forgive myself for the past pain I've caused myself and resolve not to hurt myself any more.

One Day at a Time . . . .
I give myself the gift of forgiveness and amends.

~ Jeff

NEGATIVE THINKING

"Condemn the fault and not the actor of it."
William Shakespeare

How many times do we beat ourselves because we have failed to attain the goals we have set? We are human and we suffer from a disease that renders us helpless and out of control. Is it any wonder that we fail in trying to conquer such an unforgiving beast?

It is not ourselves we should be angry with, but the disease and how it affects our actions and reactions. Our inability – or unwillingness – to realize that we cannot achieve recovery alone is our only true failure. We need help. Without it we are weak and defenseless. This disease would have us believe we are failures ~ but in reality, all we have done is open the doors to our enemy. These doors can be closed again. Our disease not only manifests itself in the form of uncontrollable eating, but also in our negative thoughts and actions towards ourselves and towards the people around us.

It takes no more time to think positively than it does to think negatively. Our only job is to remember that we have a disease. We can choose to forget it, we can choose to beat ourselves up when we leave the door ajar, or we can choose to forgive ourselves and begin again.

One Day at a Time . . . .
I will work on forgiving myself.
I am worth forgiving.
You are too.

~*Sue.*

Meditation 213

THE PAST

*"Our past is a story
existing only in our minds.
Look, analyze, understand, and forgive.
Then, as quickly as possible, chuck it."*
Marianne Williamson

Before I came into program I had the tendency to beat myself up over the things I'd done while in the throes of my disease. I would relive everything I'd done – especially my misdeeds. Guilt ruled my life.

Then I found Twelve Steps that set me on the road to recovery. And I found promises ... promises that told me that if I were to rigorously and honestly work the program, I would find a new freedom and a new happiness. I was told that I would not regret the past nor wish to shut the door on it, (as found on page 83 of the Big Book).

For me, the Big Book reminds me of where I came from and that I never want to go back. The Williamson quote (above) tells me that I don't need to wallow in the guilt of yesterday.

One Day at a Time . . . .
I remember my past, release it and move on.

~ JAR

CONTROL

*"I know God will not give me anything I cannot handle.
I just wish He didn't trust me so much."*
Mother Teresa

There was a time when I asked God to handle only the impossible. How dare I ask someone as busy and important as God to help me with a simple thing like food? After all, this was just a matter of using a little will-power ... of pushing myself back from the table. Or so I had been told.

As I began to trust my Twelve Step program more and more, I found myself turning over to God the issues which triggered my compulsive eating. It was with great relief that I began to surrender my food and other problems to Him. It was with enormous gratitude that I realized what a gift it is to finally be able to give up control and put my life in my Higher Power's hands.

One Day at a Time . . . .
I relinquish control of my food.
I relinquish control of people.
I relinquish control of my life.

~ Mari

WORKING IT

*"For the things we have to learn
before we can do them, we learn by doing them."*
Aristotle

When I walked into my first Twelve Step meeting I had absolutely no idea what was going on. I knew nothing about the program, the Steps, or how to work them. But I listened, asked questions, and I learned.

One of the most important lessons I learned was that I couldn't just sit around waiting for recovery to take place. I couldn't just ask God for help and do nothing else. I had to put feet to my prayers, as they say. I had to do something. So ... slowly, with the help of my sponsor, I took the First Step. And then the Second.

I found that I could talk a good game around program folks because I'd learned the lingo. But the saying, "you've got to walk the talk" tells me that I have to do it. I can't just speak my recovery into existence. I found I didn't have recovery until I began working the Steps. It was only when I started "the doing" that the real learning – and the real recovery – began.

One Day at a Time . . . .
I will take what I learn about recovery and put it into practice ... I'll work the program.

~ JAR

Meditation 216

OTHERS

"In the deepest part of a compulsive eater's soul ...
is the realization that recovery begins when we find one another."
Anonymous

Growing up in the deep South in the 1950's, I witnessed things I never dreamed could happen. It taught me lessons I have never forgotten. Little did I think that someone like me could ever be discriminated against. After all, I was the right color, the right size, the right religion and lived on the right side of town.

Messages began to be taped early on in that little girl's brain ... into the psyche of that teenager who worked so hard to achieve ... and into the young woman who had the world by the tail. In adulthood those messages began to play ... and food made the messages easier to hear. So began the life of a compulsive eater. So began discrimination because of my weight.

Years later I would be grateful for my life as an overweight adult. I would look back and see that the God of my understanding was preparing me to see discrimination as a disease of the soul. But what happened to give me serenity and peace and contentment? I found another compulsive eater. And then I found another ... and another. And recovery began.

One Day at a Time . . . .
I will overwrite those taped messages;
I will not regret the past;
And I will cherish my fellows forever.

- Mari

Meditation 217

PAIN

"Your pain is the breaking of the shell that encloses
your understanding. Even as the stone of the fruit
must break, that its heart may stand in the sun,
so must you know pain."
Kahlil Gibran

There was much to be unhappy about in my childhood. There was also a lot of unhappiness in my adult life. Until I found The Recovery Group online, that unhappiness was the driving force in my life. That force robbed me of the ability to see and enjoy the many wonderful things that I had experienced. I wore a cloak of sadness, bitterness and resentment ~ I had been short-changed. It was the old glass-half-empty, glass-half-full story....poor me.

Being able to share the pain and unhappiness I have known has freed me from the power it had over me. Clearing away the wreckage is enabling me to see my part in some of the unhappiness I've known. It has enabled me to see more clearly that there is so much for which I can be grateful. It has enabled me to see that I truly AM the person of value which I had represented myself to be towards others. I am integrating that person into the "unacceptable" being I carried within. I have seen others here endure challenge, pain and hardships with so much grace. I have learned that pain is, indeed, inevitable. I have the choice whether to dwell on the pain morbidly, or to instead focus on the joy of this day.

One Day at a Time . . . .
I will live in the joy of this day and I will strive to share this wonderful gift of self-acceptance to others in program.

~ Karen H.

SELF-ESTEEM

"No one can make you feel inferior without your consent."
Eleanor Roosevelt

I always used to feel "less than" everyone else, so I'd eat and feel even worse. Without true love for myself I was dead in the water. I would compare the facts I knew about myself against the impression I had of you. I never seemed to measure up. Without self-love, I was unable to ask for, expect or accept love from others.

When I love myself and treat myself lovingly, it doesn't matter what others think of me; what matters is that I do not think less of myself.

One Day at a Time . . . .
I ask my Higher Power to show me little ways
to act lovingly toward myself and to know deep within
that I am worthy of being loved by others.

~ *Melissa S.*

Meditation 219

SERVICE

*"You cannot do a kindness too soon ...
because you never know how soon it will be too late."*
Ralph Waldo Emerson

So many people in program sit silently in meetings because they don't think they have anything of importance to say. Perhaps they haven't been in program very long, and feel that, because they aren't a seasoned veteran, they haven't the right to speak up. But everyone's experiences and insights are different, and I would appreciate hearing from those who are quiet. They just might say something that will keep me from losing my serenity and abstinence. It would be a kindness for them to speak up.

I've had people tell me, "Oh, I can't pick up the phone and make an outreach call to someone I just met." To that I say, "Why not?" It would be a kindness to let someone know that you're there and you care about them.

Sometimes a person will say, "But I'm having a bad day myself; how can I offer hope to someone when I'm in such a shape?" It would be a kindness to share your struggle, for you would be giving others the chance to serve. I think it's as much a selfishness on our part to deny someone the opportunity to serve us as it is to deny our service to someone who is hurting.

Ours is a fatal disease. I don't want to risk missing the chance to serve someone who may not be with us tomorrow. I want to do that kindness today in case it's YOU who isn't here tomorrow. I hope you would do that kindness today in case it's ME who isn't here tomorrow.

One Day at a Time . . . .
I will perform an act of kindness,
for I never know when I may forever lose that opportunity.

~ JAR

HAPPINESS

*"Happiness is never something you get from other
people. The happiness you feel is in direct
proportion to the love you are able to give."*
Oprah Winfrey

I learned a great lesson while grieving the loss of my three-year-old son. It was Christmas time. I had three other children who were looking forward to a wonderful day with all the trimmings, but my heart was despairing. I came to the realization that I could take the experience one moment at a time. Some of those moments would be very sad, but some of those little periods of time would be joyful. I found out that happiness is moments, not a state of being. We can take those joyful moments and treasure them until they accumulate into happiness. We have the choice to treasure them or to allow them to disappear in our lack of gratitude and appreciation.

Every day there is joy that we miss because we aren't looking for it. When I look back at the end of the day and add up the good moments, I often realize there is so much joy in my life. I learn to appreciate the little things.

That Christmas is remembered more for those little moments of joy. The love in my heart for the other children helped me to rise above the despair and reach out to give them a gift of happiness on that treasured holiday.

One Day at a Time . . . .
I strive to see the good in each moment.

~ Dottie

ANSWERS

"There is no need to run outside
For better seeing,
Nor to peer from a window.
Rather abide at the center of your being."
Lao Tzu

I always looked for answers outside of myself. I did not put the trust in myself and thought someone, anyone, always knew better than me. I believed the advertisements and compared myself to polished pictures of beautiful thin women.

As I recover from compulsive overeating, I am learning that all of the answers are inside of me. I need only to get quiet and listen to that still small voice. I pray that my Higher Power will give me the willingness to go inside where my truths lie.

One Day at a Time . . . .
I look within and wait patiently ... knowing the answers, however big or small, are all within.

~ *Melissa S.*

LOSS

"The act of giving something up is painful.
But as we negotiate the curves and corners of our lives,
we must continually give up parts of ourselves.
The only alternative is not to travel at all on the journey of life."
M. Scott Peck

As I look back over my life, I can remember many losses. Some came about by death, some by the circumstances of life, and others by choices I made. All of my losses were painful, but only three were traumatic. Whenever I gave something up there was a period afterwards when my life wasn't the same as it had been before. The amount of pain I experienced and the length of its duration were not contingent upon the seeming "severity" of the loss. Death was final, but not the most traumatic for me. Letting go of something takes many forms.

Though my most traumatic losses were those I experienced at the end of a relationship, there were other losses, too. I lost my youth and I mourned that. I lost a part of my life when a decades-long career gave way to retirement. I lost my role as mother when my children grew up and I found myself with an empty nest. I lost my identity when the disease I have had for a lifetime caused me to reach bottom and, in the process, took the "me who was" along with it. And I lost another part of myself when I accepted the reality of my marriage and let go of the storybook dreams I once had.

My Twelve Step program has enabled me to go through a mourning process for each loss I experienced. I have allowed myself to grieve and feel the feelings. And when all this was done, God's grace allowed me to heal.

One Day at a Time . . . .
I will learn from those things I had to give up ...
and I will continue my journey in serenity and peace.

~ *Mari*

THE THIRD STEP

*"Any concern too small to be turned into a prayer
is too small to be made into a burden."*
Corrie Ten Boom

Like many people, I used to feel that surrendering to God would be an act of weakness. There was a time when I also felt it was inappropriate because I felt God just didn't have the time to spend on the lesser issues of my life. But later I discovered that those "lesser" issues became some of the biggest challenges with which I would ever have to deal.

One of these most difficult struggles was my addiction to compulsive eating. How dare I ask God to handle that! This was MY problem. MY weakness. MY Hell. What right did I have to inflict that on God? And now they're telling me to turn not only my will, but my very life over to Him?

The bravest thing I ever did was to get down on my knees one day with tears streaming down my face and beg God to help me with this compulsion that was taking its toll on the quality of my life. For the first time I told Him that I gave up and that I could no longer deal with this. I told Him that I was turning this, and my life, over to Him to do with as He could ... and would. From that day to this I walk hand-in-hand with God and try to do what I believe He is telling me to do in all areas of my life, whether it be food, relationships, or anything else. I have to do this because I remember the feeling I was experiencing that day when I first surrendered and I never want to go back there.

One Day at a Time . . . .
I will walk hand-in-hand with my Greater Power.
Each morning, each evening, and often in between,
My Higher Power hears these words ...
"I love you, God."

~ *Mari*

Meditation 224

SAFETY NET

"Leap, and the net will appear."
Julia Cameron

I am an analyzer. Given the opportunity, I can analyze something to the point the original context has been lost. This was exactly what I did when I was first introduced to the Twelve Step recovery program. With each Step, I tried to discover a hidden meaning, an excuse not to work it. I spent more energy not doing the program than I ever would have following it.

When I finally made the leap into that First Step, my life began changing direction from the downward trend it was in. It was a leap of faith, and the net of my Higher Power caught me. This net will not break, nor will it fall. As I discover truths about myself that enable me to move forward in life and become a better person, I need the safety of that net of faith.

One Day at a Time . . . .
I will take a leap of faith towards my recovery,
knowing I'll be safe, and the miracle will happen.

~ *Trish*

JOY

"Joy is not in things, it is in us."
Richard Wagner

Growing up in a household of people in need of recovery, one of the things I learned early on is that things can bring happiness. None of us realized that the happiness was very temporary, never seeing us through what feeling we were wanting to stuff or what hurt hole deep inside us needed filling. I had so many feelings and so many holes inside me that I didn't have near enough money for the things I needed. What hurting 7-year old in a sick family does?

Given that, it seems natural that I turned to food to help fill holes. Just another "thing," but at least the fridge was always too full, and I didn't have to worry about the money aspect.

But things caused pain too. I learned that my parents gave more expensive and better things to those people they liked more and wanted to please. I was not one of those people; my brother was. I noted every gift and compared, and set myself up for more hurt that could only be soothed in the kitchen because I didn't know any other way.

The food "things" I ran to have caused less joy in my life than any of the things I've bought. I've been fat since I was four, torturing my body over the years by alternating starvation with massive bingeing and with purging. I was never good enough because I've never been thin enough except for that growth spurt when I was nine.

Then I found the Twelve Steps. As a result of working the Steps, I've found me. As a result of finding me and learning to fill hurtful holes by feeling rather than with things or food, I've truly found the joy that is in me.

One Day at a Time . . . .
I will remind myself that things and food do not bring happiness; joy is within.

~ *Rhonda H.*

LISTENING

"I have learned silence from the talkative,
tolerance from the intolerant,
and kindness from the unkind.
I should not be ungrateful to those teachers."
Kahlil Gibran

Verbosity is one of my personal characteristics ... especially in my past. I remember so well discussions in which I found great joy in talking. I also remember my prayers to the God Of My Understanding in which I had a litany of things prayed for.

As I became more and more entrenched in my program, I noticed that I began to listen more and talk less. I also began to really hear what God was saying to me. Praying is our talking to God and meditating is listening to Him. So now meditation has became a way of life for me.

As I go through my life encountering the talkers of the world, I now try to listen to those who are silent but who have much to say. The loud voices of my past life were just loud. It is, however, the quiet, calm voices that have spoken to me in volumes.

One Day at a Time . . . .
I will listen carefully to those who speak.
I will listen especially carefully if it's God who is speaking.

~ *Mari*

Meditation 227

LOVE

"Love conquers all things.
Let us, too, surrender to love."
Virgil

Learning to love myself has been one of the hardest lessons I've had to learn. I had to discover my capacity for self-care. I had to listen to the way I talked to myself and to learn to speak in more affirming ways. Learning to smile – and then laugh – when I made a mistake helped me to be less self-centered and more able to just have fun.

Life is a great experience when I surrender myself to the love around me. Expressing my love to others increases its quantity and quality inside of me. We all need to know that someone loves us and that we are lovable. Everyone needs to know that they are sufficient. I've discovered that as I give love to others, it is returned to me many times over.

One Day at a Time . . . .
I will work at expressing unconditional love.

~ *YAL*

SELF-KNOWLEDGE

"The world we have created is a product of our thinking.
It cannot be changed without changing our thinking."
Albert Einstein

The world I created before finding the Twelve Steps of recovery was a world in which I had no responsibility. Everything bad in my life was someone else's fault: my parents', my husband's, society's, and, when there was no one else to blame, it was God's fault.

As I worked Step Four, I learned that I had been a part of all of these things for which I blamed others. I learned that I had defects of character that kept me from taking part in my life. As I recognized these defects, I asked my Higher Power to remove them, and that gradually happened.

One of the things I had tried to do for many years was bury my feelings of grief and pain. I seemed to have managed that fairly well, but in doing so, I had also buried all the other emotion. I no longer took enjoyment in anything. My child's smile evoked no feeling and I felt no pride in anything I did. I felt none of the love that others gave to me. As I started dealing with the painful feelings, the positive emotions emerged as well.

The promise the Big Book speaks of became true for me: I no longer regretted the past nor wished to shut the door on it. I was able to feel my hurt and grief. Now I am also able to feel love and happiness. I have learned how to change my thinking through the process of working these wonderful Steps.

One Day at a Time . . . .
I do a daily Tenth, Eleventh and Twelfth Step and am reminded that it is my responsibility to listen to my Higher Power and do my part in creating the world around me.

~ *Nancy*

Meditation 229

TRUST

"'Come to the edge', he said.
They said, 'We are afraid.'
'Come to the edge,' he said.
They came. He pushed them.
....and they flew."
Guillaume Apollinaire

Whenever things look bleak I remember how dark and dismal my life was before my Higher Power led me to this Twelve Step program. Before program I was afraid to reach for recovery. I was afraid to try to be an over-comer and I was afraid to come to the edge. But slowly I inched my way over to that edge and my Higher Power gave me a gentle nudge. I was flying! I wasn't chained by my disease anymore. I wasn't trapped in the darkness. I'd come into the light. That day I received a gift from my Higher Power ... I received a taste of recovery.

One Day at a Time . . . .
I come to the edge and trust my Higher Power to give me wings to fly.

~ Jeff R.

FEAR

"Some of your griefs you have cured
And the sharpest you still have survived ~
But what torments of pain you endured
From evils that never arrived."
Ralph Waldo Emerson

As a compulsive overeater I have lived my life in fear. I feared the apparent cruelty of the surrounding world. I feared to challenge the unknown and chose instead to seek safety in familiar "surroundings." I was afraid to have ambition and dreams.

My whole life I've battled an increasing waistline. I realized that I was stagnate in a world of pain and darkness because my fears of responsibility as a "slim" person sabotaged my efforts to lose weight.

I've learned that worrying about a situation doesn't change the outcome! My fears simply prevented me from moving forward. They clouded the real issues and hid the answers to my problems. Instead of expending so much energy into worrying and fearing an event, I could put it to much better use by dealing with the present realities in my life.

Surviving a situation provides added armor for the next battle. Overcoming a fearful predicament puts confidence in my stride towards my next goal. Faith is the opposite of fear. Having faith in my choices, abilities and ambitions will provide the steadfast pathway ahead.

One Day at a Time . . . .
I try to remember that fear and worry only serve to chain me to the present. Faith can break the shackles and enable me to walk on to where I was heading.

~ *Nancy*

Meditation 231

ANGER

"Anger is only one letter short of danger."
Eleanor Roosevelt

Before I began to work the program anger was a dangerous emotion for me. Anger was my excuse to react negatively without thinking. I let anger cause me to judge others, say or do hurtful things, turn away from my Higher Power, and to overeat.

I came to realize that I felt angry even when there were other emotions brewing on a deeper level. I felt angry when I was actually feeling afraid, embarrassed, hurt, tired, forgetful, or stressed out. As I work the Twelve Steps, I welcome my Higher Power's guidance in feeling my true feelings; in accepting myself and the situations in my life; in acting on life – rather than reacting; and in having the compassion to understand myself and others. By doing this I no longer fear anger and I no longer find it a danger in my life.

Turning to my Higher Power, I use the Serenity Prayer and the Twelve Steps to process anger in healthy ways. When I feel angry at myself, I give myself a break! I treat myself with kindness, acceptance and forgiveness.

One Day at a Time . . . .
When I feel angry, I wait before I act.

~ *Lynne*

AMENDS

"If you have behaved badly, repent;
make what amends you can and address yourself to the task
of behaving better next time. On no account brood over your
wrongdoing. Rolling in the muck is not the best
way of getting clean."
Aldous Huxley

I grew up with high expectations of perfection and a constant feeling of failure. I seldom recognized truly bad behavior in myself, but instead I apologized for the things I had taken on as my responsibility that were not under my control. I apologized when the weather spoiled plans. I apologized for an adult family member's poor behavior. I felt intense shame when I accidentally slipped and fell, sure that I'd embarrassed the people with me. Yet I was oblivious to how I snapped at people simply because I was in a HALTS (Hungry, Angry, Lonely, Tired, Sick) place. My temper was quick to rise and explode, but I always told myself I had a "good" excuse or cause.

On the other hand, I could feel so mortified over my behavior that it haunted me night and day for weeks, and even months, after the incident; long after any witness could recall it. Years later a phrase would bring the memory back to the forefront and shame me all over again as though it had happened mere minutes before.

I couldn't seem to find a truthful middle ground until I began working the Twelve Steps. In studying the Steps I learned how to uncover and acknowledge the wrongs for which I am sincerely responsible, how to make proper amends, and how to let go and move on.

One Day at a Time . . . .
I will remember that I am responsible only for my own behavior and actions. With the help of my Higher Power, I will acknowledge my wrongdoings quickly and make loving amends.

~ Rhonda H.

Meditation 233

I AM

"I yam what I yam."
Popeye, the Sailor Man

When did I start believing that being myself was bad? Was it the first time I did something 'wrong' in the eyes of an adult? Do I remember the day I went from being a bright-eyed child to a shadow of a being? Whenever it occurred, as time progressed, I began to trust that being myself was somehow shameful.

It's hardly a wonder that I turned to food and other addictions. After all, food never spoke badly of me, yet it did darken my spirit. Every compulsive bite dampened my light.

Thank God for this program! It has taught me that those people of my past, however well-meaning, were wrong. Being me is good. In fact, it's better than good. It's wonderful! Without me, this world would be a little darker, a little more lost. That is why I am here, why God created me, to be a light for the world.

One Day at a Time . . . .
I realize that it is through God and this fellowship that I am able to shine.

~Debbie

PREPARING

"Failing to prepare is preparing to fail."
John Wooden

Every morning I make a decision. I decide to prepare for a day of recovery, or I decide to not prepare for a day of recovery. It comes as no surprise that on the days I prepare I do better.

I have to take responsibility for my decisions, even my indecision. If I do nothing to help myself today, I have no one to blame but myself. If nothing else, I can take five minutes in the morning to invite my Higher Power into my life.

One Day at a Time . . . .
I will prepare for a good day today. I will take responsibility for my recovery.

~ Q

FAILURE

"Accept that all of us can be hurt,
that all of us can – and surely will at times – fail.
Other vulnerabilities, like being embarrassed
or risking love, can be terrifying, too."
Dr. Joyce Brothers

The prospect of failing ~ or worse yet, " Being A Failure" ~ was a crippling monster which held me in its cold and unforgiving stranglehold. If I thought I could not do a thing perfectly, I would not do it at all. If I didn't know the "Right" way to act or to be, I was paralyzed. One day my therapist shocked me by suggesting I make a mistake on purpose. She wanted me to practice giving myself permission to make mistakes and to survive the experience.

I vividly recall intentionally dropping a gum wrapper on the ground and leaving it there. The Fearful Perfectionist inside of me screamed, "Pick it up! You never litter! This is wrong!" Yet I also heard a whisper welling up from within: "It will be alright. Just let it go."

As part of my Recovery, I am exploring with brutal honesty the mistakes I've made in my life: the ways and the people that I've failed. Though doing so is embarrassing, humbling, and frightening, I am surprised to find a budding sense of relief. My attempts to avoid Failure never made me Perfect; rather, they caused me to be more entrenched in my pride, insecurities, fears, and stunted growth. A young girl I know is an expert skater. I asked her how she learned, and her answer stopped me in my tracks: "Mostly by falling down."

One Day at a Time . . . .
I will practice accepting my failures as necessary steps towards my healing. I will remember that the word "practice" honors the fact that we gain our progress by making attempts, failing, and learning from our mistakes.

~ *Lisa V.*

Meditation 236

ADDICTIONS

There are addictions to feed and there are mouths to pay so we bargain with the devil but we're O.K. for today.
Georgia

But am I really? When I am actively feeding my addiction, how can I possibly be O.K.? Before I started on my road to recovery, the price I paid to stay in my disease included sacrificing my mental health, my social life, my relationship with my family, my physical health and a myriad of other things. I really did feel the in order to stay alive I had to make daily bargains with the devil. I remember thinking things like "I know this isn't good for me but I need to have that one extra bite." I had even progressed to the point that I didn't realize I was eating to make myself feel better. I ate simply because I didn't know what else to do. My addiction, my devil, exacted the price of my awareness, my happiness and the quality of my life. What's worse is, I was so blinded by my dysfunctional thinking that I couldn't even conceptualize the price I was paying. Coming into recovery gave me back the gift of awareness. Working through the Steps and using the tools helped me to re-establish my life, relationships, and health. Living my life while practicing my addiction meant that the best I ever felt was O.k. and the worst? Depressed, discouraged and at some points suicidal. Today, in recovery the worst I ever feel is O.K. and the best is Happy, Joyous and Free!

One Day at a Time . . . .
I ask my HP to help me to remember that I am one compulsive bite away from the slavery I once lived in. I trust that by the daily maintenance of my spiritual condition I never have to go back to my addiction.

. . Mari

Meditation 237

LISTENING

Listen or your tongue will keep you deaf.
Native American Proverb

Sometimes it really feels as if talking too much and eating too much are connected. They're both done with the mouth, is that why? Is my compulsion about doing something, ANYTHING, with my mouth? Is it because hearing the drone of my voice is just as good an escape as eating, eating, eating? Maybe one day I'll find out. But I don't need to know the why before I stop talking, just as I don't need to know all the reasons why I'm overeating in order to become abstinent. There is a wonderful serenity that comes with eating moderately. And there is a wonderful serenity that comes with being quiet and listening. There is so much to listen to! Others? words, rain falling outside, children playing, my cat purring. I cannot hear those things when my tongue is loud and makes me deaf to anything but my own voice.

One Day at a Time . . . .
I can realize that I do not need to talk all the time just as I do not need to eat all the time. I can take time to be quiet, to listen.

~ *Unknown*

Meditation 238

LOVE

"When you love you should not say,
'God is in my heart,' but rather,
'I am in the heart of God.'"
Kahlil Gibran

What is love? And what does it mean to love myself? I've found from my experience that it is easier to describe what love is not. Through many failures – and with my Higher Power's help – I have discovered that to love myself means choosing to not hurt myself by overeating. Self-love means choosing to no longer ignore my inner-child who sometimes screams to be heard and must have a tantrum to get my attention. Self-love means not isolating or allowing the hurtful, grieving, angry, fearful thoughts to possess my mind to the degree that the disease overtakes any sanity I may have. This list could go on – focusing on the failures and the negative – but my Higher Power has given me the desire, strength and power to feel, express and give love. Our Higher Power offers the freedom and joy of self-love to each of us who are willing to receive and practice it.

The more I am able to receive the love of others, the more I am able to love myself. And conversely, the more I love myself, the more I am able to receive love from others. As I work this Twelve Step program to the best of my ability each 24 hours, I am shown love through meetings, my sponsor, meditating, journaling, spending time with my Higher Power, and sharing my experience, strength and hope with another person. Some days, "the best of my ability" may be to just get out of bed and say the Third Step prayer. Other days, "the best of my ability" will seem like I'm working the program close to perfection. Regardless of my ability on any particular day, I've found that love can be gleaned from each day.

As the quote above states, "I am in the heart of God." I experience this when I am willing to surrender daily to the will of my Higher Power and to be completely and absolutely surrounded and protected by the heart of God.

One Day at a Time . . . .
I will seek to see love in as many moments as possible by looking to my Higher Power and then reaching out to others.

~ *Ohitika*

Meditation 239

PERFECTION

*"People throw away what they could have
by insisting on perfection, which they cannot have,
and looking for it where they will never find it."*
Edith Schaeffer

Time and time again I have felt like I was suspended from two ropes, being flogged for my imperfections. The tragic fact of that vision was that I was the person wielding the whip!

Before my heart and mind were opened by the Twelve Steps and Traditions, I sought perfection in everything I attempted. A simple letter would be written and rewritten until I was satisfied that perfection had been achieved and the letter could be sent. Frequently the goal was not reached and I would abandon the project in frustration and bitter disappointment with myself. Events that I organized had to be executed with the utmost precision. If, God forbid, a mistake was made, I would berate myself for days until sheer mental and emotional exhaustion prevailed.

Ironically, I never sought perfection in others and accepted that it was okay for them to be human. However, seeking perfection from myself became an obsession tangled with the search for self-acceptance. Needless to say, a rainbow cannot be seen through closed eyes, and I never found that which I sought. Through the teachings of the Twelve Steps I have come to appreciate that the beauty within myself is that I am not perfect. I can grow through my mistakes, and in my imperfections I can find serenity and release from the struggle.

One Day at a Time . . . .
I will accept that I am perfectly imperfect.

~ Sue G.

FIT SPIRITUAL CONDITION

*"... the problem has been removed. It does not exist for us.
We are neither cocky nor are we afraid. That is our experience.
That is how we react so long as we keep in fit spiritual condition."*
The Big Book, p.85

These words, read every morning during prayer time, teach me to live as I am meant to live. Sanely and peacefully. Laid back. Patient and forgiving of myself. I am no longer a part of the war of the worlds. Anger can be dealt with or walked away from. Eating over it is no longer an option. Compulsive overeating is a problem I can live without, just for today.

One Day at a Time . . . .
I will remember where I came from and how I got here so long as I keep in fit spiritual condition.

~ Jo

STAYING PRESENT

"First you need only look."
Anne Hillman

My disease of compulsive overeating is fueled by my regrets of the past and my fears of the future. The more I try to rewrite the past, (which of course I cannot do); the more I try to devise a future plan, (which usually does not come to pass), the less I am present for my life.

I learn much from my three-year-old son. Sometimes when running to get a ball, he suddenly stops to look at an unusual insect he sees on the ground. His life flows and he abides by this pattern. He follows his heart and is "there" for life.

When I consciously stay present for life – when I savor each moment and stay with my feelings – I am alive and living. In the present there is no worry, no fear, no regrets.

One Day at a Time . . . .
I ask my Higher Power to help me to stay present for my life, to stay with whatever is happening at any given moment. I feel feelings. I am spontaneous and life is exciting and inspired.

~ Melissa S.

SERVICE

*"Ask not what your country can do for you
but what you can do for your country."*
John Fitzgerald Kennedy

At one of the first program functions I ever attended, there were a large number of pots and pans that needed to be washed in the kitchen. My sponsor told me that we were going to go in there and wash all those dirty pans. When I asked why, she said, "Because this stuff keeps us abstinent." That was good enough for me. Service is essential to my recovery. As our primary purpose states, "we carry the message to the compulsive overeater who still suffers." The essence of my program is that of committing to service.

Since then my service in program has been of paramount importance to me, so I sponsor and serve at the group and Intergroup levels, I attend all events I can, and I am in service at most of the meetings I attend. I encourage sponsees to serve their fellow sufferers also and ask them to sponsor newcomers as soon as they have worked Steps One through Three. This action gets them working on Step Four as well.

One of my favorite ways to give service is to be available to talk to newcomers by telephone. As our responsibility pledge states, "Always to lend the heart and hand to all who share my compulsion, for this I am responsible." A commitment to service is as vital to my recovery as are my commitments to abstinence, working the Steps and a daily food plan. These components mesh together and give me purpose I never had before.

One Day at a Time . . . .
I will find a way to be helpful to others in program.

~ *Jill C.*

Meditation 243

FRIENDSHIP

"The ideal friendship is between good people,
and people who share the same virtues.
Leading a good life for the sake of friends,
is the utmost of friendship itself."
Aristotle

When I first came into recovery I had no idea how to be a friend. I thought that people liked me because of what I did for them, what I gave them, and how nice I was to them. It never occurred to me that being a friend could mean taking care of myself. I didn't realize that friendship also consists of holding fast to my program no matter what, being gently honest to others in all things, being loyal to my group, and being true to my program and to myself. But the part that escaped me the most was that there were those who counted me as a friend just because I am me.

One Day at a Time . . . .
I will be a friend by being loyal to myself, my program and my ideals.

~ *Judy N.*

EGO

"Whenever I climb I am followed by a dog called 'Ego'."
Friedrich Nietzsche

Ego can be defined as the consciousness of our own identity. It works by judging and establishing limits on everything it sees. I do not consider myself to be an egotistical person. My ego, however, is like a yo-yo at the end of a string. When my program is going strong, my sense of well being rises up, and almost all things seem go be going my way. At the same time, that yo-yo of emotional ego begins to be pulled right back towards me. My sense of confidence and well being turns into self-importance and over-confidence My ego is fed, continues to grow and draw closer.

Do I find it hard to be humble? No. I find it hard to STAY humble. Humility feeds my Higher Power. My Higher Power, however, rewards me with success in so many ways, and my mind loves the validation success brings..

Humility is the only real defense against humiliation. It is the false pride, vanity and arrogance that set me up for a downfall. Nothing in this life is perfect, and it is the embarrassment of losing face that makes it so hard to swallow.

One Day at a Time . . . .
I will remind myself that I must continue to work my program so that the channels to my Higher Power are wide open, can show me truth and remind me of the peace and wisdom of humility.

~ Marilyn S.

ISOLATION

"A great hope fell, you heard no noise,
The ruin was within.
Oh, cunning wreck that, told no tale
And let no witness in!"
Emily Dickinson

When I was young, I was unable to negotiate situations that were too big for me to understand. I went within and hid. I lost hope and was filled with despair. I soothed myself with food that was always there for me. In time, I felt so isolated that I felt completely separate from the human race.

As I recover, it is important for me to use the tools of the program which reconnect me with other people. This connection tells me that I am okay. I always have a choice to isolate or connect. Today I choose to connect.

One Day at a Time . . . .
I ask my Higher Power for the ability and courage to reach out and connect to others by using the tools of the program.

~ *Melissa S.*

SPIRITUAL GROWTH

"I have defined love as the will to extend oneself
for the purpose of nurturing one's own
and another's spiritual growth."
Scott Peck

In my disease I had this terrible need to control everything and everyone in my path. Like the actor in the AA Big Book, I was forever arranging things the way I thought they should be, only to find that when I was done, I had ripped through the area like a tornado on the plains.

Often I would claim that my actions were done out of a spirit of love. When I didn't get my way, I would announce to the world that I was not loved and would head for the solitude of my binge foods.

Today as I work my program, I find that by taking the Third Step, I am truly extending myself for not only my own growth, but for those around me as well. When I decide to turn my will and my life over to the God of my understanding, I don't have to be the director of the world! As I once heard in a meeting, "The position of God is filled. They did not ask for resumes, they did not take applications, there was no ad in the classifieds. So what makes you think you can apply for the job?" By not extending myself into God's role, I am extending love.

One Day at a Time . . . .
I pray that I may stay out of my Higher Power's way, and by doing so, extend myself
for spiritual growth.

~ *Mark Y.*

Meditation 247

ACTION

"Men at some time are the masters of their fates."
William Shakespeare

When I first approached Step Four I did so with fear. To make "a searching and fearless moral inventory" of myself seemed like an impossible task. I had so many resentments and fears I did not know where to start. I felt very overwhelmed. When I shared this with my sponsor, she sat down with me and I took a pen and paper and we started. Just seeing something down on paper gave me the courage to go on. I took the inventory person-by-person for my resentments and sex conduct, and fear-by-fear for my fear inventory. At first it was hard to see my part. I wanted to be a victim. But with the help of my sponsor I began to see my part. I began to take action.

No longer was I the victim, but I became the master of my fate for the purposes of my recovery. I chose to make a searching and fearless moral inventory. No, it wasn't easy, but step-by-step, I completed it. It wasn't nearly as overwhelming as I thought it would be. Step Four requires much action, and I must choose to take it.

One Day at a Time . . . .
I will choose to take action in my recovery and be fearless and thorough no matter where I am on my journey.

~ Carolyn

Meditation 248

SERVICE

"The world is full of willing people;
some willing to work ... the rest willing to let them."
Robert Frost

There is a time when we first come into program when we need to just sit back and receive. We come in a desperate state, empty of love and acceptance, with nothing to guide us and no place to go. We learn to feel our emptiness and to accept resting on others and being supported.

Then we begin to "get it." The tingling excitement of hope is aroused in us. A source of power to live is discovered inside of ourselves.

At that point, a change must take place if we are to continue our success. While we will always remain a receiver, we must move into the ring of the givers. It requires a new role of courage and boldness to take this step. Fear of what to say, how to sound, and quality of performance must be overcome. This is called Step Twelve.

One Day at a Time . . . .
God, grant me the courage to take Step Twelve, however imperfectly, to grow in my
ability to share what I have so generously been given.

~ Mary Clare

RISK

*"And the day came when the risk to remain tight in the bud
was more painful than the risk it took to blossom."*
Anais Nin

I think that many people, like myself, come into Twelve Step Programs out of desperation. I had just begun to realize that the price I was paying to continue eating compulsively was way too high. For me, I noticed I was a very distracted and impatient mother. I saw my children getting more and more out of control because I had neither the time nor the energy to discipline myself, let alone them. I started to wonder what kind of lives I was training them to live. I saw my husband disappear more and more into books and work, and retreating from me. My body was beginning to rebel against what I was doing to it. I was sleeping in a recliner because I could not breathe well enough to sleep in my bed. My knees and my feet were beginning to hurt. I was unable to do even routine housework and shopping without great effort and discomfort.

I began to realize this was no way to live. I was consumed with both the fear of living and the fear of dying. I had a friend who was in a similar condition, and together we gathered up the courage to attend a few program meetings. I also discovered a wonderful community of program members online and here is where I found the courage to move forward and to begin my recovery journey. It was also online I found the fellow sufferer in recovery who became my sponsor.

I am so thankful my Higher Power made me realize that I could move through the fear I had about living. With the help of my program and my Higher Power, I became a blossoming flower who did not die in the bud.

One Day at a Time . . . .
I accept that fear may be in my life and that my Higher Power is stronger than anything I fear. I move forward today trusting my Higher Power to draw me to my highest good. I know that growth comes with action and I am willing to risk moving through the fear into positive action.

~ *Janet H.*

HONESTY

"If it is not right do not do it;
if it is not true do not say it."
Marcus Aurelius

Honesty of all sorts is important, but honesty with ourselves is foundational. With everything that was in me, I resisted the notion that I had an eating disorder. Everybody else had a problem with my eating, not me. But when I finally faced the painful truth, I began the journey to freedom, from not merely overeating, but from all the underlying bondage that had caused me to stuff my feelings.

The same thing happened when I acknowledged that my relationship with God was in need of correction. Sure, my whole life was a mess, but that had to be God's fault, right? I had to own up to the fact that God did not fail me; I had failed myself. I had to be open and receptive to His way. What power comes from honesty! I used to be afraid of truth, but truth is becoming my friend.

One Day at a Time . . . .
Today I will not let myself hide from truth simply to be comfortable; I will use truth as a tool for freedom.

~ *Deborah H.*

DREAMS

*"You've got to have a dream
in order to make a dream come true."*
Oscar Hammerstein II

Since first hearing this saying many years ago, I have come to believe in it. I have always had the dream of being happy, healthy, helpful and whole, but it wasn't until I found this program (or it found me) that I am learning I can have all of these things. Through the program I am being shown a way to achieve them.

When I first joined the program, I just wanted to lose weight. But as I continue to understand and learn about the program, my dream is slowly coming true. It's a slow path for me right now, but as long as I keep the dream alive in my mind, heart and soul, I know I'll be able to accomplish it one day at a time!

One Day at a Time . . . .
I ask my Higher Power to keep me on the right path toward my dream of being happy, healthy, helpful and whole. And right now, in this moment, I am grateful for my dream and for the opportunity to fulfill it.

~ *Lorraine*

Meditation 252

CONNECTION

*"We all have God's phone number
but the only number we tend to use is 911.
We only call in an emergency
instead of calling just for daily connection with God."*
Mary Manin Morrissey

When I first came into the program, my goal was to lose weight. It's still my goal, but now it's not the main focus of my program of recovery.

I've learned that my spiritual and emotional fitness are every bit as important as my physical fitness. In fact, I'm finding that for me the spiritual aspect is the most important. If my relationship to the God of my understanding is in order, then everything else seems to fall into place. If I leave my Higher Power out of my life, then everything falls apart.

There's an old program saying, "If you feel apart from God, then who moved?" Whenever I feel like God is a million miles away, I know it's because I moved away from Him, not the other way around. When I am feeling separated from God, I see my disease of compulsion start to take over. That's why it's very important to me to maintain a conscious contact with my Higher Power. If I let things get too far out of hand and I start to move away from Him, then I need to pray. But my intention is to keep in constant touch with God so that a spiritual emergency isn't the only reason I check in with Him.

One Day at a Time . . . .
I will do all I can on a daily basis to connect with my Higher Power.

~ *Jeff*

Meditation 253

FAITH

*"Faith has to work twenty-four hours a day
in and through us, or we perish."*
The Big Book

The Big Book states that if we are rigorously honest we will receive release from our addictive compulsions. Working the Steps is what keeps us honest. I didn't believe this with my whole heart and I lived within my disease. My sponsor told me to just "do it" and see what happened; to "act as if it were true."

What is faith? It is the belief that if we stay close to our Higher Power we will be where we need to be. It is the guarantee that we do not walk through this world or this disease alone. Faith requires commitment to a belief that is greater than what we can see, hear, taste or smell. It's knowing that there is a God who loves us as we are, and Who will journey through this life with us. And faith requires that we act on that knowledge. That is faith.

I did the Steps and the compulsion was removed. A miracle? Absolutely! I had faith that the program would work. Putting the faith to work by diving into the Steps released me from the grips of the disease, one day at a time. The beauty of the program is faith in a Higher Power who will walk us through one hour, one day and one miracle at a time.

One Day at a Time . . . .
I will act as if there is a God who loves me.

~ Sara H.

THE PRESENT

"Real generosity towards the future
consists in giving all to what is present."
Albert Camus

Fear ruled my life until two years ago. I was paralyzed with fear about the future and what would happen when "they" discovered how bad I really was and how little they could trust me. I was terrified that the past would catch up with me and I'd be found out. The guilt and shame of my last binge came along for the ride as I replayed the scene compulsively and beat myself up for screwing up yet again. This made it impossible for me to stay in the present.

In program I learned that I wasn't really paralyzed by the past nor the future; rather, I was paralyzed by fear of losing control. The only way to release that fear was to admit, every hour of every day, that I was powerless over people, the past, the future and the food. When I wrote it down and put it in my God box, I could live in the present time. It was hard at first, and I'd grab it back when the fear crept in. But I'd let it go a little more each time, allowing me to be free of fear and enjoy moments of the day. The moments turned into hours and soon I was experiencing a full day without fear. The fear of the past and the future held less sway over me as I worked the Steps, surrendered my fears, and did service.

Service is the most important tool for me. The more service I do, the more I am fully alive in the present and I worry less about the past and the future. The peace and serenity that replaced the fear are blessed gifts allowing me to explore more of the present day. With them, I can honestly share myself with others and rebuild relationships. I now know the freedom of "giving all to what is present" and I pray for the willingness to stay in the present and be generous toward my future.

One Day at a Time . . . .
I live fully in the present, easily and effortlessly surrendering the past and the future to my Higher Power.

~ Anne L.

Meditation 255

LOVE

"Love yourself first and everything else falls into line.
You really have to love yourself to get anything done in this world."
Lucille Ball

It took me a long time to learn what love truly means. I thought love included pleasing others, saying "yes" when I meant "no," swallowing my true feelings and putting myself last. What I didn't know is that I was practicing resentment, anger, fear, jealousy and everything but love. I could not love others because I did not love myself.

Then I decided to take care of myself first. I considered no one but me, took care of myself, (or so I thought) while actually alienating myself from those close to me. I ate compulsively to tame the self-loathing I felt inside. And I loathed myself because I did not treat myself with real love and kindness.

Today I know that loving myself must come first. If I love myself, I am better able to love everyone in my life because I do things from a place of honesty. If I treat myself with respect, I treat others with respect. Everyone wins when I love myself enough to accept myself, flaws and all.

One Day at a Time . . . .
I will ask my Higher Power for the ability to accept and love myself for where I am this day, knowing I am a work in progress like a tree that grows from self-care and nurturing.

~ *Melissa*

ABSTINENCE

"It's a funny thing about life.
If you refuse to settle for anything less than the best,
that's what it will give you."
W. Somerset Maugham

When I first came to program, I was in the diet mentality. After a few "slips" I had to face the facts: I was in relapse, and I had never really surrendered. With the help of the program, I gained an increasing awareness of this progressive disease. Did I really want to recover? Was I really willing to go to any lengths to find relief from compulsive eating?

When I finally surrendered the food and began working the Steps, I didn't know what to expect. All I knew was that food could no longer be the answer. With seven months' abstinence, I now know that I have a long way to go in my recovery. However, one day at a time, I am willing to find my answers in the Steps instead of in the food. Thank you, Higher Power!

One Day at a Time . . . .
I choose abstinence and will listen for God's calling in my life. God's will for me is the safest and most loving place I can be, and I know God wants me to live a life free from the compulsion to eat.

~ *Christine S.*

Meditation 257

SLOW SUICIDE

"He who does not use his endeavors to heal himself
is brother to him who commits suicide."
Solomon

Rather than a regular, sudden suicide, I have subtly entertained the idea of slow suicide. I have neglected myself: my health, my vision and my gifts. I have either taken actions that have harmed me, or I have neglected to take actions that would have helped me to live a longer and more productive life. I have stuffed my face with garbage, accepting that as my fate.

Today I have a program that teaches me that I can't take care of myself alone and that I can, and will, receive help. I accept that help with humility, taking the Steps I am shown and using the tools I am offered. I begin to see that I have something to offer others and my life takes on new meaning and purpose.

One Day at a Time . . . .
I pray that I will say "yes" to my own life today, and take actions which represent that "yes."

~ Q

STEP SIX

"The Spiritual lift, the nearness to our Creator
that is experienced from humble invocation of His help,
and our willingness to be freed from old willful thoughts and habits
are essential to successful attainment of these steps."
The Little Red Book

I am a compulsive overeater. I eat three moderate meals each day without exception. In between, I have nothing except sugar-free gum, water, diet soda, and black coffee. Today I am working hard to allow my Higher Power to remove my imperfections. The focus is on the removal of blame, resentment, fear, and self-pity. I want to blame. I do resent. I have a lot of fear, but with surrender it is not paralyzing. I easily feel sorry for myself and cry about it. All of this threatens my abstinence, which is about sanity. The weight loss is an extra reward. The ability to approach responsibilities and feelings is the life force which I cannot take for granted.

When food was my higher power it was hell. I take my disease and recovery seriously. It's choosing life over slow, torturous death. All my problems are the same, yet somehow they are livable. Continually asking for removal of my defects results in a decrease of anxiety. I believe fully that my Higher Power will remove my problems in a time and way which I have no control over, as long as I remain willing. Today I am completely willing. I am grateful to have been chosen for recovery.

One Day at a Time . . . .
I can eat three weighed, measured and committed meals without exception. I enjoy
my meals and feel satisfied by them.

~ *Ellen*

Meditation 259

REDISCOVERY

*"When you come right down to it,
the secret of having it all is loving it all."*
Dr. Joyce Brothers

In dealing with compulsive eating issues, we tend to lose ourselves to the darkness of low self-esteem and self-criticism. We are our own worst enemies and we don't know how to nurture ourselves. We don't like who we have become. We feel like failures to ourselves and to all of those around us.

In working through the program, we learn to surrender and to accept the things we cannot change. We gain wisdom and strength. As we learn to take care of ourselves, we begin to feel good. We become self-aware. We recognize our needs and work aggressively to make sure they are being fulfilled.

We realize that we can choose how to react to the things around us. We accept our true selves, we voice our opinions, and we make changes. We realize that people do accept us the way we are and we don't have to hide anymore. For the first time, we are able to re-discover our true identity.

One Day at a Time . . . .
I learn something new about myself. I accept myself for who I am as I surrender myself to my Higher Power. I prioritize my needs and all of the responsibilities in my life. I find the courage to change the things I can, and I accept the things I cannot. I look in the mirror and, with each passing day in recovery, I like who I see.

~ *Lori*

Meditation 260

AGING

"We turn, not older with years,
but newer every day."
Emily Dickinson

Until I found Program, I used to think that being young was good and that being old was undignified. But working the 12 Steps helped me find the natural wisdom that comes from living over time without practicing addiction.

Now that I'm middle-aged, I feel a power, wisdom and dignity I've never felt before. Youth was good. This is good, too. For me, in fact, it's better. I know myself at last. I have so many more resources inside me. I am grateful to be in my middle years.

As I get older, I seem to be getting more innocent. I no longer need to fit in, please others, or do things just because everyone else is doing them.

Somehow this has cleared my vision and it is easier for me to see and appreciate things the way they really are.

In the end, it is easier every day to see myself for who I really am and to accept and love myself.

One Day at a Time . . . .
I am willing to be innocent and new; to go wherever my Higher Power leads me next.

~ Juno V.

Meditation 261

OVERWHELMED

"Fear is a sign –
usually a sign that I'm doing something right."
Erica Jong

When I first came into the Twelve Step program, I felt overwhelmed. Life overwhelmed me. My eating disorders overwhelmed me. My inner-pain overwhelmed me. Before I walked into my first meeting, I felt very alone.

My Higher Power has been good to me. When I entered my first meeting, I learned I was not alone. As I began to work the Twelve Steps, I learned that, while I had a lot of healing and learning to do, I would not be doing it alone. I have many friends who help me, but most of all, I have a relationship with my Higher Power that assures me constantly that I am loved.

Today, I don't often feel overwhelmed. When I do, I turn to my Higher Power and my friends, all of whom help me to focus on doing the best thing for my mental, emotional and physical health.

One Day at a Time . . . .
I will remember that even when I feel alone, I have the love and help of my Higher Power.

~ Rhonda H.

SERVICE

"We must give alms.
Charity wins souls and draws them to virtue."
Angela Merici

An important lesson in life is that in order to get something we need or want, we first have to give some of it away. If we want friends, we have to be a friend. If we want to be loved, we have to love. If we want recovery, we have to help others recover.

Then we begin to "get it." The tingling excitement of hope is aroused in us. We discover an inner-source of power to live.

Giving service is as important to our recovery as are abstinence and working the Steps. It includes everything from organizing materials at a face-to-face meeting to hosting meetings online. It's sharing our problems and our solutions on the loops, as well as sponsoring. Recovery is incomplete until it is shared by giving service to the program or to individuals. It's remarkable how service brings us closer together, allows us to make friends, helps to end our isolation and gives that feeling of self-worth and confidence that we so desperately need. Simply put, service is as much a lifesaver to us as it is to those we reach out and touch.

I want to be a giver to the program so it is always available to those who will come after me seeking their freedom from this dread disease.

One Day at a Time . . . .
I strive to give love, support, comfort, cheer and encouragement, knowing it will come back to me pressed down, shaken together and running over.

~ *Dottie*

Meditation 263

FILLING THE VOID

"You can't have everything.
Where would you put it?"
Steven Wright.

I had thought marriage alone would heal all the hurts I had gathered up in my life. My husband, also the product of a dysfunctional family, felt the same way. We quickly learned that our love for each other was not enough to our emptiness.

I was used to using food to temporarily fill my inner-holes; he was used to abusing another substance to fill his. Neither worked well, and we soon discovered that buying things we didn't need would help to temporarily fill some of our hurts. Pretty soon we had a house that was full of things we'd bought that had given only a few moments of pleasure at best.

One of the benefits of program life is that I've learned to fill the holes within me in ways that really work. I want to make my life more simple and less cluttered. Three years later, I'm still getting rid of things we bought and never used again. But the best part is we can go to the mall when we really do need something and not feel the compulsion to buy something we don't need.

One Day at a Time . . . .
I will use the lessons I've learned working the program to finally heal the hurts within me instead of looking for material things to repair these inner-holes.

~ Rhonda H.

CHANGE

If you always do what you always did,
then you'll always get what you always got.
Anonymous

Initiating change has been the hardest part for me as I reach for recovery. How could I possibly change the thoughts and behaviors that have carried me through the past 25 years? How could I deal with those feelings that I had been trying to avoid for so long? Why did I even consider giving up my coping mechanisms, even though I knew how deadly they had become?

I realized that I could change the distorted thinking and behaviors by taking each day, one at a time. I didn't have to eat today, as I did the day before. I didn't have to isolate myself. I could choose what I was going to put into my mouth and when. I could try alternate ways to cope, such as calling a friend, going for a walk, screaming out loud if I had to. I didn't have to binge anymore.

Some days are easier than others, but I continually pray for the strength to get through the difficult ones. By working the Steps and giving it all to my Higher Power, I am initiating change. I am asking for help. I know I can't do it alone, so as I work at not doing what I've always done, I see a new life developing in front of me. I am experiencing new thoughts and behaviors. I am making healthier decisions about my life. I am detoxing my body and spirit. Change brings with it fear, but also many new moments of serenity and happiness.

One Day at a Time . . . .
I will be aware of the changes I need to make, while at the same time realizing that change comes slowly, quietly, and sometimes unexpectedly. I will know that I have some responsibility in helping my Higher Power, by working the program. I will experience change one moment at a time, as I choose not to comfort myself with food.

~ *Lori*

Meditation 265

ACCEPTANCE

*"And acceptance is the answer to all my problems today.
I need to concentrate not so much on what needs to be changed
in the world as what needs to be changed in me and in my attitudes."*
The Big Book of Alcoholics Anonymous

Dissatisfaction has been part of my disease and it played a significant role in bringing me to recovery. It is the human condition to dislike where we are. Like many of us, I used to think that only some mystical, non-existent person, place, thing or situation would make me happy. If only my spouse loved me as I want to be loved; if only the boss would see and appreciate my contributions; or if only my house and children were perfect. I sat year after year speculating and fantasizing my life away.

The Serenity Prayer tells me to ask God for the wisdom to know His will for me. I lived in darkness and despair until I learned that my Higher Power is here. He is in charge. I must, through prayer and meditation, seek God's will and do the next right thing. I need to cooperate with my Higher Power to change my attitude. To that end, I do the footwork just for today.

One Day at a Time . . . .
I will seek and accept God's will for my life.

~ *Danny*

EMOTIONS

"A life lacking the emotional upheavals of depression and despair,
fear and anxiety, grief and sadness, anger and the agony of forgiving,
confusion and doubt, criticism and rejection, will not only
be useless to ourselves, it will be useless to others."
Scott Peck

Because I have always thought of myself as such an ordinary person, as life moved along I was surprised to find so many emotional events happening in it. I have had severe periods of depression and despair; I have known fear, anxiety, anger and doubt. I have wrestled with grief and known the agony of rejection. I have been subjected to criticism and experienced firsthand the difficulty of forgiving those whom I once thought I would never be able to forgive.

What I have learned about life and recovery is that no one is ordinary, that everyone experiences emotions of all kinds, and what is important is that each of these upheavals are instructive and not wasted.

Whereas once I would block my feelings, I now allow myself to feel them. Instead of sweeping my emotions under a rug, I express them. Rather than blocking grief from my soul, I experience it ... then heal from it. When I am rejected, I try to move on by exploring the reasons why.

One Day at a Time . . . .
I will turn my negative emotions into positive ones by transforming them into useful
learning experiences both for myself and for others.

~ Mari

Meditation 267

THE FUTURE

"When I look into the future, it's so bright it burns my eyes."
Oprah Winfrey

I receive the gift of abstinence one day at a time. I am relieved from the obsession to eat one day at a time. With the help of my Higher Power, I can live life on life's terms... one day at a time.

As my recovery builds and builds, I start to imagine all the possibilities for my life. Things I never had the confidence or emotional stability to pursue are options for me. Now that I am free from the despair and self-destruction of overeating, there is space to actualize new adventures. But before I become overwhelmed or grandiose in my thinking, the Program gently reminds me that it is STILL just one day a time.

One Day at a Time . . . .
I will work my program so that I have a future.

~ *Christine S.*

Meditation 268

COURAGE

"Courage faces fear and thereby masters it."
Martin Luther King, Jr.

I have never been a brave person and was always very fearful. I would watch movies where the hero would rescue the heroine, someone would climb Mount Everest or perform some feat of daring, and I would be totally in awe. I was afraid of the dark, of rejection, of failure and of most other things that I was convinced took courage. There's no way would I go parasailing or deep sea diving as that seemed to require the courage that I lacked.

I didn't understand then that people who do those kinds of things are not totally without fear, but they have a way of overcoming their fear and still doing it anyway.

When I came into the program and learned that I would have to do an inventory and then, worse still, make amends to the people I had harmed, I was paralyzed by fear. Eventually I realized that, even though I feared doing these things, all I had to do was ask my Higher Power for strength and guidance and then do the things I'd most feared. Perhaps these weren't the feats of daring that I had seen heroes perform, but for me they were great victories and in being able to do them, I knew that I was developing courage.

One Day at a Time . . . .
I will continue to walk through my fear with my Higher Power at my side, knowing that I am developing the courage that I thought I lacked.

~ *Sharon S.*

LETTING GO

"We must be willing to get rid of the life we've planned,
so as to have the life that is waiting for us."
Joseph Campbell

It is hard to give up old habits. Although my former solutions to dealing with stress, anger, and emotional and physical pain had never worked and only made the problems worse, they were familiar. I had high hopes the results would be different each time. I wasn't too surprised when it didn't happen because this was familiar ground.

Then I heard about this program, half-heartedly joined and began working the Twelve Steps. It was scary! Things began happening to me that I'd never dreamed possible. I was given abstinence! I had not planned for that to happen. How could I, when I had no idea what abstinence would really be like?

At first I felt very anxious, sure the abstinence would be snatched from me just as I was beginning to feel comfortable with it. While I enjoyed abstinence and not having to focus on my eating disorder's requirements, I often felt like I was in foreign territory without a map. I couldn't plan my life like I had before because my life was busy evolving in ways I couldn't imagine.

But the longer I worked the program, the happier my life became. To my utter shock I've recently discovered that I, a control freak and ultimate planner of everything, have begun to enjoy the unpredictability that my Higher Power has so graciously put in my life.

Before the program I never appreciated spontaneity; I couldn't. Now, a day without plans is an opportunity.

One Day at a Time . . . .
I will pray to let go of my will and instead to be open to my Higher Power's will for me.

~ Rhonda

Meditation 270

PATIENCE

"Patience and perseverance have a magical effect
before which difficulties and obstacles vanish."
John Quincy Adams

When I first walked through the meeting doors, I wanted recovery and I wanted it now! Give me the magic wand, I'll wave it, then get on with my life. At least that's what I thought.

One of the most difficult things I've had to learn is the art of patience and allowing God to work within his own time while I do the footwork to the best of my ability. It is my belief that the universe and my Higher Power will order the next level of my physical recovery. Physical recovery does not grow without spiritual progress. This Program is a journey, not a crash-course in fad dieting.

When I struggled with bouts of pride connected to my levels of patience and God's timing, I knew I was uncovering yet another character flaw that could delay my spiritual recovery. Spiritual recovery, as "Old-timers" have told us again and again, is the actual foundation of the program. The inner-person will eventually make its way to the outer-person.

One Day at a Time . . . .
Today I will slow down, take a deep breath, and just remind myself that my Higher Power is in control and that my natural pattern will develop under His nurture, care, and control.

~ January

Meditation 271

OTHERS

"Those who have learned by experience
what physical and emotional pain and anguish mean
are a community all over the world...
One and all, they know the longing to be free from pain."
Albert Schweitzer

Whether we isolate or are on the go constantly, whether we're in the disease or out of it, whether we've found all the Promises or we haven't, we are bonded for a lifetime by the disease of our addiction.

I was alone until I found other compulsive eaters. Yes, I had a family and friends and relatives and doctors and church and careers, but I was emotionally alone with this intricate, enigmatic, hellhole of a disease. The moment I met and connected with other compulsive eaters, my "real" life began.

One Day at a Time . . . .
I share what I have learned with those who haven't.
I give what I have to give, and I get so much more.

~ Mari

Meditation 272

TOGETHERNESS

*"Take my hand, and no matter how dark the night,
the light of day will come, and we will share the tomorrow."*
Ken Grant

When we first walk into our recovery rooms, we are all afraid: afraid of more rejection, afraid of more failure, and afraid of more loneliness. Once we sit and listen, we realize that we are not much different than the other people there. We ease up, start sharing, begin trusting our Higher Power and ourselves more.

Our darkness of the past is drawn out by our sharing with other addicts. We realize our deep, dark secrets are not as bad as we thought.

We are not alone! Then hand-in-hand, we begin climbing the ladder of recovery and the light of day begins to shine brighter and brighter.

One Day at a Time . . . .
When we let our guard down and let Higher Power and other people in, we learn that at the end of a dark day is the light of our next today. We learn that together we can do what we can never do alone.

~ *Jeanette*

Meditation 273

SERVICE

"A single sunbeam is enough
to drive away many shadows."
St. Francis of Assisi

There are many tools I use to maintain my abstinence, but none of them is as important to me as service. I do a lot of service, but it's not for fame or glory: I do service in order to keep my program strong. I came into program for the first time back in college, and got there only because someone offered to give me a ride.

When we first walk into these rooms, we often feel lost and alone in the dark world of addiction. But at that very first meeting we hear people talk about their experience and strength, and a small glow of light comes into our view. All it takes is that "single sunbeam" and we have hope again and our world seems brighter.

As we keep coming back and working the Steps, we encounter lots of different sunbeams, and slowly the shadows in our lives are cast away and the world becomes bright again. It is then our responsibility to let our own light shine. One of the beauties of this program is that everyone can find a way to give service. Whether it be on the group or Intergroup level, whether by sponsoring or just making a call, whether by serving as secretary, treasurer, or just by helping to put chairs away after a meeting, there is a job for everyone.

No one should feel "unimportant." I'm sure that the lady who gave me a ride to my first few meetings didn't feel like she was doing anything special, but she was the first sunbeam in my life. All these years later, her act of giving has ignited in me a burning desire to give back to others the miracle of this program.

One Day at a Time . . . .
I will be unafraid to let my light shine. Any act of service that I can give will not only help another, but will ensure that my own light does not burn out.

~ *Laurel*

Meditation 274

THE FEAR OF FAILURE

"It is not because things are difficult that we do not dare;
it is because we do not dare that things are difficult."
Seneca

I was full of excuses: "I can't start a food plan. Won't it be the same as a diet? I'm a free spirit! I don't like such restrictions! If I can't do something perfectly, why should I even start? I do it perfectly, or I don't do it at all! I have gone too far to ever go back to being anywhere near healthy. I don't have time to plan my Food. I am young. I have plenty of time to worry about taking off the weight!"

These were my favorite excuses. Underlying all the excuses was the fear of failure. I did not know that true failure comes about by not ever having tried. My life circumstances never got better by ignoring my problems with food. Ignoring my condition began to complicate every aspect of my life.

This moment I have a choice. I dare to choose in the next few moments even one small thing that I can do to make my life better or more healthful.

One Day at a Time . . . .
If I cannot think of anything, I will pause and ask my Higher Power to help me learn to choose.

~ *January K.*

COMPULSIONS

"All human actions have one or more of these seven causes:
chance, nature, compulsion, habit, reason, passion, desire."
Aristotle

When I was eating compulsively, it was similar to taking nitrous oxide at my dentist. Like a heavy anesthesia, the food comforted me and gave me an extraordinary sense of well-being. Like many short-term cures for what is bothering us, it took its toll. Any resemblance to reality while in the fog of compulsive eating is purely coincidental. While there may be times in my life I needed anesthesia, to use it day in and day out to block emotional pain is a burden only compulsive eaters know about.

Compulsion is self-will gone berserk. I try to think of it as the opposite of effortless abstinence. Between the two are miles and miles of varying experiences. For me there was never moderation ... only the two extremes. It took several years of squeaky clean abstinence to trust myself and begin to try moderation in eating. At that point I had learned to recognize and be aware of the dangers of that first compulsive bite. There have been times when this cunning disease always waiting to pounce has sent me straight back to hell as a result of that one single compulsive bite.

One Day at a Time . . . .
I will pray that my actions are caused by anything except compulsions.

~ Mari

TRUTH

*"The truth will set you free,
but first it will make you miserable."*
James A. Garfield

After years of therapy, I thought I knew myself fairly well. I prided myself on my integrity, honesty and responsible nature; however, my morbid obesity and compulsive overeating reflected the exact opposite of these values. After breaking many resolutions to myself, starting and stopping countless diets, and continuing to have no control over my eating, I began to doubt my integrity. How could I keep a commitment to everyone I knew and yet break my promises to myself over and over again? It wasn't until in a moment of frustrated clarity I blurted out, "I'm acting like an addict!" Finally I experienced my own truth.

I am an addict. I am addicted to food. I use food to fill the gaping black hole within me. I use food to anesthetize my pain. As a compulsive overeater, I stuff my face rather than face my stuff.

Working the Steps allowed me to see that even though I thought I valued honesty, I was constantly lying to myself about my compulsive eating. Becoming abstinent from compulsive eating removed the veils of delusion and dishonesty that I had over my eyes. Living this program, one day at a time, freed me from compulsive lying to myself as well as compulsive eating. Telling the truth, while sometimes very difficult, has let me live happy, joyously, and free.

One Day at a Time . . . .
I will work the Steps honestly, tell the truth about my life, and be the person of integrity my Higher Power always intended for me to be.

~ *Bernadette B.*

Meditation 277

SHAME

*"It is not the criminal things that are hardest to confess,
but the ridiculous and the shameful."*
Jean Jacques Rousseau

I had a very strange childhood filled with lots of emotional and physical neglect. Combine that with moving about once a year and being deemed as "unacceptable" by each new community we moved into, and how could I help but feel a great sense of shame about everything about me?

As an adult I left home and became a well-respected part of a new community. I have lived in the same nice house, with a beautiful yard, and had well kept-children. In spite of all the evidence to the contrary, internally I was still that "unacceptable" child. I had not told anyone about my childhood because I felt it to be a shameful secret. I thought that much of my adult unhappiness was deserved because I truly believed that even though no one knew the truth about me, deep down I really was still unacceptable.

Since coming to TRG, I have been releasing something far more important than the 60 pounds of weight I have lost. I have begun to release the shame, the sense of being unacceptable, and the sense of being unworthy and unlovable. I have shared my secrets with wonderfully-loving, accepting people. By sharing my secrets I am releasing my pain. My request that my name not be revealed at the end of this meditation, though, clearly states that I still have work to do. TRG, the program, and the Steps are offering me the means to recovery and I will gratefully accept the offer!

One Day at a Time . . . .
I will remember that the old false self-perceptions are no longer relevant in my life. I am learning new ways of self-acceptance and new ways of self-nurturing that will serve me far better.

~ *Karen H.*

Meditation 278

HABITS

"A habit cannot be tossed out the window;
it must be coaxed down the stairs a step at a time."
Mark Twain

How grateful I was when I read that quote – even though I had to translate it a bit. It has always been difficult for me to start good habits. I've heard all kinds of things about that – that it takes 21 days, 40 days, or an x-number of weeks to start a habit. It always made me feel bad and different because I swear for me, it probably takes at least two years. Until then I'd be biting my nails, knowing that even if I did practice good habits, they might disappear at any time. It was supposed to be so much faster, so much easier! A few weeks of eating healthy, and magically I would be cured! Well, that never happened.

Now I can look at good habits – like eating healthy, exercising, meditating, paying my bills on time – as tender, shy little animals that need a long time before they can be coaxed up the stairs of my life. They need patience, a lot of quiet time, and a willingness to be understood and studied. How do I feed, nurture and care for this habit?

I cannot do it alone. I do not have the patience, the willingness, nor the nurturing to do this by myself. I need the help of the fellowship and the help of my Higher Power. This help is freely given to me ~ all I need to do is accept it, and together we can make my habits more and more comfortable in the house of my life.

One Day at a Time . . . .
With the help of my Higher Power and the program, I can patiently learn to practice healthy habits.

~ *Isabella*

Meditation 279

LONGINGS

*"The great question - which I have not been able
to answer - is, 'What does a woman want?'"*
Sigmund Freud

All my life I have been searching for what I "really want". I tried sports, different jobs, friends, lovers and traveling. I even tried therapy. None of these ever worked. Once I had what I thought I wanted, I didn't want it anymore. The urge to want – to long for the best things – was an inner, unsatisfied hunger. Excessive food became my sedating drug. When using food, I was numb to my longings. I felt it was impossible to fill this void. It seemed I would never know or receive what I wanted.

The Twelve Step program of recovery taught me that I could have anything I wanted – if God gave it to me. When I stopped wanting everything so badly, and I surrendered to be His child and employee, I learned that what I'd thought of as "wanting", was actually what I was "missing". I missed everything important in my life, so I wanted everything. It was never enough ~ never the right thing or the right person. I felt that even I was "wrong" because I was without love, patience, tolerance or companionship. In OA I found all of that. With God's help, I now have those things in my life every day when I ask for it and accept it as part of me today.

One Day at a Time . . . .
I no longer want so much, and I am thankful for what I receive. I am receiving more than I have ever dreamed of.

~ Trine

Meditation 280

WISDOM

"Wisdom ceases to be wisdom
when it becomes too proud to weep,
too grave to laugh,
and too selfish to seek other than itself."
Kahlil Gibran

When I heard the serenity prayer at the first OA meeting I attended, I didn't understand what it meant to accept what I couldn't change, have courage to change the things I could, and wisdom to know the difference. I said it at each meeting and hoped that eventually I would somehow find that wisdom. It was quite some time into my recovery when I finally understood what having wisdom really meant.

Before Program, I never accepted things or people the way they were. I felt paralyzed by my fears about what wasn't working in my life. This fear kept me from seeing what I could change, or even try to change, in my life.

I finally realized that before coming into the Program I had put on a mask and never let anyone know the real me. I didn't know how to laugh or cry, and I certainly never knew how to reach out to others because it was always about me and my unfortunate life.

But once I finally allowed myself to be real and vulnerable with others, miracles began to happen. I became more willing to accept people and places as exactly the way they should be at that time. I was able to walk through my fears and learn what I could change in my life. To my delight, when I became more vulnerable to others it didn't make me weak; rather, I felt a strength and power flow through me and I became more able to know the difference between what I could or couldn't change, and for me, that is wisdom.

One Day at a Time . . . .
May I always be willing to know the difference between what I can and cannot change.

~ Sharon S.

Meditation 281

WISDOM

*"Rarely have we seen a person fail who has thoroughly
followed our path. Those who do not recover are people who cannot
or will not completely give themselves to this simple program."*
The Big Book of Alcoholics Anonymous

I always believed that I had to control every aspect of my life or I would be a "less-than" person. This attitude even crept into my attempts to learn the art of watercolor still life and portraits. Even my art could not escape the effects of my character defects! In order to learn something new, I have to be willing to follow the rules of the very thing I want to learn. I shared this with an experienced artist and best friend, "I find myself still wanting to control the outcome of the colors."

"Isn't that the way we try to control our lives? She replied. "Drop the paint where you want it to go, then drop the second color into that one and let it go! You can take your brush and guide it, but don't mess with it!"

My life is like learning to watercolor. I have to trust that doing the footwork of recovery as others have done will bring about a beautiful portrait of growth in recovery.

One Day at a Time . . . .
I will do the footwork by making good choices, letting each build upon the other, and I will stand back to see what God will create.

~ *Sharon S.*

BALANCE SHEET

"It is amazing what you can accomplish if
you do not care who gets the credit."
Harry S. Truman

Before I came to OA, I kept an emotional account of all my positive actions. I didn't really do that many good things, but the few I did were meant to show how great and kind I was. I even "wrote down" smiles, talking politely, giving a hand in the house, or filling in at work. I expected a great reward one day for all of my good actions ~ especially considering all of the things I put up with. I wanted people to speak well of me. I wanted people to grieve in great sorrow at my funeral for losing the fantastic person I was. Because I felt I never got back half of what I had put into this balance sheet, my resentments started to block me from acting nicely. Why help out, when nobody ever does anything for me? I didn't have an honest focus on reality. I felt worn out, bitter, used and angry. Why was I never paid what I deserved?

I learned in OA that I have a terminal disease which will kill me sooner or later – if I do not change my thinking and acting. I am powerless over this disease. The only thing I can do is to admit I'm powerless and surrender. As I see it, this disease is the primary reason I have gotten into trouble all my life. I am self-centered, bitter, immature and insecure. Before I entered these rooms, I didn't know how to have a real friend, or brush my teeth on a daily basis. In this program, I learned that I am worthy, loveable, and an ordinary woman – with my positive and negative sides – just like everyone else. When I am accountable today to God as I understand him, I do not need an emotional balance sheet. I do not need to grow bitter or hate other people.

One Day at a Time . . . .
Because I have so generously been given a new life in this program, I choose to give service to my home group and to give time and patience to my sponsees. I choose to give of myself, for that does not have a price, in money or in diplomas. I no longer need the credit for what I give.

~ *Trine*

TOLERANCE

*"I have learned silence from the talkative,
toleration from the intolerant, and kindness
from the unkind; yet, strange, I am ungrateful
to those teachers."*
Khalil Gibran

Two of my biggest character defects are arrogance and fear. I used to have a hard time tolerating people who are not like me. When I was driven by fear, anger, and shame, I believed they threatened my social position. A normal day for me was filled with frustration and anger at people I didn't like. Gossip was my language.

After I decided that I was truly powerless over my addiction and that my life had become really unmanageable, I surrendered. I started writing the suggested Step work and had a great awakening. In the Fourth Step inventory, I came to the conclusion that I did not like "different people" because I was afraid to be like them. And what were they like? Just like me. I didn't like myself. That was one of the most revealing acknowledgements that were given to me. I have no reason to pick a fight anymore, nor discuss or judge any person. When I meet people I do not like, I know why.

One Day at a Time . . . .
My greatest teachers are those who have shown me what I do not like or accept about myself. I understand that I would never have appreciated these lessons as precious gifts without the understanding, growth and tolerance within the Twelve Step fellowship. Today I make a living amend by never judging or disliking any person. Every human being is a creature of God as I understand him, and who am I to judge?

~ Trine

FAITH

"Faith is not belief. Belief is passive.
Faith is active."
Edith Hamilton

I always believed that God could relieve my suffering if He chose; however, I was overlooking the distinction of the required "partnership" between my choices and his strength. God is not a magician who, with artful finesse, will relieve me of the bondage of my free-will choices. He requires my attention – and then my ACTION – in order to work through and in my life.

One Day at a Time . . . .
I am willing to test my faith by putting forth the required action(s) that will help me move toward my share of miracles that abound in this Program.

~ January K.

GRIEF

*"To spare oneself from grief at all cost
can be achieved only at the price of a total detachment,
which excludes the ability to experience happiness."*
Erich Fromm

In the years before program I lived in a bland state of non-feeling and I ran away from all painful emotions, especially loss and grief. Of course my drug of choice was always there to keep the painful emotions at bay. Whenever I experienced any kind of loss, I was always able to focus my attention on other things. Instead of feeling my own emotions, I focused on being strong for someone else whose loss I perceived to be greater than mine. For some strange reason I didn't think I had the right to grieve.

After losing a beloved cat recently, I was overwhelmed by all the painful emotions of loss and grief. It was almost as though all of my previous losses were combined into this latest loss, but instead of running from my feelings, I allowed myself the luxury of grieving for my cat who was so special to me. This time I didn't need to run away into my addiction. Of course it was hard and painful, but I know that allowing myself to feel even uncomfortable feelings like this is part of being alive and that means allowing myself to feel both the positive emotions and the negative ones.

One Day at a Time . . . .
I will allow myself to feel both the good emotions and the bad ones. Because I have a program, I don't need to blot them out with addictive behavior.

~ *Sharon S.*

HONESTY

"Honesty is the first chapter of the book of wisdom."
Thomas Jefferson

Throughout my ups and downs in life and in working the Steps, I have discovered the importance of complete honesty. No matter what I feel or think, being honest about it with myself, others and God helps me to stay in a healthier state of physical, emotional and spiritual wellness. When I first started in the program, the idea of telling my Higher Power how I really felt was foreign to me. Sure I asked for help and "explained" what I was going through, but I didn't often pour my heart out. I didn't want to offend or burden God with complaints or weakness.

With the help of the Steps, I have let go of the formal prayers I learned in my youth and I more often tell God the way my life really is. Sometimes that includes sharing my negative attitude, crying, or just conversing casually with God. My Higher Power is full of acceptance and understanding and is pleased every time I share my honest thoughts and feelings with Him.

The years of denying and burying my feelings have resulted in an automatic reaction to not allow myself to feel or think straight in lots of situations. If I can take the time to identify exactly where I am and then honestly admit that to God and others (when needed), I have made progress.

Sharing my true self with a sponsor or in a meeting helps, too. It lifts the blinders from my eyes so that I can see my reality and proceed from there. If I hide from God, fool myself or deceive others, I rob myself of honesty which is the foundation of my progress towards serenity and wisdom.

One Day at a Time . . . .
For today I will embrace my reality, the good and the bad. I will honestly admit my thoughts and feelings to myself, to another person and to God.

~ *Susanne*

Meditation 287

COURAGE

Courage is not the absence of fear,
but rather the judgment that something else
is more important than fear.
Ambrose Redmoon

In the program, I've heard you have to hit bottom before things can start getting better. I thought I'd hit bottom when I attended my first meeting, but apparently I hadn't. A few weeks later things got worse, and I reacted by becoming agoraphobic. It's awfully hard to attend a meeting when you have panic attacks every time you try to leave your house.

Finding Twelve Step meetings online was a blessing. Even though things had gotten much worse, I knew I'd hit bottom and needed the program more than ever. I'm so glad my Higher Power allowed me to know from my short stint with program that it was what I needed to survive. I persevered until I found meetings I could attend ... online. Then I wanted more. I wanted to be able to walk into a face-to-face meeting. With the help of a sponsor, I was able to see that what I wanted and needed was bigger than my phobia, and I walked into my first face-to-face meeting in two and a half years.

I've battled the agoraphobia. It's been more than a year since my last panic attack, and it was laughably minor, thanks to the tools I've learned in the program. I have plenty of other fears that the Steps have helped me to slay, one by one, and a few more I face daily. Just today I was shown I can ask for help, without fear, and feel worthy of that help. Just another miracle of the program.

One Day at a Time . . . .
I will work my program to the best of my ability, remembering my fears can be overcome with the help of my Higher Power, my sponsors, and my fellow Twelve-Steppers.

~ *Rhonda H*

LEARNING NEW IDEAS

"I can't understand why people are frightened of new ideas.
I'm frightened of the old ones."
John Cage

When I look back upon my life before I heard of food being a compulsion, I remember my old thinking – which was not very thoughtful at all! I performed the task of feeding myself without any conscious forethought or planning. It was whatever was in sight, available, or easiest to fix. I never stopped to think why I eat what I eat. I don't know what I was thinking when I consumed something that I knew would leave me feeling as though I were in a stupor or would send me crashing into naps that lasted hours.

My old ideas were mindless, thoughtless. I was an unhealthy automaton who had never been taught how to think about the "what" and "why" of her food choices. I have learned to listen to others who have recovery, take what I need from their stories, and apply some of their actions to my own life.

One Day at a Time . . . .
I am willing to put aside old ideas as I discover them, to lay groundwork for the new ideas that have been presented to me, and to continue on a journey of personal growth. My mind is like a garden. I have to pull the weeds so that new flowers can begin to grow.

~ January K.

Meditation 289

FELLOWSHIP

"When we honestly ask ourselves which persons in our lives
mean the most to us, we often find that it is those who,
instead of giving advice, solutions, or cures, have
chosen rather to share our pain and touch our wounds
with a warm and tender hand."
Henri Nouwen, Out of Solitude

When I first came into The Recovery Group's online meeting room nearly a year ago, I was bankrupt of mind, body and soul. I felt so unlovable that even I couldn't stand myself! I casually observed at the first few meetings and I was intrigued by the warmth of the fellowship there. After a few meetings I finally opened up and shared, "spilling my guts" about what it was like to reach bottom and to desperately need a hand to lift me up. After they heard my share, they told me they would love me until I could learn to love myself. That really blew me away! They told me they had been where I was and that they had found a means to recover. They assured me this program would work for me, if I really wanted it, and to follow their steps ~ their beloved Twelve Steps.

Shortly after joining, I got an online sponsor with whom I have been walking the path of recovery ever since. I eventually shared with her things I had spent a lifetime desperately longing to be able to tell another person, but had needed to keep shrouded in secrecy. Being heard and understood was the gift of a lifetime. The weight has been falling off, I have experienced a lot of emotional healing, and I am in a much better place spiritually. This fellowship, their Steps and meetings, and my Higher Power have brought me a long way in a year's time!

One Day at a Time . . . .
I will emulate those warm, wonderful people by welcoming newcomers with love and by helping them get started on the road to recovery. I will sponsor with the love and dedication that my sponsor has shown me.

~ Karen A.

SELF SABOTAGE

"The truth is that our finest moments are most likely to occur
when we are feeling deeply uncomfortable, unhappy, or unfulfilled.
For it is only in such moments, propelled by our discomfort, that
we are likely to step out of our ruts and start searching
for different ways or truer answers."
M. Scott Peck

For the last fifteen years I have been an avid and restless student of "self-help." I read popular books, spent years in therapy, and attended various support groups. Because I didn't see any improvement in my life, I was consumed with anger, shame, bitterness, and a pervasive sense of injustice. I blamed my Higher Power, my family, my partner, and my life circumstances. Only since joining The Recovery Group have I discovered the source of my toxic stagnation. It was myself. When doing a thorough examination of my life, I was absolutely shocked to find that I had been repeatedly practicing destructive acts of self-sabotage.

I was in love with my suffering. I was addicted to my misery. Sometimes we cling to our illnesses and weaknesses because they are so familiar to us. Though they hurt us, we find them oddly comforting. It's what we're used to. And change is scary. The unknown is scary. I found that my self-sabotage stemmed from shame, anger, low self-esteem, my lust for being a Victim – and even a Fear of Being Well. I had to reach the profound darkness of depression before I could admit that the damage I did to myself had become unbearable.

Now I make a choice each day to not sabotage myself. It's not easy. Rather than being my enemy, I choose to be my friend and advocate. With the help of this program and my friends in recovery, I have come to like myself and to truly want good things for myself. The changes are gradual and require me to be patient and gracious with myself. Now I can celebrate each baby step and forgive myself when I fall back into old patterns. I now know that when I do make a mistake, I can admit it, learn from it, and press forward with my Recovery.

One Day at a Time . . . .
I will choose to accept myself as a person of worth. I will resist temptations to sabotage my recovery and I will choose good things for my life.

~ *Lisa*

Meditation 291

LOOKING FOR LOVE

"The most important thing in life
is to learn how to give out love,
and to let it come in."
Morrie Schwartz

As a compulsive overeater I was always looking outside of myself for love, yet I was terrified of letting it in. "What if it hurts me once I let it in?" I was just as afraid of giving out love. "What if I lost myself or was taken advantage of?" My life was ruled by fear, and at a very young age I discovered the false security of food. I used food as a source of companionship and as a way to numb out my pain. It became a substitute for love.

As the disease gained control, the more I ate and the more shut down I became. I built huge walls around myself. As the weight came on, I was convinced that this was the reason people didn't love me the way that I wanted to be loved. I believed that "if only I was thin enough" I would get what I wanted. It never occurred to me that I was already so full of the food that there was no room inside to receive anything else.

When I came into program and began to put down the food, I slowly discovered that this love that I was searching for was within me all along. My Higher Power is love and dwells within and all around me. In recovery I am graced with the freedom to act out of love and therefore be with my Higher Power.

One Day at a Time . . . .
I will choose to act out of love and to keep my heart open to the love that my Higher Power brings into my life. If I just open my eyes, my ears and my heart, it is everywhere.

~ Jessica M.

Meditation 292

LIVE AND LET LIVE

*"If I knew for a certainty that a man was coming to my house
with the conscious design of doing me good,
I should run for my life."*
Henry David Thoreau

I have gleaned from the OA program that I can let others be themselves and make their own decisions unless an issue involves me as well. What a powerful concept. I have struggled long and hard with the issue of letting others live their lives as they choose without the benefit of my wise, profound advice. I really believed that I had all the answers and that by listening to me, one could get his or her life on the right track and be forever grateful to me for the magnanimous favor I had done them. I really believed this! I was also deeply frustrated when people did not immediately do whatever it was I had "advised" them to do. How could they be so dumb?

More importantly, how did I overlook the fact that my own life was heading downhill at a remarkable clip? Thanks to the OA program, I have slowly learned to keep my mouth shut. My motto for relationships is simple: sweep off my side of the street. It makes being me so much easier and it makes the lives of those around me a bit better too.

One Day at a Time . . . .
Today I will accept and love those around me without acting on the urge to make their lives "better." I will live and let live as I continue to realize the freedom the program offers me.

~ *Pete*

LIMITATIONS

*"You cannot help men permanently
by doing for them what they could and should do for themselves."*
Abraham Lincoln

I love the idea of helping people. Seeing the other person shine after my input gives me a great feeling. The flipside of this peak experience is the sadness and bleakness I feel when the person I am helping does not succeed. When it is all about me, I have to accept responsibility for everything: the good and the bad.

Thank You, God, that it is not really me who is the source of all help, it is You. I can point the way and make suggestions, but I cannot make someone change for the better. What causes people to change is something for which no person can take credit. It is simply divine!

The real question is whether or not the person I want to help will turn to his or her Higher Power and use the help that is offered. I cannot actually take these steps for others. I can pretend to do that, and perhaps offer some temporary relief, but lasting recovery will come only to those who make a quality decision to take the necessary steps on their own.

One Day at a Time . . . .
I will realize the limitations of my help. I will not try to do for others what only they can and should do for themselves.

~ Q

READY

"If we wait for the moment when everything,
absolutely everything is ready, we shall never begin."
Ivan Turgenev

This was one of my biggest obstacles in recovery: I wanted everything to be perfect. This type of thinking kept me stuck for many years in the disease. Instead of my program being One Day At A Time, it was always "one day later and I will do your will God."

Now I know that today is all I have. I have no guarantees for tomorrow. So I let go and let God, and do the best I can. I have discovered that I do not have to work a perfect program. Not everything has to be just "right."

One Day at a Time . . . .
One day at a time I do the footwork that is required of me and leave the results to God.

~ *Terri*

Meditation 295

ACCEPTANCE

"Life has no other discipline to impose, if we would but realize it, than to accept life unquestioningly. Everything we shut our eyes to, everything we run away from, everything we deny, denigrate or despise serves to defeat us in the end. What seems nasty, painful, and evil, can become a source of beauty, joy and strength, if faced with an open mind."

Henry Miller

I used to have a difficult time accepting even the positive things in my life. I was great in a crisis but had a hard time with people being nice to me. It seemed that I was doomed to misery and could never experience joy. The idea that the world was to blame for all of my problems was the attitude that kept me eating. This attitude almost killed me. I had tried to change the world and everyone in it to better suit my tastes. Somehow that got me nowhere but exhausted and frustrated.

In the course of working the Steps I started asking myself hard questions about what my role was in creating the unacceptable life I was living. I found that what was often needed was a change in my own attitude and actions. This was a completely new realization for me. I needed to change myself: not the people, places and things around me. I also discovered that a lot of things that had seemed so important before recovery, actually weren't important at all. It was like getting rid of all that excess junk you keep in the closet for no reason other than it is yours. I gave all that stuff to my HP.

One Day at a Time . . . .
I pray for the wisdom to know what can and can't be changed. Once I see the truth, I pray for the willingness to change. I learn to gratefully accept life on life's terms.

~ Danielle

PAIN

"People are taught that pain is evil and dangerous ...
Pain is meant to wake us up ...
You should stand up for your right to feel your pain."
Jim Morrison

I am what some might call a "pain expert." Inside, outside, stuffed, unavoidable ~ there are so many kinds of pain. I used to think that if I were really strong, I would never let pain affect me, regardless of its source. And there were plenty of sources. I walked around with this smile on my face and this wall built around me, trying to ward off the pain.

Then one day I cracked. I lost someone very close to me. When I actually accepted that, I just broke down. There was so much pain I had been avoiding for years. At that moment I was confronted by all of it!

That was when I started to realize that I couldn't go through life avoiding pain. It was still there and it would come back. And it would be worse. Joining this program and reading the Big Book helped me to recognize my pain and feel it. I'm now able to not fear it, but to see it for what it is: a piece of me. I grow from what I feel, including pain. Without it I wouldn't be me.

One Day at a Time . . . .
I will feel my pain and I will do what is necessary to accept it. Together we are
bound by pain. Together we can see our strength.

~ *Miranda G.*

Meditation 297

FEAR

"Fear is not created by the world around us,
but in the mind, by what we think is going to happen."
Elizabeth Gawain

There are different kinds of fear. Certain fears are good, because they help preserve our lives. Babies, for example, have a fear of falling. It just seems to be a natural instinct. Any fear that protects us from harming ourselves is a good fear.

However, when fear becomes an obsession, it is getting out of hand. Why do we go looking for trouble? There is a saying, "Don't let clouds of fear of the morrow hide today's sunshine." We can get so anxious about what's going to happen in the future that we don't enjoy living today.

Life is a precious gift to be lived one day at a time, and it is to be shared with others.

One Day at a Time . . . .
This is how I will live my life: One day at a time, one moment at a time, sharing my precious gift with another through Twelve Step giving.

~

COURAGE

"If you're going through hell, keep going."
Winston Churchill

Recovery work takes great courage. Everyone who tells you differently has not explored themselves in great depth.

It takes great courage for many of us to get up each morning to face a day of physical challenge. Others feel the pull of emotions, job, or family issues.

If but for today, reach inside and give yourself a big hug for being willing to hang on one minute longer. That minute will turn into moments, and before you know it, you will have lived out the Program message, "One day at a time."

One Day at a Time . . . .
I will honor and celebrate the courage shown in working this program.

~ January K.

Meditation 299

PATHS

"I shall be telling this with a sigh
Somewhere ages and ages hence:
Two roads diverged in a wood and I –
I took the one less traveled by,
And that has made all the difference."
Robert Frost

As a compulsive overeater, I longed to find a solution to my problems. Like so many of us, I tried all the heavily traveled roads ~ the endless means to lose weight and to alleviate my indulgent eating behaviors. But at the end – and there was always an end – of every new "method of weight loss" I returned to walking my old path of destructive compulsive overeating. I always went back to the old eating behaviors as well as the consequences of those behaviors. I had heard of OA but did not know anyone who belonged to its groups. It seemed like the whole world was on the latest fad diet – diets that I could never continue for more than a few days or weeks.

Since joining The Recovery Group, I now walk a new path and have abandoned the old roads and the diet of the week. I have been on this road nearly a year now, and it is a wonderfully pleasant trek. I indeed believe "I shall be telling this with a sigh, somewhere ages and ages hence." I have found an incredible amount of recovery spiritually, emotionally and physically. I am traveling on "the one less traveled by, and that has made all the difference!"

One Day at a Time . . . .
I will enjoy this road less taken...a path of acceptance and surrender. It is a path of spiritual, emotional and physical recovery!

~ Karen H.

Meditation 300

LIVING IN THE PRESENT

"As long as you are seeking to find happiness somewhere,
you are overlooking where true happiness is."
Gangaji

Happiness is always somewhere else, isn't it? It is all too human to put off our happiness until a more appropriate or perfect time. Ideally, we know that happiness is not a matter of timing; it is a state of mind caused by even the smallest actions that we take (or fail to take) each day. However, I often used to remark to others that, "One day I will be happy when I get thin." I got much thinner, but never thin enough, it seems. "One day I will take a night course." I was so busy working, "on-call", and doing things for others that I never managed to find the time.

"One day I will start this new food Plan," I'd promised myself. It had worked for others. I truly wanted to give myself a chance to see if it could work for me too, yet I approached it haphazardly, at first. On paper, any food plan is just a diet, unless, you have a Sponsor, use the Tools, and work the Steps! I'd been told this over and over, and later–lived the actual experience of doing it my way. As long as I told myself, "One day I will find the time for me," it didn't come about!

One Day at a Time . . . .
I now realize that as long as I keep looking to the future in order to allot myself wonderful challenges and small joys, I am choosing to postpone my happiness until my life is perfect, which is never in the realm of reality. I believe that this is why those who have gone before us in recovery suggest that we live life on life's terms to the best of our ability just "One day at a time."

~ January K.

Meditation 301

HOME

"My home is not a place, it is people."
Lois McMaster Bujold

I have spent most of my adult life feeling very alone in the world. My disease of compulsive overeating separated me from others due to my isolation, embarrassment and shame. I was always the outsider looking in at others.

It wasn't until I walked into a Twelve Step meeting that I found a home for myself. Here these people knew me, heck they WERE me. Whatever I thought, whatever I felt, and whatever I had done in my life, so had others in OA. I am accepted in my totality. OA is the only place where I feel truly safe and at home. I am not alone anymore. The entire Twelve Step fellowship is on my side ~ and what a great feeling that is!

One Day at a Time . . . .
I will make OA my home.

~ *Cindi L.*

TRIAL AND ERROR

"Anything worth doing at all is worth doing poorly."
Joachim de Posada

Imagine my shock the first time I heard this statement, which happened to be in a Twelve Step (OA) meeting. I had been reared in an environment in which anything worth doing at all was worth doing well. In fact, in my world this concept was practiced as if it had religious authority. It was perfectionism given flesh and bones.

Perhaps the idea that "anything worth doing at all is worth doing well" worked for some folks. For me, it was paralyzing. There were many things that I needed to do that I simply could not do well. These included things like trimming the hedge, praying, and making good investment choices. So how did my sick, obsessive-compulsive self respond? Predictably, of course: I just didn't do those things I felt I couldn't do well. I was rarely willing to take the chance of acting and being wrong, so I did not act at all. Soon I was living a very restricted life – a life hemmed in by the fear of messing up. I needed to be perfect or just not be at all.

Then I found the program. There I learned that I am human and that making mistakes is part of being human. I even learned that making mistakes is a good thing, because in doing so I have acted. This is a program of action. I learn by acting and by making mistakes. How liberating! How freeing. I can't tell you how much my constricted, warped life began to open up. I acted and did things poorly, and people responded warmly and in a helpful manner. I took their advice and I joined the human race. I now consider this simple concept – act, even if it means doing a thing poorly – as one of the greatest gifts of the program. My life is really my life now. Perfectionism occasionally rears its ugly head, but when it does, I simply remember where I came from and then I go ahead and make a mistake and set myself free again.

One Day at a Time . . . .
Today I will do what I need to do, and I will do it as well as I can. When I make a mistake I will not conclude that I am a mistake. I will accept that I am human and I will ask for help. Perfection has never been a goal of this program and it is not a goal for my life.

~ *Pete M.*

Meditation 303

TRUTH

*"The truth that makes men free is for the most part
the truth which men prefer not to hear."*
Herbert Agar

I spent thirty-five years of my adult life running from the truth. It wasn't until I came to OA and began to work through the Twelve Steps that I had enough emotional support to turn and face the truth. What is my truth? I am a food addict.

Once I was able to face and accept that truth, surrender to my Higher Power was immediate. At long last I was free of cravings, free of bingeing, and free of obsessive food thoughts. That freedom allowed me to work toward the goal of becoming the person I had always wanted to be.

The way I see it, I can be an addict in recovery or I can be an addict in hell. I choose recovery.

One Day at a Time . . . .
I will seek the truth in my life by working the program of recovery.

~ *Cindi L*

SERVICE

"Service is the rent that you pay for room on this earth."
Shirley Chisholm

Midway through my first Fourth Step someone asked me to sponsor her. I was thrilled and eager to share my experience, strength and hope. As my work with my sponsee progressed, something began to happen in my own program. All that I had learned and was sharing with my sponsee reminded me of where I came from and how far I had progressed. I found that my recovery was strengthened through this process of giving away my experiences in program. This service allowed me to keep what I had received.

It is vital for me that I serve the program of OA in all different manners: as a sponsor; as a leader of a Step meeting; as treasurer of a local meeting; and by reaching out to newcomers, people in relapse, and others in the OA fellowship. The more I give, the more I receive.

One Day at a Time . . . .
I will give service to the OA fellowship so that I may remain in recovery.

~ Cindi L.

Meditation 305

ACCEPTANCE

"Acceptance is not submission; it is acknowledgement
of the facts of the situation. Then deciding what to do with it."
Kathleen Casey Theisen

Before program I kept wishing that I had a perfect body, spouse, mother, child, or whatever. My dissatisfaction with the things in my life kept me from really accepting that things were exactly the way they were meant to be for that time. I always used the excuse, *"If you had a spouse, ex-husband, mother, or whatever like I did, you'd also have to eat."* I never took responsibility for my compulsive eating and I lived in blame and guilt.

When I came into program and heard the Serenity Prayer at my first meeting, I didn't fully understand its meaning. What I have finally come to understand is that I cannot begin to change the things within my control until I accept my powerlessness over food and over the people and circumstances in my life. I have now come to accept the fact that there are some things I cannot change, but I can change my attitude towards others. As I do so, I am learning to take responsibility for my part in the things that happen to me. What a difference that is from the past.

One Day at a Time . . . .
Only when I acknowledge and accept the reality of what is in my life, can I begin to change the things that are within my control.

~ *Sharon S.*

TODAY

"Finish each day and be done with it.
You have done what you could;
some blunders and absurdities have crept in;
forget them as soon as you can.
Tomorrow is a new day; you shall begin it serenely
and with too high a spirit to be encumbered with your old nonsense."
Ralph Waldo Emerson

For a long time I went through therapy, dealing with the past. But working the Steps has helped me to focus on today. What happened is over. It is my choice how I allow it to affect my life now. When I cannot seem to let the past go, I have to remind myself that I need only to let God have the past. Yesterday is beyond my ability to change. Today is my charge.

Today I write before I eat compulsively. Today I give service to others in recovery. Today I choose to not eat compulsively and to seek all the support I can find to hold to that choice. I put aside yesterday, reflecting on the lessons learned. Like a hiker looking ahead to mark the next point on the trail, I look to the future that is stretching out before me. But it is today that I act. Today I do not worry about what I have not done, but rest in the knowledge that I have done what is before me to be done. Day after day will add up to recovery, to serenity, to living.

One Day at a Time . . . .
is all the time I have within my control so I choose to live in the now.

~ Tassy

Meditation 307

INNER STRENGTH

"Troubles are often the tools
by which God fashions us for better things."
H. W. Beecher

I often wondered why so much seemed to happen to me. Why was it that no sooner had I picked myself up from some trauma or tragedy than another one came along. Most people had never had car accidents, but I'd had two, one almost life-threatening. I'd been through an unpleasant divorce; I lost a brother and a stepson, both dying unnatural deaths at an early age, and could not understand why these kinds of things were always happening to me. I used to be so angry with God. *"Why me?"* I'd ask. It just seemed so unfair. Everybody else appeared to have lives that were so much better and free of all this trauma. For a long time I retreated into depression and food to cope with what seemed to be a miserable life.

But God must have had other plans for me. I truly believe I must have been guided to my first meeting so that I would not only find a way to live free of my compulsive eating, but would also be able to learn some lessons from my seemingly tough life. I have been very blessed in that, because of all my experiences, and the fact that I was literally brought to my knees and had to seek God out, I have learned the meaning of true spirituality. I have also learned some valuable lessons from all these experiences that have made me a much stronger person. I have so much more to offer than I would have had my life been the nice easy one I always wanted. Because of what I have learned as a result of my many struggles and difficult times, I am now able to pass on that wisdom to others on this journey of recovery.

One Day at a Time . . . .
I will try to remember that when God sends me difficulties, I must view them as lessons He wants me to learn so I can become a better and more useful person.

~ *Sharon S.*

SERVICE

"When people are serving, life is no longer meaningless."
John Gardner

I used to always think that I was kind and helpful, and that I was always there for other people. Well, of course I was. I was a people-pleaser, and the payoff was to be liked. That never happened, or at least I didn't think so, and I became more resentful and full of self-pity. The truth was that I was so self-absorbed and self-seeking that I didn't know how to really be there for other people, not even my own children. I'm sure that for a long period, even though I was always doing things for them, I was emotionally absent and unavailable when they really needed me. The focus was on me and how fat I looked, or how nobody fulfilled my needs, instead of looking outside of myself to what I could REALLY do for others.

This recovery program has taught me, first and foremost, how to love myself so that I am able to love others, especially my children. I was spiritually and emotionally empty before, but now I am being constantly filled and nurtured spiritually. Now I am able to give back what has freely been given to me. I am learning for the first time the pleasure of giving of myself, of my time and my experience, strength and hope, that others may walk this beautiful road to recovery as I have. In giving what I have, I am strengthening my program and my own recovery. What a joy that has been!

One Day at a Time . . . .
I remember that when I do service and give away what I have, I will experience the promises of the program on a daily basis.

~ *Sharon S*

Meditation 309

FOCUS ON OTHERS

"I had the blues because I had no shoes
until upon the street I met a man who had no feet."
Denis Waitely

I find that when I am stuck or feeling sorry for myself I just need to reach out and help someone who is worse off than me. When I pray for someone to help, someone always shows up. This past weekend I was feeling sorry for myself. I went to church and prayed for God to bring someone for me to help. Alas, as I walked in to school this morning I was greeted by a tearful friend whose husband was just diagnosed with lung cancer. I hugged her and told her I was there for her. It took the focus off of ME and I was able to help someone else feel better.

One Day at a Time . . . .
Allow me to be of service to others. I need them as much as they need me.

~ Sue

Meditation 310

FREEDOM

"There is no such thing as a little freedom.
Either you are all free, or you are not free."
Walter Cronkite

In the past, when I was threatened by another person's thoughts, beliefs, actions, or desires, I simply deemed them completely unacceptable and worked hard to convince the other person just how wrong they were. I cited all kinds of religious doctrine and politically correct ideas to try to convince the other person why their ideas were unacceptable.

This *"convincing"* was nothing more than an attempt to control another so I wouldn't have to face myself or any of the things that caused me anxiety and fear. All I succeeded in doing was forcing others to help me lie to myself. Of course, this also created its own anxiety and fear, so I had to do something to cover it up. What did I do? I compulsively overate, I binged, I purged, I exercised, I starved myself, I abused laxatives, and on and on.

Today, because of my Higher Power and the gifts of this program, I can look at why some thoughts, feelings, beliefs and desires threaten me. I can be gentle with myself as I look at which of my *"boo-boo buttons"* have been pushed. I can ask myself how I've been hurt by these ideas in the past and learn how those *"boo-boo buttons"* were produced in the first place.

Just like a wound, exposing my hurts to the sunlight helps them heal. Bringing them out into the light helps me see all the truth about them–not just the distorted parts I felt in the darkness. I can see what my part was and I can see what the part of others may have been. Through working the Twelve Steps, I can find peace with these hurts and experience the promise of not regretting or wanting to close the door on the past.

One Day at a Time . . . .
I can set myself free from the darkness by looking at past hurts in the light of truth.

~ *Sandee S.*

Meditation 311

FAITH

"Hold faithfulness and sincerity as first principles."
Confucius

As a child, I believed in God, but the God of my childhood was a punishing God. I often felt that the reason for all the tragedies and misfortunes that I went through was because I didn't adhere to all the traditions and rules of my given religion. Perhaps the fact that I wasn't a good enough daughter to my parents, a good enough mother to my children, or a good enough friend was another reason why I was being punished. I would pray to the God of my childhood for what I wanted, but God never answered me or gave it to me, so what was the use of praying? I eventually stopped praying because my prayers were never answered.

I now know, having been led into this beautiful fellowship of the spirit, that God is a loving and forgiving God who always gave me what I needed, even if it didn't at the time seem to be what I wanted. The trouble had always been that I was filled with fear and found it hard to believe or trust in something or someone that I couldn't see or hear. I am a logical and rational person so it was really hard for me to have faith and trust that God would take care of me. It's said that the opposite of fear is faith, and so I am now learning to let go of the fear and put my faith and trust in a Higher Power of my understanding. I realize that He knows what's best for me, and will always be there for me if I only let Him.

One Day at a Time . . . .
I will trust that my Higher Power knows what's best for me, and I put myself in His care. My faith is growing stronger each day and I am able to release fear.

~ *Faith*

DROWNING TROUBLES

"You can't drown your troubles,
because trouble can swim."
Margaret Millar

My feelings have always been too large for me to handle alone. Whenever I felt troubled or had a problem too big to handle, I always turned to my friend and comforter...FOOD. This friend and I went everywhere together and with it, I figured that I could handle anything thrown at me. This friend made me feel good. I was drowning my troubles one by one.

Then someone said to me, *"Don't you know that eating too much, drinking too much or even working too much won't solve your problems! Troubles usually reproduce themselves rapidly when you try to drown them."*

I really didn't understand what she was trying to tell me but kept the thought tucked inside my hat. My friend food and I just kept batting these troubles deeper and deeper in my sea of tears, but sure enough, they would bounce right back up at me again later only twice as bad. What was happening? I was using my friend more each time and I began to hate it. Why was food trying to hurt me? I really thought it was my friend.

Finally, after many bruises, I realized what that person was trying to tell me. She was right. My troubles were swimming and I was drowning. I was using one of my addictions to try and fight the others, and was only going in circles. I was caught in a tidal wave and unable to get out alone. Each of my other addictions were throwing me back to my primary addiction of compulsive eating...my former friend, FOOD.

But where could I go? What could I do? The wonderful person who warned me led me to my recovery meeting and stayed with me. She helped me to find a Higher Power who was always there to help. I learned to share my experiences with my recovery family of choice. I got a wonderful sponsor who also knew me as well as I know myself. Together we looked at all the problems and troubles of the past and they weren't so heavy any more. I moved out of the deep sea that I couldn't swim in, and on dryer, more sturdy ground. What a relief!

One Day at a Time . . . .
I remember that my troubles are strong and can drown me in the sea of food if I try to handle them alone. Troubles may be able to swim strongly, but they are NO MATCH for me, my Higher Power, my sponsor and Program. Together, we are strong, but alone we are weak. Together we can do what we can never do alone.

~ *Jeanette*

Meditation 313

HOPE

"Hope is the feeling you have
that the feeling you have isn't permanent."
Jean Kerr

I pray for hope today, and I am receiving hope today. Hope is something that comes more and more readily to me as I stay abstinent and continue working my program of recovery.

In the past, many of my feelings of hope were centered around the next diet or the next fix for my bingeing. However, now that I am abstaining and practicing the Twelve Steps, I have been freed to hope for bigger things. There is now space in my head where the food and diet obsession used to be!

One Day at a Time . . . .
I will abstain. One day at a time I will direct my attention to the Steps when I am in need of a solution.

~ *Christine*

SELF-WILL

*"Our whole trouble has been the misuse of willpower.
We had tried to bombard our problems with it
instead of attempting to bring it into agreement
with God's intention for us."
The AA Twelve and Twelve*

I want the answers to all my questions and the solutions to all of my problems RIGHT NOW. Furthermore, I want to tell my Higher Power what I want those answers and solutions to be. I think I know what's best for me and what will bring long-lasting peace and serenity to my life.

My self-will has gotten me hurt and possibly caused me to hurt others. It has convinced me I could do things my way and everything would be just fine. My self-will has helped me lie to myself about my disease of compulsive overeating, anorexia, or bulimia; it has convinced me that darkness was light and that I should have what I want exactly when I want it.

How grateful I am that my Higher Power loves me enough to not take my advice! How grateful I am that, after I've plunged head-first into the same wall at least one hundred times as I tried to force my own answers and solutions, my Higher Power is waiting patiently to bless me by leading me where He would have me go. How grateful I am that I don't have to run into the wall of my self-will as often or as hard as I once did. One day, maybe I won't run into it at all.

One Day at a Time . . . .
I can let go of self-will and remember that the Third Step says we "made a decision to turn our will and our lives over the care of God as we understood Him." The care of God ... God can take better care of me than I can of myself.

~ *Sandee*

HUMOR

"Don't take yourself too damned seriously."
Rule #62, AA's Twelve Steps and Twelve Traditions

In the years of my existence, before I got into recovery, I would run from one self-important crisis to another. Everything was so important, so heavy! What laughter there was ended up directed derisively at others. I treated my life with self-importance and pomposity.

It took sitting in the rooms, day after day and night after night, listening to how recovering people were able to laugh at themselves. Oh, they were deadly serious when it came to working the Steps and the traditions. After all, if not for them, they'd be dead or crazy. But as they would share things where they had shown the heavy-does-it attitude, they would see the folly of their ways and start a good belly laugh that would cascade through the room and have us all wiping our eyes.

As I work my program, I realize that there are some things that need more prayer and meditation than others. Then there are those things in my life that, under the light of my recovery, are just plain flat-out silly. My Higher Power gives me the ability to cry and grieve where appropriate. My Higher Power also has taught me that laughter, indeed, is often the best medicine.

One Day at a Time . . . .
I learn that healthy laughter is just as important to my recovery as are the healthy tears.

~ *Mark Y.*

HITTING BOTTOM

"My life closed twice before its close."
Emily Dickinson

Doesn't every addict, sooner or later, face some kind of incomprehensible end to something they hold dear, all because of their addiction?

I certainly did. In my late thirties, in the plum Ivy League job that was the envy of all those I'd gone to graduate school with, I was fired. The fact was, though I'd tried to put a good face on it, I was up to my eyebrows in my disease of compulsive overeating and was consequently seriously depressed. Or was I seriously depressed and consequently...?

No matter. I had been in a hole the width and depth of which I could not overcome. Day after day I would sit in my office with the door closed, work piled on my desk, unable to make headway. I had done this for over a year. Then the axe fell, and there I was, a depressed, overweight workaholic without work.

Fortunately for me, by this time I had already found program, and although I was a newcomer of only six months, I knew enough that I was lucky to have lost my job. Although I would never have quit it, it would have eventually led to the loss of my health and sanity, what was left of them. I was in that important and prestigious job for all the wrong reasons, but mainly as a balm to my tiny and broken self-esteem.

The fact was, the healing for my self-loathing wasn't in a fancy title or professional honors. It was in the spiritual life and the recovery of mind, body, heart, and spirit that I found in program.

I learned for myself that hitting bottom is not the end. I let my Higher Power into my life, and it was the beginning of a more honest and worthy way of living.

One Day at a Time . . . .
I turn my life over to my Higher Power to make of it what She will. It makes every day a good day.

~ *Roberta*

Meditation 317

GRATITUDE

"Feeling gratitude and not expressing it
is like wrapping a present and not giving it."
William Arthur Ward

Since I first walked into these rooms, I was welcomed with open arms. Everyone said, *"Welcome home."* In my gut I felt welcomed into the fellowship, but only now, after years of accepting it, do I finally get it.

Who is this God everyone is saying cares about us? I felt God was too busy creating and managing the universe to concentrate on any one individual, let alone each and every one of us. Now, I don't know how anyone else acted while in the clutches of their disease, but I do know how I reacted. I was not a very nice person to be around. If you said the sky was blue, I would say it was black. Nothing was right in my world and I refused to trust anyone or anything; I was rebellious. That is how I treated God! I dared God to fix me, to take away my desire for food, to come into my life so I would know it.

Well, people told me God meets you where you are. I learned the hard way that God does reveal Himself to you in whatever way works for you. For me that has been by learning to listen to people share in meetings and verbally state what God has been trying to get through my thick skull. When I read program literature, I hear little voices of recovering people speak of how God is doing for them what they couldn't do for themselves. I watch people in recovery living a new kind of life, in which they are participants. I learn from them how to live rather than bouncing off the walls because I only reacted to life. I am beginning to see all the little things that I have been given from God through my interactions with fellow compulsive overeaters. My soul feels welcomed in this fellowship. I feel I have a new family in which to heal my wounds from my family of origin. I am filled with immense gratitude to a God that cares enough about each and every one of us.

One Day at a Time . . . .
I will stop and take inventory of all the blessings I receive, each and every day, from a loving, supportive fellowship and a God of my understanding who loves me enough to put up with all my baggage.

~ Judith

CONTENTMENT

"Everything has its wonders, even darkness and silence,
and I learn, whatever state I may be in, therein to be content."
Helen Keller

I spent most of my life dreaming and wishing for the stars, always hoping that something wonderful would happen to change my life. If only my mother were more loving; if only I had more friends; if only I had a better husband or smarter children; and, more especially, if only I were thin. I was never satisfied with what I had because someone else always seemed to be better off than me. It was like I was always being short-changed in life, and what expectations I had had as a child just didn't materialize. I never realized that what I had was exactly what I needed at the time, even though it may not have seemed to be what I wanted.

I know now that, even though I may have less than a perfect life, I have many wonderful things. I have so much more than many others, and instead seeing my cup as half-empty, I can now see it as half-full. I can see the miracle of the changing seasons, the beauty of a sunset and the changing moods of the sea. I can hear the beautiful music that feeds my soul, a baby's cry and the crash of thunder. I am surrounded by loving friends and family who care for me as I care for them. I can look at those less fortunate than me and know that I am truly blessed. More and more I am becoming aware that I have exactly what I need for today, and in that I am content.

One Day at a Time . . . .
I am content knowing that I have many blessings in my life ... may I always be
willing to see that.

~ *Sharon S.*

Meditation 319

STEP TWO

*"The definition of insanity is doing the same thing over
and over again and expecting a different result."*
Henry Wadsworth Longfellow

While in the grip of my disease I tried many things to deal with my compulsive overeating. I tried many, many diets, fasting, exercise programs, treatment, therapy, church and even resorted to weight loss surgery. I did the same thing over and over again – I tried outward solutions to fix an inward problem. And the sad thing was I somehow thought that I would get different results: a permanent change of my compulsive overeating. But it did not work that way. It was acting with insanity. I was frustrated and very, very sad. All along, I knew there was something wrong with me, that I was not *"normal"*, but I didn't know what to do about it.

Then the blessing of the program came to me. I learned about Step Two: *"Came to believe that a Power greater than ourselves could restore us to sanity."* I came to believe that was true. I finally was doing something different. Never before had I approached my compulsive overeating on three levels all at the same time. I had never seen my disease as a physical, emotional and spiritual disease that needed addressing at the same time, one day at a time. I began to slowly learn how to do this through the Steps and the tools, with the help of sponsors and friends in the program. I found myself doing something different and getting different results. I found my sanity returning, piece by piece.

One Day at a Time . . . .
I will do something different, knowing I will get different results.

~ *Carolyn*

HONESTY

"Whatever games are played with us,
we must play no games with ourselves,
but deal in our privacy with the last honesty and truth."
Ralph Waldo Emerson

When I began to study Step One in OA I learned that the principle behind the Step was honesty. That was difficult for me because I had spent so much time lying to myself and others about my eating. I was so ashamed of my eating habits and behaviors that when asked about them, it never occurred to me to tell the truth. I couldn't conceive of being accepted, or even cared for, if anyone knew the truth.

Then I came into the program and began to hear people share. The denial and shell of lies began to melt. For the first time I found myself in a fellowship where I felt like I could tell the truth because I was surrounded by people whose stories were similar to mine. Most importantly, the people in the fellowship loved me and cared for me when I told my truth, no matter how ugly it seemed to me. I call this the magic of the fellowship. It makes me want to be that kind of loving, caring person for the newcomer taking his or her First Step.

One Day at a Time . . . .
I will honestly confront the reality of my compulsive eating, knowing that I am in a fellowship where I am unconditionally loved and cared for.

~ *Carolyn H.*

AVOIDING FAILURE

*"Many of life's failures are people who
did not realize how close they were to success
when they gave up."*
Thomas A. Edison

I love this quotation because it reminds me of how close I was to giving up on my program when the miracle of recovery happened to me. For two and a half years I worked program, yet I was unable to maintain abstinence. I worked my way through all Twelve Steps and used as many of the 8 Tools as possible each day ... but it wasn't working and I didn't know why. Depression hit me hard when I suffered a personal loss. My motivation to keep working program was waning. I had had enough and wanted to take a break from program, but my sponsor absolutely refused to allow me to do so. She said that if I left, I might never return. She told me that she saw potential in me and that she wanted me to stay with the program. I stayed and continued working program every day ~ whether or not I felt like doing so.

Six months later I made a formal commitment to the Twelve Step program. I gave up my self-will and my life to the care of my Higher Power. That was two years ago and I have been naturally abstinent since that day. My miracle of recovery had happened and I am a new woman. Program is ingrained in my daily life and I am so aware of the blessings that I have received by working a strong program. I choose every day to continue working my program.

One Day at a Time . . . .
I will be grateful for the miracle of recovery that is given to me as I work my program.

~ Cindi L.

Meditation 322

HONESTY

"You never find yourself until you face the truth."
Pearl Bailey

I was brought up to be scrupulously honest, or so I thought. I still remember how my father would go back into a shop if he'd been given too much change, a practice that I adopted too. I found it hard to tell a lie, even a white lie, and I would never contemplate cheating on a test. But when it came to food, I only realized later, I was totally dishonest. I was even dishonest when it came to telling people how I felt, or for that matter who I really was. The person who did these things was a totally different person to the upright person I liked people to see.

I know now that all the things I'd hidden around food were obviously what I felt ashamed about. I wanted people to see only the *"good"* side of me and not the person who did all these devious things in secret. I kept thinking that I was a bad person and the shame stopped me from being totally honest about what I had been doing.

It has taken time, and the love and acceptance I have found in the fellowship, to be able to get totally honest with myself. It has taken time to look at all the things about me that I felt ashamed of. In the housecleaning necessary in the Steps, I have been able to face my shame. I learned that I am human, and that I have a disease. Some of the soul searching has been very painful, but at the same time it has been totally enlightening. I am amazed how I am beginning to know a new me, with faults and all, but a loveable me nevertheless. As I peel off more layers of the onion that represents the sum total of what makes me unique and truly one of God's creatures, I am actually beginning to like the new me. I know now that I am not a bad person trying to get good, merely a sick person trying to get well.

One Day at a Time . . . .
I will keep being honest about who I am, what I eat and how I am behaving in my relationships, so I can learn more about me. Even when I don't like what I see, I know I am still a loveable person and a child of God, created in His image.

~ *Sharon S.*

Meditation 323

THE PROMISES

"We will intuitively know how to handle situations
which used to baffle us. We will suddenly realize that
God is doing for us what we could not do for ourselves."
The Big Book of Alcoholics Anonymous

When I first came into program and heard these words I couldn't grasp their meaning. Life baffled me. I had no idea who I was or what I was doing. I was completely in the grip of this disease. I felt like I was the disease. Why would God do anything for me?

Initially I thought these people were crazy and even worse off than I was. My opinion soon changed when I noticed wonderful differences between them and myself. They seemed calmer, verbalized their feelings more clearly, appeared to have their act together, and seemed to enjoy life. I was hooked! I wanted what they had. I finally wanted to want to live. I was drawn to those who demonstrated traits I wanted to have. I talked to them and listened when they shared. I asked them how to work the program and how to find my Higher Power. I started working the Steps. I began my search for a God I could relate to. I found online recovery loops and people who shared how they worked their program.

Then I had a crisis develop which almost overwhelmed me. Yet as I read the Big Book, I realized that the promises God had given to the other program people were given to me too. I had been so busy working this program that I needed to pause and examine all I had received. Yes, it does work when you work it. I proved it to myself by allowing God to prove it to me.

One Day at a Time . . . .
I will remember that the promises really are for everyone and that they come into my life as I work my program to the best of my ability.

~ Judith A.

PATIENCE

"Patience is the key to paradise."
Turkish proverb

I used to be the queen of the *"quick fix."* Anything I wanted done had to be done today, if not yesterday. I'd even do a job myself because I couldn't wait for someone else to do it in their time. I ended up chasing my tail most days, and trying to run the show myself, simply because I couldn't wait. Even all the many diets that I went on had to get results fast or they weren't worth their salt. Small wonder, being the compulsive person that I was, that when I wanted to eat, there was no such thing in my vocabulary as delayed gratification. When I wanted it, I had to have it right then.

Imagine my horror at coming into the program and seeing that people who had been in the fellowship for years were still there. Surely they should have gotten it right by now and graduated from this program. But I soon learned that this is not something we graduate from. Recovery and abstinence happen in God's time, not mine. I've had to learn that this a journey. Progress can sometimes be painfully slow, but the rewards for those who wait for the miracle is a gift I wouldn't want to be without. Not only am I offered freedom from compulsive eating, but also sanity and serenity to live my life the way I was intended to do.

One Day at a Time . . . .
Even when progress seems slow, I will keep coming back and working the program to the best of my ability, knowing that recovery will come to me if I wait.

~ *Sharon S.*

Meditation 325

WILLINGNESS

"If you have decided you want what we have
and are willing to go to any length to get it
then you are ready to take certain steps."
Big Book of Alcoholics Anonymous

Willingness was one of the hardest concepts to get through my disease thinking. I was only willing to have my disease cured so I could continue indulging in my allergic substances of choice. According to the dictionary, the definition of will is *"the power of choosing what one will do"* and *"willing, favorably inclined; ready."* My disease was in control and chose for me.

I didn't want to stay stuck in the food. Then I found this program. Still, I had trouble with the concept of willingness. Then I relapsed, but the food didn't cure anything. This program, like the Big Book says, had ruined it for me. So, when I found some online recovery loops I found renewed hope. Hope led me to learning about willingness from others' sharing. Then I figured, ok God, I don't want to give up the allergic substances, they are too strongly imbedded in my fibers, but I am willing to ask You to grant me the willingness to let go of those substances that aren't healthy for me.

I kept up this prayer for weeks. One day I discovered that it had been a week since I had thought about or eaten one of those allergic substances. I figured this must be what was meant by God doing for me what I can't do for myself. So I changed my prayer and asked God to keep making me willing, just for today, to go without those foods. It is working, not because of me, but because I was finally ready to ask for willingness. As the saying goes, *"Try it, you'll like it!"* I tried it and I liked the results... A God-given abstinence. Now, as I go about my day, it's becoming easier to be willing to turn more and more of my will over to the God of my understanding.

One Day at a Time . . . .
I will go to the God of my understanding and ask for the willingness to live
according to His will for me; so that I may have a life, and not self-will run riot.

~ *Judy*

FAMILY

"Call it a clan, call it a network, call it a tribe, call it a family:
Whatever you call it, whoever you are, you need one."
Jane Howard

As an only child of parents who immigrated and left their own families behind, I have always felt that I was missing out on the great wealth of sharing and caring that I saw other people have in their families. That was before recovery.

Today, I have an extended family – not only by marriage – but by the simple fact that my Higher Power led me to the great wealth of caring and sharing that I have found in perhaps the strangest place of all – cyberspace – in the form of online recovery loops.

Being prone to isolation, my disease first led me to seek out others who have struggled with compulsive overeating, and that, in turn, led me to my new 'family.' As someone so wonderfully expressed it to me recently, it's a *"family of choice."* What a concept! My family of choice not only has sisters and brothers, it also is filled with mothers and fathers, aunts and uncles – more than I could ever have dreamed of before, and each brings into my life more experience, strength and hope than I could ever have imagined.

One Day at a Time . . . .
I thank God that I have found this huge, loving family that constantly offers me hope,
inspiration, understanding ... and most of all love.

~ *Lorraine*

Meditation 327

SUCCESSFUL RECOVERY

*"I always remember an epitaph which is in the cemetery
at Tombstone, Arizona. It says: 'Here lies Jack
Williams. He done his damnedest.' I think that is
the greatest epitaph a man can have."*
Harry S. Truman

No matter what their drug of choice, compulsives all have one thing in common. If we don't practice our program, we run the risk of relapsing back into the disease.

What separates those who find recovery and those who don't is this: those who don't find recovery slip and fall, and don't get up again. They figure, *"I've already relapsed, so why not just continue using my drug of choice? Why not wallow in my disease?"*

Those who recover are like Jack Williams...they do their damnedest. They continue to read program literature, they continue to do service, they continue to reach out to others and to their Higher Power. The winners in this program don't wallow...they pick themselves up, dust themselves off, and keep on keeping on.

One Day at a Time . . . .
*I will do my damnedest. I will work my program to the best of my ability, and if I fall,
I won't stay down.*

~ Jeff

Meditation 328

GRATITUDE

*"If the only prayer you said in your whole life
was, "Thank you," that would suffice."*
Meister Eckhart

I spent most of my life blaming my circumstances and those around me for the way I felt, for my eating problem and for my terrible life in general. There was nothing good in my life at all and I viewed everything through a dark cloud of negativity. I couldn't see anything good in my life, and life became totally unbearable. Poor me, I thought. It really wasn't fair that I had been made to suffer the way I had, and I felt awash with self pity. The more sorry I felt for myself, the more I ate, and the more I ate, the worse I felt; it became a vicious circle.

When I was brought to my knees by this disease and came into the fellowship, I was forced to take stock and look honestly at my life. For the first time ever I considered the losses and difficult situations in my life that I had perceived as unfair and negative. In each case there had been amazing gains. For example, the car accident I'd been in hadn't been my fault at all. In fact, it became the catalyst that enabled me to change careers. One of the bereavements that I had brought a wonderful and special friend into my life. And so it went. Before, I had bemoaned my fate as a compulsive overeater. Now, I am actually grateful to be a compulsive overeater, because without my disease I never would have a wonderful program that helps me to live my life sanely and serenely, nor would I have all the very special people who love and support me through thick and thin.

One Day at a Time . . . .
I am grateful for all the wonderful miracles that have happened in my life as a result of this program ... may I never forget to thank my Higher Power for all these wonderful blessings.

~ *Sharon S.*

Meditation 329

CHOICE

"The strongest principle of growth lies in human choice."
George Eliot

I spent most of my life blaming others for my woes and the fact that I was a compulsive overeater. I thought, "If you had had a mother like I did, an ex-husband or a tough life like mine, you would also have turned to food for comfort or to block all the painful feelings." I was sure that had I had an easier life like I perceived others to have, I wouldn't have had to do the things around food that I did. I never took responsibility for my part in all this because, in truth, I was the one who chose to react to my life in that way. Nobody forced me to behave the way I did and nobody held me down and forced food into my mouth.

I never used to realize that I do have choices in life. I can choose not to eat foods that are harmful to me; I can choose not to surround myself with unhealthy relationships; I can choose not to let other people's problems become my own; in fact, I have choices in most things that I do. I can choose to have a more positive attitude today, instead of focusing on all the negatives. I do not have to react to life's adversities with destructive behaviors. I can choose to be active in my life rather than being reactive, like a sailing ship in a stormy sea that is totally at the mercy of the weather. I can choose to seize life with both hands and live it the best I know how.

One Day at a Time . . . .
Today I choose to work this program of recovery knowing that, even with life's difficulties, the promises of the program will come true in my life, and I will know serenity and peace.

~ *Sharon S.*

Meditation 330

VISION

*"The greatest tragedy in life
is people who have sight but no vision."*
Helen Keller

The miracle of recovery has given me new vision! I lived for many years with eyes that viewed the world through fear, pain and resentment. These were the factors that shaded the lenses of my eyes. Because they clouded my entire perspective, they prevented me from seeing reality as it was. Instead, I lived in fear of the distorted realities of my world.

When I took my Fourth Step I began to see with new vision and clarity. It was amazing for me to realize how skewed my perception of life had been all those years. I discovered that my vision hadn't been focused on the truth! The shades of this illness had cast many shadows upon reality and I had spent my life reacting to those shadows instead of responding to life.

I had years of experience looking at the world through illness, and I was not sure if I could really keep this new vision which was promised through recovery. I was a little worried that it would soon fade away into those old shadows … as had happened in other awakenings I had experienced.

As I continued to take the Steps, I found that my new vision not only remained, but grew broader and deeper every day. As I continue to work a daily Tenth, Eleventh and Twelfth Step and to practice these principles in all aspects of my life, I continue to celebrate life with the vision that recovery brings. This vision is one of deep joy, gratitude, serenity, and love!

One Day at a Time . . . .
I will practice the Steps of recovery in all aspects of my life and I will continue to receive and share the gift of vision that recovery brings.

~ *Cate*

NEW BEGINNINGS

"There will come a time when you believe everything is finished.
That will be the beginning."
Louis L'Amour

During my life I've always found it hard to start anything. I don't know whether it comes from being a compulsive overeater, but I do know that I took my time in starting a recovery program. Maybe it was a fear that, if I didn't succeed, I could never start over.

Luckily, this is a very forgiving program. If I slip, I can get up and start over. I don't have to stay down. In fact, I can be down, but I can never be counted out, because all I need to do is begin again. My Higher Power helps me stay on track, and it comforts me to know that, if I fall, I can be picked up and allowed to continue my journey to recovery.

One Day at a Time . . . .
I will remain "higher powered" and start over if I need to.

~ *Jeff*

GOODNESS

*"Above all, let us never forget that an act of goodness
is in itself an act of happiness."*
Count Maurice Maeterlinck

While in the disease, most of the goodness I tried to do was for ulterior motives. It was only in recovery that I learned to give unselfishly and without strings to help another. In doing so, I have found happiness beyond measure. I can create my own happiness in the service of my Higher Power and other compulsive overeaters. I can make the promise of a *"new happiness and a new freedom"* come true.

One Day at a Time . . . .
I will do acts of goodness.

~ Judy N.

Meditation 333

TO THINE OWN SELF BE TRUE

"Hide not your talents, they for use were made.
What's a sun-dial in the shade?"
Benjamin Franklin

In the cups of my illness I was a chameleon and people-pleaser. I was afraid to stand on my own opinions and be myself. My fear of rejection kept me always looking for ways to fit in. I was running from life because I was afraid that I would be found to be a fraud and a compulsive eater. I played dumb in school and with my friends. I was afraid to be smart. I was afraid to have differing opinions. Shame kept me hiding inside of myself and inside of my suit of fat. I was afraid to be me.

Since coming to the program I am learning more each day that it is okay for me to be me. It is more than okay; it is essential. I can spread my wings and let myself out of my self-imposed cage ~ and I can go for a flight gliding on the breeze with ease. My first steps were wobbly, but this program promises me that the sunlight is there and it is okay to come out of the shade and be whom I really am. I have something to offer the world. We all do. It is up to us to find it in our deepest heart's desire.

One Day at a Time . . . .
I can take one small step to match my insides to my outsides.

~ Lanaya

BOUNDARIES

"People are lonely because they build walls instead of bridges."
Joseph Fort Newton

When I was growing up I remember always being lonely and I never had many friends. In order to protect myself from the pain of rejection, or perhaps because I didn't have self-esteem or believe in myself, I gave the impression that I didn't need people. I was probably thought of as a snob. I thought that people didn't like me because I was shy and introverted, but I had built up around myself an impenetrable protective wall which didn't invite anyone in. It was small wonder that I spent many lonely nights buried in a book or food or any other solitary pursuit for that matter.

In my adult years I became a people-pleaser in the hopes that people would like me more. That even spilled over to include my children as well, which meant that I wasn't able to say no to them or anyone else unless they stopped loving me. I would say yes when I really meant no, and consequently I was always filled with resentment and felt even lonelier than ever. I didn't know how to set boundaries and was terrified that if I said no, people wouldn't love me anymore.

I now know that when I set boundaries, it is an affirmation of my worth, and in most cases I am respected and liked by those people who are really my true friends. My children, too, have benefitted from my having set boundaries with them, and they have more respect for me than before. I am beginning to realize that it is just fine to do what is right for me, and that it doesn't have to jeopardize any of my relationships.

One Day at a Time . . . .
I am learning that it is right for me to define my boundaries with those that I love, knowing that I set these boundaries in love and friendship, rather than hostility, and that I am still a lovable person.

~ *Sharon S.*

Meditation 335

SPIRITUALITY

"When the heart weeps for what it has lost,
the spirit laughs for what it has found."
Sufi proverb

Before I came into this program, I had thrown God out the window. In fact, I was plain angry at Him. Where was He when my only brother was killed in a car accident, when my only nephews were lost to me for many years as a result? Where was He when my parents died, when I went through my ugly divorce, when my step-son committed suicide, or when I had two major car accidents? I didn't know how to deal with all the feelings around the grief, loss and pain. I was spiritually bereft, although I didn't know it then. All I knew was that I was depressed a lot of the time, and had this great big hole in my soul that I had to keep feeding so I wouldn't have to feel the pain or deal with anything in my life. But the truth was that no amount of food could relieve that constant ache, and all that happened was that I felt more and more fat, bloated and miserable. The food that was supposed to take away all the pain of living was really causing me more pain.

When I came into program and heard the three letter word, God, I nearly ran away. I'm a very rational, logical person so it was really hard for me to believe what these crazy people were saying, but I was desperate enough to keep coming back. I had to act as if I did believe that I could recover and that a Higher Power might help me. When the miracles started to happen, my faith began to develop, and I slowly realized that my Higher Power was always with me. I now have a far better way to fill that hole in my soul, and it is a far more satisfying and saner way than filling it with mountains of food.

One Day at a Time . . . .
I pray to keep my Higher Power in my heart and in my soul, because if I do, my life will be enriched immeasurably in ways that food could never do.

~ Sharon S.

Meditation 336

FAITH

"I try to avoid looking forward or backward,
and try to keep looking upward."
Charlotte Bronte

If only I would remember to keep my focus on God and today, not yesterday and not tomorrow. The past is just that ... the past. I can't change any of it, the good memories or the bad. They are just memories. I don't have to forget my past; I just have to stop hurting myself by constantly agonizing over what I consider mistakes and failures.

Tomorrow is in God's hands. What better place for it to be! I have to learn to trust God to hold me in the palm of His hands, the same way He holds tomorrow. He isn't going to drop me or close His fist around me so tightly that I can't breathe.

We are all created with the ability to make choices, and He gives us that freedom. He will hold us securely, and help us make the right choices, if only we let go and let Him.

One Day at a Time . . . .
I will forget yesterday and tomorrow. I will not look backward or forward. I will look up and put myself in God's care, knowing He will hold me safely in the palm of His hand.

~ Debbie K.

INTUITION

*"Don't listen to friends when the Friend
inside you says, 'Do this!'"*
Mahatma Gandhi

The Oxford dictionary describes intuition as *"immediate apprehension by the mind without reasoning."* Well, I certainly never acted on intuition for most of my life because, in order for me to make any decision, it had to be based on cold hard logic. I would literally make a scientific *"if - then hypothesis"* based on all the possible consequences of any action I was contemplating, and by the time I'd looked into all the possible negative outcomes, I'd more than likely have talked myself out of it. Part of the problem was fear that if it didn't turn out well, I would not be taken care of. How could I trust that my Higher Power would take care of me, seeing I had for a long time been angry at God and believed that He was definitely not there for me?

One of the miracles of the program has been my returning belief in a Higher Power who is always there for me when I need Him. I am slowly learning that I just need to turn my will and my life over to Him on a daily basis as it tells me in Step Three, and amazing things are beginning to happen. Because I wasn't able to do this for many years, I had blocked my intuition, which we are told is the way in which we are in direct contact with our Higher Power. The intuitive thoughts are slowly returning as I work on a daily relationship with my Higher Power, and I am now more able to act on them, knowing that I will always be taken care of.

One Day at a Time . . . .
I will continue to turn my will and my life over to my Higher Power knowing that my connection with Him, my intuition, is getting stronger each day, and that I am more able to do God's will for today.

~ *Sharon S.*

Meditation 338

COURAGE

"Courage faces fear and thereby masters it."
Martin Luther King, Jr.

I have never been a brave person and was always very fearful. I would watch movies where the hero would rescue the heroine, or where someone would climb Mount Everest, or perform some feat of daring, and I would be totally in awe. I was afraid of the dark, of rejection, of failure and of most other things that I was convinced took courage. No way would I go parasailing or deep sea diving as that seemed to require the courage that I lacked. I didn't understand then that people who do those kinds of things are not totally without fear, but they have a way of overcoming their fear and still doing it anyway.

When I came into the program and learned that I would have to do an inventory and then, worse still, make amends to the people I had harmed, I was paralyzed by fear. Eventually I realized that, even though I feared doing these things, all I had to do was ask my Higher Power for strength and guidance and then do the things I'd most feared. Perhaps these weren't the feats of daring that I had seen heroes perform, but for me they were great victories, and in being able to do them, I knew that I was developing courage.

One Day at a Time . . . .
I will continue to walk through my fear with my Higher Power at my side, knowing that I am developing the courage that I thought I lacked.

~ *Sharon S.*

Meditation 339

ACTION

"The principle of life is that life responds by corresponding;
your life becomes the thing you have decided it shall be."
Raymond Charles Barker

Action is an important part of my program today. Before I came to the program, I believed that many things in my life just happened. I didn't know that when I did not take action I was acting by omission. I was making decisions by not deciding.

Now that I have been taught by the program to act, I have tools to take positive action on a daily basis. I have tools given me by the program that help me shape my life into something useful and beautiful – if I choose that for myself. I can attend a meeting, make a phone call, serve, read literature, do some writing, pray, meditate or one of many actions available to me to work my program. And I know as I work my program my life takes shape – into the shape my Higher Power has for me.

One Day at a Time . . . .
I will live life based on the principle of action and watch my life become something beautiful.

~ *Carolyn H.*

Meditation 340

FORGIVENESS

"We realized that the people who wronged us were spiritually sick.
When a person offended we said to ourselves,
'This is a sick man. How can I be helpful to him?
God save me from being angry. Thy will be done.'"
Big Book of Alcoholics Anonymous

This has been one of the most important paragraphs for me in recovery. I have used it for any type of hurt I have in reaction to another person. Besides my asking God to save me from anger, I ask God to heal all feelings I have toward that person that block me from having a closer relationship with the God of my understanding. For me, this has meant I have had to learn to forgive everyone who my thinking told me had injured me in some way. I was unable to do this no matter how hard I tried. I prayed to the God of my understanding to teach me how to forgive those others and to work with my heart to create that forgiveness. It involved a long process of discovering my part and the other's part; separating acts from people.

Once I had done this work and knew in my heart that God had given me the miracle to forgive these people, an interesting thing happened. During Step Four and Five work, my sponsor told me I also had to forgive myself. I discovered, by going through this process, that working through the anger and pain, I ended up also having forgiven myself. For me, it wasn't enough to tell another person all my Fourth Step. I had to feel the feelings in my heart and give them to God to heal. Then, after I truly forgave others I could forgive myself. I wasn't able to forgive myself until I gave it away to others.

One Day at a Time . . . .
I will remember that God will help me in anything I ask, the answer just may be different than I expected. When the miracle occurs I will be able to see God's hand in it.

~ *Judy A.*

CHANGE

"If we don't change, we don't grow.
If we don't grow, we are not really living."
Gail Sheehy

Throughout my life, I have been terrified of change. To me, change meant abandoning one set of experiences which, although adverse, were at least familiar. I thought I'd be replacing them with another set of experiences which would surely be at least as bad, and which had the additional disadvantage of being unknown.

In this program, I was appalled to see a whole room of people who spoke enthusiastically, joyfully, about the changes that the program was bringing to their lives –not just in terms of released weight, but in so many areas of day-to-day living. Panic-stricken at the idea that I, too, would change, I talked about it after the first meeting with a dear friend.

"Hey," she smiled. "No one's forcing you. If changing gets too scary, you can always decide you want to stay put." Armed with that slight reassurance, I decided I would go with the program until it got too scary.

In the course of the next weeks, as I maintained strict abstinence and began to work the Steps, strange things began to happen. I found myself looking forward to getting up in the morning and adding all kinds of things to my morning ritual: body lotion, foot care, cosmetics. Amazingly, my life-long habit of nail-biting disappeared, and my nails are not only well-tended, but polished!

On the professional level, I started keeping a list of projects due, instead of relying on my sketchy memory. I hired someone to answer phones and to help keep my eternally messy desk more or less clear. Most important, I have started an honest reassessment of my relationship with my life partner, and have decided that it's not enough that this is the first relationship of my life that is free of physical abuse; I deserve to be loved and desired, and to have that expressed.

At a face-to-face program meeting this week, I read the Promises. I was amazed to hear a strong, confident voice–mine–saying "Our whole attitude and outlook upon life will change," and I realized that I was changing. I love it!

One Day at a Time . . . .
I will welcome change, for change is growth, and I will know that, now that I have placed my life in the hands of my Higher Power, any change will be for the better.

~ *Sharon N.*

Meditation 342

ENOUGH

"One day at a time - this is enough. Do not look back and grieve over the past for it is gone: and do not be troubled about the future for it has not yet come. Live in the present and make it so beautiful that it will be worth remembering."
I. Scott Taylor

As a practicing compulsive overeater, I was obsessed with getting my *"fair share"* and stockpiling everything from food to friends. I was afraid there wouldn't be *"enough"* in the future. One of the Promises of the program states that *"Fear of people and of economic insecurity will leave us."* But just how can I calm down when the thought comes that there isn't enough, or that there won't be enough in the future?

At a recent meeting, the speaker said that when he began to worry about his finances, he would ask himself, *"Do I have enough money between now and the time I go to bed?"* Since we're only alive in the moment, that's really the appropriate time frame. To me, that sounds like the best example of *"One Day At A Time"* thinking I've heard so far! Additionally, this could be applied to anything else I might worry about: *"Do I have enough FOOD between now and bedtime?... enough LOVE?"* You-fill-in-the-blank, because it isn't always just economic insecurity that haunts us!

One Day at a Time . . . .
I'm learning to trust my Higher Power, which always supplies my needs. Whenever I start to worry, I can ask myself if I have enough to last between now and the time I go to bed, and cultivate trust and appreciation for the gifts I receive daily.

~ *Marilyn*

LIFE

"Life is the movie you see through your own unique eyes.
It makes little difference what's happening out there.
It's how you take it that counts."
Denis Waitley in "The Winner's Edge"

L ife is a very precious resource. Everyone has a different interpretation of reality, and people who are happier in life make the most of what they have been given, no matter how good or bad it may seem at the time.

Everything happens for a reason. Although we may not understand something at first, we must seize the moment and make use of every single second that our Higher Power has blessed us with. Enjoy all the good times that you deserve, but remember to accept those down times for all the lessons that you will learn, too. It is important to remember the Serenity Prayer and keep on going.

Make the most of each day but remember to stop and smell the flowers along the way. Today only happens once.

One Day at a Time . . . .
Life is not a dress rehearsal, so have a good day, unless you have other plans.

~ Natalie

FAULTFINDING

"When You Look For The Bad In Mankind
Expecting To Find It, You Surely Will."
Abraham Lincoln

The Big Book of Alcoholics Anonymous says, *"To conclude that others were wrong was as far as most of us ever got."* It seemed as though I spent half a lifetime discovering the faults in others. I used this information as a tool or weapon against them when the need would arise, or if I needed a victory to feel superior when I was feeling low. How very sick. It took me a long time to learn that all of us have weaknesses; it's part of being an imperfect human being. We also have strengths and talents, sometimes waiting to be discovered. My job now is to search for the good in others, to overlook the pettiness, to understand that they are still growing and becoming. I am also to practice ongoing forgiveness, for them as well as for myself, to remember that God is still spiritually creating us all in His image.

One Day at a Time . . . .
Have I quit fault finding others? Myself? God?

~ *Jeremiah*

REAL LIVING

"A life lived in fear is a life half-lived."
Tara Morice as Fran,
(From Baz Luhrmann's film "Strictly Ballroom")

When I first saw this movie in 1993, it spoke volumes to my life and to my recovery. I had spent my life afraid, afraid of everything and everybody. If I crossed you, I feared your wrath. If I disappointed you, I dreaded the loss of your love. If things were going well, I wondered, often aloud, when the other shoe was going to drop. I had nowhere to go, no one to trust, nothing I could believe in, because I knew it would be taken away from me. The only safe haven I had was in the food, but I was afraid of the consequences. The biggest thing that kept me in my disease was the fear of what might be on the other side.

The bravest thing I ever did was walk through the doors of my first program meeting. I had been shamed into it by a therapist, but once I got there I sensed that my fears would be vanquished. I saw people who had been there, done that, and designed the t-shirt of fear that I was wearing. They showed me, through the Steps and Traditions, that there was more to life.

The program of recovery has taught me that a life of fear indeed is a life half-lived. Living in fear, I only succeeded in quashing the joy, the adventure, the zest for life that was naturally planted in me. It also eliminated the biggest fear ... that of a Higher Power. It has given me faith, the diametric opposite of fear. Faith shined its light on the darkness of my life, and allowed me to live a fuller existence that cannot be taken from me, save for retreat into fearful despair. I am so immensely grateful for what I have been given: life, instead of mere existence.

One Day at a Time . . . .
Faith in a Power greater than myself is a powerful antidote to a fearful, half-lived life. I pray to keep the light of faith shining brightly in my life.

~ *Mark*

GOD IS

"Open your eyes and the whole world is full of God."
Jakob Bohme

When I was a child, my family never talked about God. I never knew the light of God, never felt His love or power, or recognized His presence in my life. When things were rough, I could only see the darkness. When I was lonely, I didn't know He was with me all the time. When I was weak or scared, I thought I had to overcome and be strong, and not be afraid. I didn't feel His presence with me, or believe that He was watching over me. Then, for twenty years I was married to a religious man who did talk about God. I tried so hard to believe as he did, but his words soon lost their meaning. The abuse began to overshadow the hope that things would change, and the belief that God would make everything okay, if only I believed like my husband. For years I have struggled with my faith, trying to believe in a God that was willing to light my way, love me, and protect me ... not just in the good times, but in the painful times.

When I first came into recovery, I was still struggling, but I became *"willing to believe"* that God cared about me. I started watching for signs that He was there, ready to light my path when I could see only the darkness, ready to enfold me in His arms when I felt unlovable, and ready to protect me when I was scared. I became willing to recognize His presence in my day-to-day life.

Now that I am willing, I can find God's love everywhere ... in a friendly smile, in the kind words of a friend, in the beauty of a flower, and in a child's eyes. Sometimes, when life gets rough, I have to look a little harder, but it's there. I only have to remain open and willing to see it and accept it. Wherever I am, God is there with me, ready to love and protect me.

One Day at a Time . . . .
I will be willing to see God's presence in my life, and know that wherever I am, God is. I will let go, and let God be there.

~ Debbie K.

Meditation 347

THE PAST

"Even God cannot change the past."
Agathon (ca. 448–400 BC)
(Athenian tragic poet and friend of
Euripides and Plato, ancient Greek poet)

Each day of recovery, I ask my Higher Power to help me stay focused on today. Although there are things I would like to change about the past, I know that it is not possible. I've let myself fall into traps, thinking *"If only I had done..."* or *"If only I'd said..."* When I think this way, I find myself wasting a lot of time and feeling bad. This doesn't seem like healthy recovery thinking. If amends need to be made, then I make them. If not, then I let go of the past.

Worrying about the past is not productive. Regret will not fix anything. It will merely keep me from concentrating my efforts on where they belong ... on the present moment.

One Day at a Time . . . .
I will stay focused on what is going on around me and leave the past in the past.

~ Teresa S.

CHANGE

"To keep our faces toward change and behave like free spirits
in the presence of fate is strength undefeatable."
Helen Keller

As far back as I can remember, I have always been fearful of change. I preferred to stay in my comfort zone, even when it became uncomfortable or painful. I suppose that was why I stayed in the disease for so long; it was what I knew. It was safe and predictable and I didn't have to deal with painful emotions such as loss and rejection. This was also why I stayed so long in a bad marriage; I was terrified of what was outside the walls of my dysfunctional relationship. In truth, I didn't really live, because fear of change prevented me from forming new relationships and doing new and exciting things. Even the move from one city to another was totally traumatic, because the old and familiar was what I knew, not because it was better. Even then, I spent so long looking at the closed door behind me that I failed to see the open door in front of me.

I know now that even when I fear change, I need only put one foot in front of the other, and do what is before me. Because I now have faith that my Higher Power will be with me every step of the way, I need only ask for help, and the help comes. Even though it still is not easy, I am aware of how many changes I have been able to make with the help of my Higher Power. In the past, I spent so much time obsessing about the outcome that I talked myself out of the change I was thinking of making. The biggest change that has happened for me is my newfound faith which enables me to take that leap into the unknown.

There have been other miraculous changes too. Now I have a more open and honest relationship with my children and others because I am able to take more risks and set boundaries, which I had never been able to do before. I have changed careers, undertaken flying overseas on my own, and in general am not the scared person I used to be. I also have a whole new family of wonderful friends in this fellowship who understand me and love me always.

One Day at a Time . . . .
I continue to grow and change as God wills me to do, and I will not be afraid because I know that He will always be there to guide and help me.

~ Sharon S.

Meditation 349

ACCOMPLISHMENT

*"The central fact of our lives today is the absolute
certainty that our Creator has entered into our hearts
and lives in a way which is indeed miraculous.
He has commenced to accomplish those things for us
which we could never do by ourselves."*
The Big Book of Alcoholics Anonymous

The one thing that I am absolutely certain of today is that our Creator, God, lives in my heart and works miracles in my life daily. The biggest miracle, I believe, is having an awareness of Him, and knowing that He is in control of all that happens in my life. His power is infinite. If I were not aware of God, then I don't believe I could work this program. It is the realization that God can accomplish anything that is helping me to work daily toward achieving my goal of continued abstinence and a changed attitude regarding food.

I cannot change what's in my heart, but God can. I cannot, of myself, break lifelong habits, but God can motivate me to change. I cannot forgive myself all the pain I've inflicted on myself and others, while suffering from this disease, but God can soften my heart, and help me to forgive by letting me know that He forgives me. There is nothing that I can't accomplish when I take God's hand and let Him lead me.

One Day at a Time . . . .
I will let God guide me into an ever-deepening relationship with Him so that I may accomplish the great feat of arresting my compulsion to overeat.

~ Joycelyn

Meditation 350

COURAGE

"Courage is the power to let go of the familiar."
Raymond Linquist
(For many years, the pastor at the
Hollywood Presbyterian Church in Hollywood, California)

A sponsor once asked me what I had against feeling good. I had no answer. I now see that in my sickness and ignorance I hung onto the familiar, what I perceived to be truth. Fear kept me from trying something new until I hurt bad enough to beg God for the courage to try a different way. I am amazed at how long I put up with a miserable existence, not even recognizing my fear of change. I understand now that, although physically full-grown, I am spiritually still growing and becoming.

One Day at a Time . . . .
Do I have the courage to change? To even look at change?

~ Jeremiah

PEACE

"We cannot find peace if we are
afraid of the windstorms of life."
Elisabeth Kubler-Ross
(Psychiatrist and author of 'On Death and Dying')

My life always seemed so filled with difficulty. I seemed to have more than my fair share of traumas and losses. Why was I always being tested like this? It just didn't seem fair. I was so wrapped up in myself and the unfairness of my difficult life that I couldn't see that each of these harsh experiences had been opportunities for growth. Instead of bemoaning my fate and blaming people or situations for what seemed to me to be the cause of the current difficulty, I never looked at what part I had played in the whole situation, or the lessons I could learn from each of these experiences.

It has often been said that God doesn't give us more than we can cope with. What I realized later, once I'd come into the program, was that each of these experiences had been a unique learning opportunity for me; they were a chance to grow and mature. I had been too stuck in self-pity and blame that I hadn't seen the wonderful gifts that I was being given with each new life experience. When I was able to open myself up fully to the lessons that I could learn from life, I became a whole person. It was then that the promises of the program begin to be fulfilled in my life, and I began to know serenity and peace.

One Day at a Time . . . .
I will look for what lesson my Higher Power wants me to learn from life. I am then able to grow and change, and by doing so, I will come to know serenity and peace.

~ Sharon S.

Meditation 352

ACTION

"You learn to speak by speaking,
to study by studying,
to run by running,
to work by working;
in just the same way,
you learn to love by loving."
St. Francis De Sales

St. Francis de Sales lived from 1567 to 1622. Isn't it amazing that a man who lived over 300 years before the birth of our recovery program could encapsulate its meaning in the above quote? Put another way, what St. Francis was saying was, *"You work the program by working the program."*

I've met so many people who had theoretical knowledge of recovery, but no practical experience. They don't work the program; they just talk the talk without walking the walk. I'm not proud to admit that I've been one of those people myself.

It's a wonderful feeling to actually work the program, to take the Steps, and to trust in the God of my understanding to keep me working it. Paying lip service to the program doesn't bring recovery; only working it does. Anything else is a waste of time and energy.

One Day at a Time . . . .
I will work the program by working the program; today, I'll take action to bring about my recovery.

~ *Jeff*

JOY

"The way to do is to be."
Lao Tzu

It is not until we can let ourselves be who we really are that we can recognize who we REALLY are! In recovery I have learned it is by embracing myself as I am today that I will become increasingly aware of my true identity. It is not by denial or pretended *"goodness"* that the Truth is revealed, but by acceptance and humility. This is one of the many gifts of recovery ... we no longer have to *"wait until."*

This program tells us we can be happy and free now. HERE AND NOW! But, my ego-mind gives me a different message. It says, *"You can be happy, joyous and free when you lose the weight, get your health back, get that job, marry that prince, receive the next degree, and on and on. In other words, *"You must wait and wait and wait, and maybe someday you'll be good enough. Then you can be happy."* Our ego keeps us in pursuit of the elusive happiness it promises.

One Day at a Time . . . .
I choose to be happy; I choose joy.

~ *Patt*

SPIRITUALITY VS RELIGION

*"Religion is a way for people to get to heaven, and
Spirituality is a way for people to get out of hell."*
Anonymous Twelve Stepper

I was raised in a home that was strongly religious. All of its standards and rules were based on religion, and on the standards of a rigid God Who is perfect, and Who calls His followers to be perfect. My mother is a person who seemed to find her mission in life by telling people how far they fell short of that perfection. I learned very early that I did not and would never measure up; that being part of religion meant accepting my inability to excel at its tenets.

But when I came into this program, I began to learn about spirituality. I learned about God from people who were not perfect, and who could accept themselves as they are. I learned about mercy and forgiveness from people with different faiths than my own; I learned about trusting God from people who did not even believe in a Supreme Being. What I learned has put *"flesh"* on the words of the Scriptures that I learned as a child. It has put life into my faith, for the first time, and it has helped me learn that I am worthwhile and acceptable just as I am.

One Day at a Time . . . .
I give my life into the keeping of the God of my understanding, and know that my best is the least, and the most, that He expects from me.

~ *Donna*

Meditation 355

BABY STEPS

"I long to accomplish a great and noble task,
but it is my chief duty to accomplish small tasks
as if they were great and noble."
Helen Keller

From as far back as I can remember, I believed that, in order to be worthy or loved, I had to achieve great things. It didn't matter what it was but I set out to be the best at whatever I did, hoping that would make me feel better. Whether it was academic or one of the many diets or diet clubs I tried, it was the same story, and failure was totally unacceptable. Delayed gratification was definitely not part of my vocabulary, and so things had to be done or achieved in record time. If I wanted something done, it had to be done today, if not yesterday. Everything I did was done compulsively. I was, as one person in a meeting described, a *"human doing,"* not a *"human being"*.

Of course the things I could never really achieve were permanent weight loss and the serenity that comes with recovery. These seemed to elude me when I first came into the program, mainly because I expected to do it perfectly and in a very short time. After all, I had lost weight before, and quickly too. I had to realize that recovery is not a race, that this is a journey, not a destination. I don't have to do it all in one day, nor do I have to be the best at it. All I need to do is to take baby steps, one day at a time, and I will recover as God wills me to do. I just need to put one foot in front of the other and do what is before me. Recovery is cumulative and I build on it, day by day.

One Day at a Time . . . .
I do the footwork and put my trust in my Higher Power, believing that, as I do what I need to do for today, God's healing power will come to me in the form of recovery.

~ *Sharon S.*

Meditation 356

RISING ABOVE

"Our greatest glory is not in never failing,
but in rising up every time we fail."
Ralph Waldo Emerson

One of the major premises of our recovery program is *"progress, not perfection."* No one but me expects me to be perfect. I have a history of driving myself in the quest for perfection. I've set goals that are so lofty that I could never achieve them. In that respect, I'm probably my own worst enemy.

However, I can also be my own best friend. I don't have to set standards that are impossible for me to meet. In fact, we're told we need to live one day at a time. If I can do that, then I don't need to live up to my impossibly high standards. My goals aren't so out-of-reach if I can see them as daily things.

What happens if I fail to meet even the *"one day at a time"* goal? I start over, knowing that I don't have to stay down. I can rise up and begin again. That, for me, is the greatest thing.

One Day at a Time . . . .
I will rise above my failures and shortcomings, and know that I'm making progress. I don't have to be perfect any more.

~ *Jeff*

FEAR

"When thinking won't cure fear, action will."
W. Clement Stone

When I first came into the program, I was told that I couldn't think my way into positive actions, but I could act my way into positive thinking. I learned that this was a simple program of action; that if I wanted what you had, I had to do what you did. None of these clichés made any sense to me; I would have to think these over. The nerve of these people telling me that they would do my thinking for me, that all I had to do was follow directions! They prodded and badgered me into working the Steps out of real love and knowledge of truth. I realize now that my actions demonstrated to God my desire to change, and He gave me the courage to try living another way. Most importantly, though, He gave me you.

One Day at a Time . . . .
Am I going to "keep on the firing line" or rest on my laurels?

~ Jeremiah

Meditation 358

REGRET

"Regret is an appalling waste of energy;
you can't build on it;
it's only good for wallowing in."
Katherine Mansfield

Before I came into the program, I allowed fear to rule my life and prevent me from trying new things. I was absent from my own life. I was emotionally unavailable to my children and I stayed stuck in a deep hole of self-pity. I never really heard beautiful music or gloried in the miracles of nature. Although I had what people might perceive as a pretty normal life, it was actually an empty shell and I merely existed. I feel so saddened now at the thought of all the wasted years. I cannot bring them back, but I can learn from them.

When I came into the program and read the Promises in the Big Book of Alcoholics Anonymous, I realized that it was futile to regret the past or to shut the door on it. Those years and all the pain I went through are what made me the person I am today. I need to always remember where I came from, because if I don't, I can just as easily go back there. I can also use my experience to help others on this wonderful road to recovery. I am able to give away what has been given to me so freely, because it's only then that I can keep what I have.

One Day at a Time . . . .
I must always remember where I came from so that I can help others in this program
of recovery and keep myself from going back into the patterns of my past.

~ *Sharon S.*

Meditation 359

HOLIDAYS

"May peace be more than a holiday;
May love be more than a season;
May the feelings deep inside transcend the calendar;
And, instead, become a way of life."
Anonymous

It is the time of Hanukkah ... of Christmas ... of Kwanzaa ... and other holidays. It is the time when the world is at its best and the hearts of all seem to be brimming with love.

It is also the time of year that my very soul finds the most difficult. My physical and emotional recovery is compromised, and memories occupy every cell in my body, causing this vulnerable addict tremendous turmoil.

These holy days test the gifts of that enigma which is my Higher Power ... the God Of My Understanding ... and when these days are over and normality returns, I smile at having once again made it through the holidays intact.

One Day at a Time . . . .
I acknowledge that in my Higher Power
I have a love that can never be fathomed,
A spiritual resource that can never be exhausted,
A peace that can never be understood,
A rest that can never be disturbed,
A joy that can never be diminished,
A hope that can never be disappointed,
A glory that can never be clouded,
A light that can never be darkened,
And a life that can never die ...
Even on holidays.

~ Mari

Meditation 360

VISION

*"A rock pile ceases to be a rock pile
the moment a single man contemplates it,
bearing within him the image of a cathedral."*
Antoine De Saint-Exupery

It never ceases to amaze me how the disease of compulsive overeating distorts the vision. Some compulsive overeaters can look into a mirror and see a fat person where there is none. Others can look into the same mirror and not see the weight that is there.

Recovery brings new eyes to the compulsive overeater. It lets us to see what's really there in the mirror. Recovery allows each of us to see the cathedral we really are, rather than the pile of rubble we think we see. Recovery corrects our vision.

One Day at a Time . . . .
As I work my recovery program, I will see myself as I really am, rather than seeing what the disease shows me.

~ Jeff

Meditation 361

JOY

"Life is no brief candle to me.
It is a sort of splendid torch which
I have got hold of for the moment, and
want to make it burn as brightly as possible
before handing it on to future generations."
George Bernard Shaw

For many years my life was filled with pain and I felt totally empty inside. I did what I had to do for my children and for the people around me, but with a heavy heart, and life seemed to be one endless day after the other. What had happened to all the dreams and hopes I had for a life filled with joy and happiness? Sometimes the pain got to be so great that life just didn't seem to be worthwhile any more. At times I even contemplated ending my life. I have often heard it said that the opposite of pain is joy but in those dark days, I certainly couldn't see that.

It is only in recovery that I see that the pain had a meaning, and it has brought me to a great appreciation of all the miracles in my life. I can appreciate the beauty in nature, and for the first time in a very long time my soul is filled with joy. When I listen to Beethoven's glorious Ninth Symphony with its last movement, the choral piece set to the poet Schiller's *"Ode to Joy"*, I begin to realize that one can create something truly wondrous out of one's pain and suffering. Beethoven wrote this magnificent work shortly before his death, when he was in tremendous emotional pain and totally deaf. Yet he created this truly amazing piece of music that lives on nearly 200 years after his death, and will probably do so for many years to come.

I now realize that there was a reason for my suffering and if, out of that, I can bring some joy or happiness to others, then my life will have had some purpose. It is only through this fellowship that I have been able to see that.

One Day at a Time . . . .
I will always remember that my pain has been a growing experience that enables me to share what I have learned with other fellow sufferers. I can now appreciate all the miracles that my Higher Power performs in my life, and I am now truly able to experience joy.

~ *Sharon S.*

MEDITATION

"God is the mirror of silence
in which all creation is reflected."
Paramahansa Yogananda

The disease of compulsive overeating is a devious one. It tries to tell me that I'm not a worthwhile person. It tries to tell me that I'm never going to recover, so I may as well eat. The disease tries to make me feel like I'm the lowest of the low.

Fortunately, there are many things in this recovery program that counteract the disease. I can use a food plan to make sure I don't eat what I'm not supposed to eat. I can read program literature to show me how to live triumphantly. I can work the Steps, do service, make outreach calls; there's so much I can do which can bring recovery from compulsive overeating.

Another of the things I can do to counteract my disease is meditation. When I meditate, I come into conscious contact with my Higher Power. Meditation helps me to see that I am a worthwhile person, that God loves me just as I am. When I meditate I gain insights into the program literature I'm reading, I learn the things I need to do to further my recovery. I also learn the things that stifle my growth, so I can stop doing them. Meditation is very important to my recovery program.

One Day at a Time . . . .
I remember the importance of meditation, and I meditate every day.

~ *Jeff*

GRATITUDE FOR ADVERSITY

"He was my greatest teacher.
He taught me patience."
The Dalai Lama on Mao Tse Tung

Whenever I feel downtrodden or disappointed by the hand that life has dealt me, I often think of this quote. It moves me beyond speech. Here was a man who had lost his homeland to communist China, yet he still had a good thing to say about the man who started it all. It forces me to come to a realization that what has happened to me is peanuts!

Too often I am caught up with feeling sorry for myself because of my disease, while ignoring the fact that I am so fortunate to have found recovery. Sometimes I feel so poor, yet I live in a large home with a wonderful spouse and delightful pets. I have a car, and enough food to eat every day. I have the luxury of obtaining my degree. Most of all, though I often complain about how unfair it all is, I am even fortunate to have an eating disorder. Because it is through admitting I have a problem that I am beginning to taste recovery, and it is sweeter than any binge item. And it has taught me that it is through our adversities that we learn compassion and patience.

I have to realize that life just isn't fair. If it were, how boring it would be! Nothing worthwhile is easy to obtain, and that includes recovery. What would it be worth if there was no effort going into it? Sometimes bad things happen, and they are unfortunate. But that's the end of it. I cannot make things be the way I want them to be. I cannot change life. I must accept life on life's terms, and learn the art of patience, so well demonstrated by the above quote. How fortunate that I have the opportunity to learn these precious skills in the safety and security of my own home, with my wonderful friends, spouse, and my program family!

One Day at a Time . . . .
I will avoid dwelling on the misery that accompanies hardship. I will develop the willingness to be grateful for the opportunity for me to learn compassion and patience.

~ *Claire*

WILLINGNESS

"Yet we finally did make choices that brought about our recovery. We came to believe that alone we were powerless over [food]. This was surely a choice, and a most difficult one. We came to believe that a Higher Power could restore us to sanity when we became willing to practice [program's] twelve steps. In short, we chose to 'become willing,' and no better choice did we ever make."
from "As Bill Sees It"

I floundered in program for a good while. I was not willing to do the Fourth Step; it scared me. Then I did it, and recovery continued.

I floundered in program again. I was not willing to do the extra work I knew I would have to do to stay in the program. I was scared of being a sponsor, so I left. The disease gradually took me over.

I came back to program. This time I was willing. No longer did the phrase "going to any lengths" scare me. I knew I needed to do whatever it took. The disease had beaten me down where I had no choice if I wanted to recover. I took the Steps ... all the Steps. I became a sponsor. I also discovered that abstinence is only the beginning of recovery - that life is joyful and free. It all began with willingness on my part. I didn't have the power to change my life, but my Higher Power was able to change it once I became willing to follow the Twelve Steps to the best of my ability.

One Day at a Time . . . .
I will ask for and receive the willingness to work this program.

~ *Julie*

LIFE IS WORTH LIVING

"These, then, are my last words to you: Be not afraid of life.
Believe that life is worth living and your belief will help create the fact."
William James (1842 ~ 1910)

I have lived my life as a compulsive eater and I have known many other compulsive eaters. I believe I can say unequivocally that life is much more difficult in so many ways for us than for many others. I denied that what I suffered from was a disease; yet I watched as over the years it robbed me of so many things others take for granted. Most of us will acknowledge early on that the manifestations of compulsive eating affect us spiritually, emotionally and physically. Volumes have been written about each of these so most reading this know the devastation it causes. When I began to inventory my life and saw how much the quality of it had suffered, it saddened me greatly.

I believe one of the most difficult ways the disease of COE, or any compulsive illness, affects us is the way society looks upon us. Because I have experienced life both ways, I know how behavior and attitudes change in interacting with a COE vs a non-COE. We wear our disease on the outside ... but the extensive damage is far more wide-spread than just the physical. The disease wrecks havoc in every area of our lives as we silently go about our life doing the things expected of us. We don't dare scapegoat the disease. After all, this is not cancer ... or heart disease. Yet it can be just as serious.

Many decades ago, a group of alcoholics gathered and, as a result, life began to change for those of us who struggled with the disease. When I reached the point in my life that I could actually acknowledge that compulsive eating was affecting it and that I had done everything possible to stop it and couldn't, it was one of the most freeing moments I've ever experienced. I learned that I was as powerless over this as I would have been suffering a heart attack. I also learned that I couldn't handle it alone. I learned that there were Twelve Steps absolutely necessary if I were to survive emotionally and, perhaps even physically.

I went from fighting the disease to acknowledging it. Because of the Steps I learned that there were tens of thousands of others exactly like me and that we all spoke the same beautiful language. I learned not to be afraid of life ... and that, despite this despicable disease, life is truly worth living. I was told to *"act as if"* and by doing this it became no longer an act.

One Day at a Time . . . .
I affirm that my life is worth living. One day at a time, I affirm that I will not be afraid of anything that makes me feel otherwise.

~ Mari

Meditation 366

Index

APRIL	MAY	JUNE
Happiness	Sharing Our Stories	Perfection
Love	Helping Others	Step One
The Future	Step One	Experience, Strength and Hope
Commitment	Light	Fourth Step Secrets
Acceptance	Choose Happiness	Honesty
Courage	Expectations	Human Emotion
Higher Power	Sublimation	Compassion
Willingness	Positive Thoughts	Togetherness
Feelings	Open Mindedness	Promises
Aging	Good Days ~ Bad Days	Growth
Meditation	Courage	Pain
Recovery	Worry	Expectations
Normality	Serenity	Loners
Fearless	Perfectionism	Peace
Success	Positive Thoughts	Perfectionism
Pain	Looking At the Stars	Mirror, Mirror
Forgiveness	The Human Spirit	Vices and Virtues
Unconditional Love	Step Eleven	Guilt
Happiness	Denial	Kind Words
The Present Moment	Avoidance	Struggle
Religion	Thoughts	A Person Of Worth
Compulsions	Faith	Sunlight of the Spirit
Birthright	Opportunity	Miracles
Loneliness	Perfection	Acceptance
Understanding	Sharing	Step Twelve
Forgiveness	Serving Others	Tools
Relationships	Balance	Efficiency and Function
Unity	Victims	Isolation
Goodness	Higher Power	Resentment
Spiritual Recovery	Home	Procrastination
	The Titanic	

The Twelve Steps of Overeaters Anonymous

1. We admitted we were powerless over food — that our lives had become unmanageable.

2. Came to believe that a Power greater than ourselves could restore us to sanity.

3. Made a decision to turn our will and our lives over to the care of God *as we understood Him*.

4. Made a searching and fearless moral inventory of ourselves.

5. Admitted to God, to ourselves and to another human being the exact nature of our wrongs.

6. Were entirely ready to have God remove all these defects of character.

7. Humbly asked Him to remove our shortcomings.

8. Made a list of all persons we had harmed and became willing to make amends to them all.

9. Made direct amends to such people wherever possible, except when to do so would injure them or others.

10. Continued to take personal inventory and when we were wrong, promptly admitted it.

11. Sought through prayer and meditation to improve our conscious contact with God *as we understood Him*, praying only for knowledge of His will for us and the power to carry that out.

12. Having had a spiritual awakening as the result of these Steps, we tried to carry this message to compulsive overeaters and to practice these principles in all our affairs.

The Twelve Traditions of Overeaters Anonymous

1. Our common welfare should come first; personal recovery depends upon OA unity.

2. For our group purpose there is but one ultimate authority — a loving God as He may express Himself in our group conscience. Our leaders are but trusted servants; they do not govern.

3. The only requirement for OA membership is a desire to stop eating compulsively.

4. Each group should be autonomous except in matters affecting other groups or OA as a whole.

5. Each group has but one primary purpose — to carry its message to the compulsive overeater who still suffers.

6. An OA group ought never endorse, finance or lend the OA name to any related facility or outside enterprise, lest problems of money, property and prestige divert us from our primary purpose.

7. Every OA group ought to be fully self-supporting, declining outside contributions.

8. Overeaters Anonymous should remain forever non-professional, but our service centers may employ special workers.

9. OA, as such, ought never be organized; but we may create service boards or committees directly responsible to those they serve.

10. Overeaters Anonymous has no opinion on outside issues; hence the OA name ought never be drawn into public controversy.

11. Our public relations policy is based on attraction rather than promotion; we need always maintain personal anonymity at the level of press, radio, films, television and other public media of communication.

12. Anonymity is the spiritual foundation of all these Traditions, ever reminding us to place principles before personalities.

Notes

Notes

Made in the USA
Charleston, SC
16 August 2011